PALGRAVE POCKET CONSULTANTS

Palgrave Pocket Consultants are concise, authoritative guides that provide actionable solutions to specific, high-level business problems that would otherwise drive you or your company to employ a consultant. Written for aspiring middle to senior managers working across business at any scale, they offer solutions to the most cutting-edge issues across modern business. Be your own expert and have the advice you need at your fingertips.

Forthcoming titles:

ATTRACTING AND RETAINING TALENT
Tim Baker

MANAGING ONLINE REPUTATION
Charlie Pownall

RISKY BUSINESS IN CHINA
Jeremy Gordon

THE NEW CHINESE TRAVELER
Gary Bowerman

CREATING A RELIABLE WORKFORCE
Ivan Robertson and Cary Cooper

THE WORKPLACE COMMUNITY
Ian Gee and Matthew Hanwell

Series ISBN 9781137396792

About the Author

Matthew Crabbe studied Chinese language, society and history at the University of Leeds and has since turned an academic interest in China into a career. As co-founder of research company Access Asia, Matthew has worked exhaustively on trying to make sense of the myriad contradictions in statistics on the consumer markets in China. He has conducted detailed analysis on China's retail sales for many years, working to highlight how China's official retail figures do not reflect the real size of the country's domestic consumer economy. He is the co-author of two books and has written hundreds of reports on China's consumer markets over two decades.

Understanding and using China's statistics

Myth-Busting China's Numbers

Matthew Crabbe

palgrave
macmillan

First published 2014 by
PALGRAVE MACMILLAN

Palgrave Macmillan in the UK is an imprint of Macmillan Publishers Limited, registered in England, company number 785998, of Houndmills, Basingstoke, Hampshire RG21 6XS.

Palgrave Macmillan in the US is a division of St Martin's Press LLC, 175 Fifth Avenue, New York, NY 10010.

Palgrave Macmillan is the global academic imprint of the above companies and has companies and representatives throughout the world.

Palgrave® and Macmillan® are registered trademarks in the United States, the United Kingdom, Europe and other countries.

ISBN 978–1–137–35319–1

This book is printed on paper suitable for recycling and made from fully managed and sustained forest sources. Logging, pulping and manufacturing processes are expected to conform to the environmental regulations of the country of origin.

A catalogue record for this book is available from the British Library.

A catalog record for this book is available from the Library of Congress.

Typeset by MPS Limited, Chennai, India.

Contents

List of Tables

Preface

This book aims to answer some fundamental questions about how China reports itself and why problems with the way the country does so are important, whilst attempting to bust some of the common myths about how reliable or not that statistical data is. The basic problems with understanding Chinese statistics remain understanding the broad issues behind the problems – be they political, methodological, corruption, etc. Understanding where and how data on China is derived is fundamental to gaining clarity about what the data really represents, whereas failing to understand that can distort the real view of the market and any business plan based on such data.

The Chinese government has historically been opaque about the country's statistics for a variety of political, defence, economic and social reasons. But the Chinese government continues to improve the situation, such as providing better statistical gathering and reporting regulations, and imposing penalties on those falsely reporting. I don't see these moves as mere window dressing, but rather real attempts to bring some order out of the chaos. The problem in China is that despite strong regulations and stiff penalties, policing the gathering and reporting of data to remove bad data is highly problematic when so many people are involved (and actively thwarting accuracy) at so many levels, leaving the system open to systemic corruption and persistent abuse.

As data improves and is reported, a new problem is created that poses problems for those seeking to understand the true trajectory of China's economy and markets. The lack of historical back-trending based on new revisions leads to practical historical data-tracking issues. This makes understanding growth trends within a single data series very difficult. Revisions and improvements also mean that data series themselves are refined ("smoothed"), but this adds even more to the complexity of historical back-tracking and comparison. Looking at data sets without understanding this means that readers can easily misinterpret what they see, gaining a false picture.

China may have become the "New Number Two" in the world economic pecking order, but the reality and significance of that position is open to debate because the measures used to define China's economic size are so suspect and widely distrusted. If we believe China's gross domestic product (GDP) figures and growth rates, it *is* already the world's second largest economy, and it might overtake the United States of America by about the year 2020. But the findings in this book point to gaps in the data used to measure China's economy. Those gaps show systemic problems that not only question the real size of China as an economy, but also its sustainability. Additionally, Beijing is keen to highlight statistics that put China in the best light – GDP growth and total output are emphasised, while on the contentious issue of global warming, per capita emission statistics are quoted over gross totals.

A large part of economic China is comprised of shadow economics (and politics and financing), and as a market it comes with concerns that much of the market is underregulated. This is not new. In the late nineteenth century, the British Consulate in Shanghai had a full-time "statistical secretary" whose job was to conduct independent calculations of China's trade data and make sense of it. Additionally, getting an independent view on China is never easy in a country with no truly free press to challenge and "speak truth to power." This lack of press freedom has been a major factor hampering the development of China's stock markets, for instance. That data from China is incorrect is not as important as the lack of discussion about why the data is incorrect, and which data is important to be correct on, and which data doesn't really matter. There are indeed (as Mark Twain, probably falsely, attributed to Benjamin Disraeli) "Lies, damned lies and statistics."[1]

The purpose of this book is to add positively to the vibrant debate about China's future economic direction, and to highlight to the reader areas of the discourse that are worth extra attention, and areas where caution needs be exercised. My aim is to encourage engagement with China, and of the positive reforms being undertaken to tackle some of the significant structural issues in the economy, and the way that China's economics is expressed in numbers. My aim is to praise the positive and constructively criticise the negative. My professional career has been (for most of my adult life) and remains tied to the country and people of China, and I wish it and its people only well on its continued odyssey out of the abyss it faced during the twentieth century.

Lastly, there are still those who get confused by Chinese units, given in tens of thousands or hundreds of millions. It is a simple thing, but I have seen data misquoted many times because people have not read the units correctly, quoting data in millions or billions when they are actually out by one or two decimal places! All too often the truth is in the missing zeros!

I would like to make it clear that the views and opinions expressed in this book are exclusively my own.

Acknowledgements

This being my first solo book effort, I must initially thank the co-author of the previous two books I have written (and my former business partner in Access Asia), Paul French, for cajoling me into believing that the contents of my head were at all worth writing down. Thanks also, for managing to persuade Palgrave Macmillan that I would be a suitable author at the start, and looking over the manuscript towards the end.

Particular thanks must also go to John Van Fleet, whose scrutiny of my initial draft and hard-nosed critical commentary proved invaluable in helping me to edge towards doing myself justice. In a world where so many people default towards proffering asinine platitudes, it is good to have someone like John who will shoot straight from the hip, with neither spicy malice nor saccharine mendacity.

I must also thank Andy Rothman from CLSA for his opinions on the importance of the human story behind the numbers. It was my fundamental endeavour in this book to show not only that statistics can be wrong, but also hide the real human story.

There are plenty of people who have helped me form the ideas for this book, probably without realising they did so. Among these must include Bill Dodson, Michael Griffiths, Liam Bussell, Gary Bowerman and Miljan Glenny.

Tamsine O'Riordan and Josie Taylor at Palgrave Macmillan also deserve great admiration, not only for taking a punt on this book and me, but also taking the risk of making it the first of a whole new series.

Finally I must of course thank my wife and children for leaving me to my evenings' writing sessions, on top of my absence due to the day job.

List of Abbreviations and Acronyms Used

ADB – Asian Development Bank
AQSIQ – General Administration of Quality Supervision, Inspection and Quarantine of China
B2C – Business to consumer
C2C – Consumer to consumer
CASS – Chinese Academy of Social Sciences
CBRC – China Banking Regulatory Commission
CCFA – China Chain Store and Franchise Association
CDB – China Development Bank
CEO – Chief executive officer
CERC – China E-Commerce Research Centre
CIA – Central Intelligence Agency
CIC – China Investment Corporation
CLSA – Credit Lyonnais Securities Asia
CNNIC – China Internet Network Information Centre
CNPC – China National Petroleum Corporation
CNY – Chinese New Year
CPC – Communist Party of China
CPI – Consumer price index
CPPCC – Chinese People's Political Consultative Conference
CREIS – China Real Estate Index System
CSRC – China Securities Regulatory Commission
EU – European Union
FLA – Fair Labor Association
FMCG – Fast-moving consumer goods
GDP – Gross domestic product

HSBC – Hongkong and Shanghai Banking Corporation
IEA – International Energy Agency
IMF – International Monetary Fund
IPO – Initial public offering
LTP – Lewis Turning Point
MIIT – Ministry of Industry and Information Technology
MoE – Ministry of Environment of China
MoF – Ministry of Finance of China
MoHRSS – Ministry of Human Resources and Social Security
NBS – National Bureau of Statistics of China
NCSSF – National Council for Social Security Fund of China
NDRC – National Development and Reform Commission of China
NGO – Non-governmental organisation
NPC – National People's Congress of China
OECD – Organisation for Economic Co-operation and Development
PBoC – People's Bank of China
PLA – People's Liberation Army
PMI – Purchasing managers' index
PPI – Producer price index
PRC – People's Republic of China
PRD – Pearl River Delta
RMB – Renminbi, the currency of the People's Republic of China
SAFE – State Administration of Foreign Exchange of China
SAMB – State asset management bureau
SAT – State Administration of Taxation of China
SCRC – State Council Research Center of China
SEPA – State Environmental Protection Administration of China
SEZ – Special economic zone
SME – Small- and medium-sized enterprise
SOE – State-owned enterprise
SPFPC – State Population and Family Planning Commission
SPV – Special purpose vehicle
UK – United Kingdom of Great Britain and Northern Ireland
UN – United Nations
US – United States of America
VAT – Value-added tax

WTO – World Trade Organization
YRD – Yangzi River Delta

Abbreviations used in Tables

bn – billion
expend. – expenditure
govt. – government
mn – million
na – not applicable
neg. – negligible
Q1 – first quarter
Q2 – second quarter
Q3 – third quarter
Q4 – fourth quarter
trn – trillion
YoY – Year on year
'000 – thousands

Introduction

China – somewhere between one and infinity

It is a simple fact that statistics on a developing country as big as China, with as many people as it has, can be a bit unreliable. Even in smaller, more economically advanced countries, statistics are an estimate of the real situation. It is therefore not the contention of this book that China's statistics, or other information, ought to be more accurate. The contention is that understanding information about China requires understanding how and why the country's statistics are defined, gathered and published, and the reason for their inaccuracies, inflations or deflations. As China's economic star continues to rise, the number of people who need to understand this also rises. Hence this book.

My own involvement in trying to interpret China's data began with, and continues to focus on, researching consumer products and services markets in China, firstly writing articles for UK-based Chinese-language newspaper *Siyu Chinese Times*, then as China market analyst at Euromonitor International, where I was hired to kick off their series of reports on consumer markets in China, starting in 1994. This then shifted to developing a specialist trade in reports on China's consumer markets for my own company Access Asia (in partnership with Paul French). It has therefore been my task to try to untangle the often contradictory information about China's economy for the best part of 20 years already.

What my experience in that time has taught me is to be extremely circumspect about any data published on or quoted about China, its sources, its method of creation, its definition, its mode of publication, its political reasoning, its timing, its interpretation, etc. It has become clear to me that the best service I can offer to those asking my opinion on China's economy is to bore them with the technical details about how they must be very careful in interpreting information about China's economy when researching markets in China, and also to challenge the accepted views that surround China and how it works. Most people, on arriving in China for the first time, will find that the country is nothing like their expectations before going there. I have been travelling to China since 1988, and it is still possible for me to suffer culture shock when there.

I have laid this book out in three parts, dealing first with the big macroeconomic numbers, second with company, trade and industrial data, and last with data on people and consumer markets. Each part aims to frame the reality in which Chinese data exists, so that readers can gain an awareness of the issues surrounding the data and can therefore approach the China market with the correct amount of circumspection. My intention is not to disparage China, nor to discourage engagement with it – indeed the opposite. What I hope for is to give examples that allow readers to train their eye to be more critical of the numbers and hyperbole that surround the "China miracle."

Information is political

Information is very political in China. Under Soviet command economy style communism, statistics was considered a political science, not a mathematical one.[1] Data has the potential to suddenly gain the epithet of "state secret" without warning. Understanding China is therefore less to do with accurate statistics, and more about understanding the reasons why statistics are collected and published, what numbers are not published and why, and what the published figures actually represent. There is political reasoning behind the choice of what data most readily reaches general circulation, just as there is a political reason behind the set of data political parties in Western democracies choose to focus on over another to promote their particular agenda. There are also different cultural and political attitudes to statistics and what they mean. China's state media and government propaganda departments manipulate the urgency of foreign media agencies to fill column inches in the same way Western democratic governments try to manipulate press interest, or deflect it. And, just as in the West, there can be those who fail to give due scrutiny to data sets offered, or challenge the accepted view.

It is also worth emphasising that local and central governments in China have a centuries-long history of mutual secrecy and figure-fudging to preserve and promote their own individual interests. This culturally engrained relationship of mutual deception among Mandarins has even entered the Chinese lexicon of oft-quoted proverbs, 天高皇帝远 – "The mountains (heaven) are high, and the Emperor is far away."

Like any government, China's has to deal with gaps in the data, and constantly shifting definitions as its economy rapidly becomes ever more diverse. There is also the problem of corruption, again not a problem that only China faces, which leads to utter deceit on the part of some politicians and business leaders who milk the system to line their own pockets and fabricate numbers to hide their misdeeds. For the Communist Party of China (CPC) national statistics are about measuring how well it is doing in providing the best it can for its 1.3 billion people, managing its economy, managing its trade and foreign relations, managing its officials and companies and managing its finances. Power may be won through the barrel of a gun, as was oft-quoted of Mao Zedong, but is sustained through the access to, control and utilisation of information. To quote Winston Churchill, "History is written by the victors."[2]

There is the misconception that because China's communist government has been in power for over 60 years, its control of the whole of China must be complete. This is to confuse the reality. China has 1.3 billion people, a people known for their entrepreneurial zeal and their historical culture of politely ignoring as much imperial edict as they can get away with. Those people are administered by 40 million or so local government officials, who are likewise prone to their own human idiosyncrasies and interpretations of the "rules" to fit their own local situations. In the realm of data gathering, there has always and will always most likely be a significant difference between what people really get up to economically, and what they report, even where they try to be as truthful as possible. I have seen enough consumer survey data from China to know that what people report they do, with all the best will in the world, does not accurately portray what they really do.

Without access to the sources and methodologies used to gather statistics, cold, hard numbers published are difficult to argue with, even where the data appears to contradict other sets of data. Government policy decisions, not just in China but everywhere with sensible governments, often hinge on key statistics to prove that policy changes are warranted, for example, figures on economic growth, on unemployment, on trade surpluses or deficits, immigration data, etc. The political arguments for or against a course of policy change will rely on interpretation of data, and that interpretation will rely on scrutiny of the way the data was collected, the definitions of what is or is not included or what data has not been collected.

In an open democracy, such scrutiny of and debate about the validity of data is not only common but it is constant, and is a process that helps to underpin the way governments try to make the right decisions for the benefit of their nations and people. That scrutiny does not need to exist in the same way where a government is not answerable to an elected opposition, to cross-party review committees, to apolitical constitutional judges, to regulators, to independent non-governmental organisations (NGOs), etc. But the Chinese government does face a strongly concerned and increasingly well-informed and vocal citizenry who are also increasingly finding their voice in challenging central and local government to provide more accountability, especially in the face of blatant corruption. The new Chinese leadership is also coming to realise that it needs its 40 million or so local officials to report data that, rather than meeting expectations laid out in top-down policy, actually reflects the reality on the ground, otherwise its own decision-making processes will be based on erroneous data.

China is not a democracy. Officially, as enshrined by Mao Zedong within the Constitution[3] of the People's Republic of China (PRC), it is a "people's democratic dictatorship (人民民主专政)" led by the working class and based on the alliance of workers and peasants with the premise that the CPC and the state act on behalf of the people and that dictatorship by the CPC is necessary to protect the state and the people of China from social elements that would threaten to undermine the rule of the CPC and the existence of the PRC. It serves well for those wishing to understand China to remember that it is still very much a communist state, and that that state continues to be subservient to the CPC.

CHINA'S KEY DECISION-MAKING BODIES

Under the rule of the CPC, as enshrined in the constitution, the following are the key decision-making bodies of government:

The State Council is the executive of the government. It is chaired by the premier and manned by the ministers of each government department.

The National People's Congress (NPC) is China's parliament.

The Chinese People's Political Consultative Conference (CPPC) is China's "House of Lords" – an advisory body of experts from various fields.

The National Development and Reform Commission (NDRC) is the top economic decision-making body in China.

The People's Liberation Army (PLA) is not an executive decision-making body within the government but is the power behind the throne and owes its allegiance to the CPC, not the State!

This is an important point, because protecting the CPC is seen as protecting the state and the people, which means that the Party controls information about itself, the state and the people with the prime motive of self-preservation of its interests. There are no formal outside checks and measures for the Party, only internal ones. Control of information is a means of protecting the rule of the Party. If the Party is damaged, so (it is claimed), by extension, are the state and the people. This is the mandate for control of information, a mandate that means the Party can decide what data the extra-Party world is allowed to see, or not see. It is important to note that in China, there is the published data and the data that nobody outside the upper echelons of the CPC gets to see. But becoming an integral part of the worldwide economy and bringing its citizens into the club of significant consumption all mean that it can no longer keep everything secret, even when it might sometimes prefer and try to do.

The July 2009 arrest of several Rio Tinto employees involved in negotiations with Chinese steel makers over the price of iron ore, and their subsequent trial in March 2010, illustrated how the Chinese state can become very aggressive in protecting its interests through information by deeming certain information as state secrets. The details of what those secrets were are not completely clear, as the trial was held in closed proceedings,[4] and that information was not published. Apparently, several of the men who were charged denied stealing state secrets but all of them pleaded guilty to accepting bribes.

Deciding what is or is not going to be viewed as a state secret can be tricky. Clearly anything to do with China's military will be sensitive (likewise, anything referring to troublesome issues like Taiwan, Tibet and Xinjiang). But would it be normal for the location or operating state of oil wells owned by a state-owned oil company necessarily to be deemed as state secrets? For naturalised US citizen Xue Feng, who was a US energy consulting company employee, his attempts to get hold of a database of that information landed him an eight-year prison sentence.[5] Oil production could admittedly be seen as strategically important for a country, but the grey legal area about what is permissible data means that interpretation of the law can be arbitrary. It could, for instance, be decided that any financial data about any state-owned company in China not included in that company's published financial reports might be regarded as a state secret, even if that data points to accounting irregularities or malfeasance, or perhaps especially so.

Even without the invocation of "state secret" as a barrier to information, the Chinese state is very careful in what it chooses to publish or not. Take the example of China's pollution statistics. Debate rages between independent observers and the government about how bad the air really is in China's cities, even though the problem is often so visibly bad that it would seem there could be no denying the scale of the problem. The government of course gathers environmental data, such as fine particle air pollution, but the readings the government publishes for the air quality in Beijing often greatly understate what the US Embassy in Beijing separately and independently measures. Even a report based on cooperative research carried out by the World Bank and China's State Environmental Protection Administration (SEPA), which has since become the Chinese Ministry of Environment (MoE), was buried when the findings were taken to be too sensitive to publish[6] by the latter.

The Devil is in the definitions

The methodologies used to create statistical data in China, and the definitions used to set what it is to be measured, can also remain frustratingly opaque. There can perhaps be no more significant instance of this than the lack of clarity surrounding China's gross domestic product (GDP) figures. This topic is explored in more detail in Chapter 1 (The Big Numbers), but is worth mentioning here because it highlights both the significance of the problem with data gathering and reporting, the seriousness with which agencies outside China take this problem (not least of which the US government[7]), and why fixating on just that one data set can blinker understanding of what is really going on in the economy.

In its 28 January 2013 Staff Research Project document entitled "*The Reliability of China's Economic Data: An Analysis of National Output*" by Iacob N. Koch-Weser (USCC Policy Analyst, Economics and Trade), the US–China Economic and Security Review Commission states that "*... there are serious deficiencies in the way the Chinese government gathers, measures, and presents its data.*" The report goes on to detail specific problems,[8] citing the overreliance on retail sales as a measure of consumption in China, in particular. This is a specific area that has been picked up as being of particular concern among other China watchers, with reference to the underreporting of data on services consumption in particular. The US–China Economic and Security Review Commission report also highlights that despite there being laws in place to ensure accurate economic data reporting, false reporting continues to be a significant problem, while official economic measures often remain unrepresentative and their methodology and their definition opaque. The problems with methodology and definition are compounded by data series being subject to revision without adjustment to historical data, rendering much historical data useless and, frankly, misleading.

The report, like many recent journal articles, indicates growing wariness about the real reported size of the Chinese economy. There is no dispute that China's economy has grown fast, or that it has become the second largest national economy in the world after the US, but it does call into question the data upon which so many business and political decisions are made in reference to China's economy. Indeed, it is because China has become such a large economy that so much importance is placed on the problems with the data and so much discussion is conducted about it.

Deconstructing expectations

China presents a deconstruction of expectations, culture shock and often defiance in the face of logic to companies arriving there to do business. During my 20 years China-watching, I have observed many foreign companies enter China only to fail, often spectacularly, due to completely misunderstanding and being overwhelmed by China. Those many past examples provide warnings to why those looking to invest in China need to be wary about how they approach the market.

Most of my experience with China data has been in working with the market sizing, sectoral breakdown and company shares of retail sales of consumer products and services to Chinese consumers, and particularly, more recently, the emerging "middle classes" of China – I use the inverted commas deliberately. In 2006, I took a sabbatical from report writing for about six months to spend time completely re-calculating all of the sectors within the China retail market, food and non-food products. The motive was growing concern, both my own and among others working on China data, that the official market size figures for domestic consumer expenditure and retail sales as published by the Chinese government were significantly wrong.

The result of that work became the backbone of my own company's reporting on China's retail markets, and was also published in the fourth quarter edition in 2006 of the *China Economic Quarterly*. One of the headline findings of that research summed up in the article was that real retail sales in China in 2005 were at most about half as much as indicated by the commonly cited official "total retail sales of consumer goods" number. So, up to that point, anyone or any business investing in a consumer product market in China using the official retail sales figures was basing their business plans on a set of numbers that were twice the size of the retail market reality! This went a long way to explaining why so many foreign companies in China were struggling to meet the revenue targets they had projected on market entry based on per capita retail sales figures that did not represent the real situation.

Another six years on, and although the reporting of data has improved much, and more data has become available, there are still significant pitfalls. The margins of error might have narrowed, but they still represent a stumbling block to real understanding. This is especially so at the micro-economic level. The big numbers have their uses, but increasingly businesses in China need to know about provincial, city or even city district retail sales, specific product market sizes, packaging trends, narrow consumer segment data by age group, gender, level of education, expendable income, etc. It is no use having just macro data any more – or perhaps, one could argue, having it at all. But with the focus now on ever narrower areas of statistical data come new sets of problems.

At the micro-market level, China is now awash with all kinds of market data from many types of sources, including local and central government, local and central trade associations, banks, trade development administrations, chambers of commerce, manufacturers, retailers, academics, market research companies and a plethora of "consultants" and "experts." They all ply their trade in creating data to suit their own profitable ends. Lots of people make their living by promoting their industry and attracting investment, and will naturally choose the numbers that best boost their chances of success, safe in the knowledge that they can probably get away with excessive positive spin on the numbers because either nobody cares to check or nobody has any better idea what the real situation is anyway. Lack of due diligence over market or company claims continues to hurt companies investing in China.

The competition to meet the growing demand for commercial market research in China has also spawned a wide variety of market research companies. There was a similar rash of new research companies opening for business in the 1990s, but many of those proved to be front operations for something else entirely, either being government agency subsidiaries using government generated data to earn an income from unsuspecting subscribers, or nefarious companies using market research fronts to launder illegal money obtained from other rather darker activities. Most have since vanished.

Many of the local market research companies that remain continue to ply a trade in bare-bones data with little added-value analysis. Much of the data produced is given scant supporting detail about methodology or definition, and most is still generic data gathered from government sources, or government-sponsored/supported trade agencies, with little regard taken to filtering that data for bias. But here, too, things are improving. Some Chinese research firms now provide much more detailed and insightful data, and more creative ways to use online and social media to test data on markets and consumer trends.

Everything you say about China is right; everything you say about China is wrong

So you have the trade boosters, from provincial statistics authorities down to dubious consultants. But there are also plenty of vested interests in China with good cause to massage the numbers downwards (or upwards, depending on need) to hide income from the tax authorities. Or to hide losses from investors. Or to hide corrupt siphoning of money into off-shore bank accounts for eventual use in paying for expensive luxuries, villas, private education for children of mistresses or gambling debts incurred on a recent trip to Macau. There are also the often less than thorough journalistic writings of those who report data without giving it due scrutiny or only framing data within a narrow context without looking at the broad picture and repercussions surrounding that data. And once it gets published, it often becomes fact merely because it is published.

There are motives at all levels of Chinese society and business to mould the data to suit a purpose, rather than have a purpose based on real data. Even where there is earnest research work into market sizes and company sales shares, there will always be a level of data pollution, almost impossible to eradicate, that will taint the figures produced. In smaller countries, with smaller populations, those marginal errors are not much amplified, but in China those errors become greatly amplified because of its sheer size.

Twenty years of trying to make sense of China's data has taught me that even attempting to claim having clean figures is a chimera and that it is better to be realistic, learn to look behind the figures that are available and try to filter out as much of the chaff as possible, then pass on any findings with all the methodological and definitional caveats necessary. On top of that is the need to apply the common sense that can be gained through direct observation. There is no use in ivory-tower research and taking published data at face value. If you really want to know what is going on in China's markets, there is no better research method than walking down the street and watching what really goes on.

China is so big and complex that it requires, demands, a more nuanced level of understanding than mere numbers can give. Perhaps the biggest myth about China is that the numbers actually mean as much, or are as important to the understanding of the country, as the amount of attention paid to them suggests. Many of the numbers we know are wrong continue to be quoted long after they have been invalidated.

But, the debate around the big numbers is not going to go away and so, before delving into the trickier, more nuanced debates around statistics in China, let's deal with the oppressively large stuff – the "heavy lifting" of China statistics.

Part I

The National Accounts

chapter 1

The Big Numbers

China's shadow province

Just as I began writing this book, the debate about China's Gross Domestic Product (GDP), and the struggle between central and provincial government over the economic numbers and the growing gap between the two, was beginning to hit the headlines, again. For me it was like meeting an old friend.

As I began to put hyper-pen to virtual paper, the *New York Times*'[1] Didi Kirsten Tatlow wrote a blog piece about how the Chinese media was widely reporting the phenomenon of China's "phantom province." The "province" was the result of the continued divergence between the central government's figure for GDP and the sum of the 31 provincial and centrally run municipality governments' local GDP figures. That discrepancy reached Renminbi (RMB) 5.76 trillion in 2012, roughly equivalent to the GDP of Guangdong province, which was the setting for China's first experiments in open economics through the setting up of Special Economic Zones (SEZs) and has been dubbed the "factory of the world" for being the source of so many export manufacturing goods.

This was one of those statistical anomalies that I had continued watching as the disparity gradually increased over the years, mainly thanks to local governments boosting their figures. The central government does occasional readjustments, such as in 2007 and 2010, to try to maintain some sort of order. However, by the end of 2012, the gap between the provincial GDP sum and the central government figure had surpassed 110% of the latter. Perhaps the most interesting thing about this blog piece was that it quoted Chinese media consternation at the widening gap, as if the yawning anomaly was somehow just too embarrassing to bear. You can see how the gap widens over the years below (Table 1.1).

The divergence of the central and provincial GDP data demands the obvious question about which set of data is correct, or whether either is correct, or whether GDP as a measure of economic size and growth in China is as relevant as the huge amount of attention given to it suggests, given its apparent unreliability. There continues to be much debate among China watchers, economists and investors about the accuracy of China's GDP data, and whether there are better proxy measures for the country's economic growth. For me personally, the top-line GDP figure is increasingly meaningless for China, as

the top-line GDP figure is increasingly meaningless for China

Table 1.1 Ten-year trend in provincial cumulative total GDP versus central total GDP, with percentage degree of disagreement, 2003–2012

	Total GDP data of provinces	Total GDP data of central govt.	% disagreement
2003	13,925.4	13,582.3	2.5
2004	16,758.7	15,987.8	4.6
2005	19,778.9	18,321.7	7.4
2006	23,048.4	21,192.4	8.1
2007	27,562.5	25,730.6	6.7
2008	32,722.0	30,067.0	8.1
2009	36,660.7	33,535.3	8.5
2010	43,273.8	40,151.3	7.2
2011	52,144.1	47,156.4	9.6
2012	57,732.2	51,932.2	10.0

Source: National Bureau of Statistics (NBS) China Statistical Yearbooks, Tables 2.14 or 2.15 depending on edition for total or provinces, and Table 2.1 for total national GDP.

it is for any country. It is telling that China (a country of 1.3 billion people) releases its quarterly GDP data two weeks after each quarter end, and never revises that data, Hong Kong (population 7 million) takes six weeks, while the US (population 314 million) takes eight weeks to publish quarterly data, and provides constant revisions.

The Chinese government remains studiously ambiguous on this point, preferring to focus on highlighting its keystone policy platform of rebalancing "social harmony" within the economy. This is important to understand as China's politicians remain in power based on how they achieve on-the-ground social and economic improvement. They give credence to economic growth that generates the wealth needed to achieve that rebalancing, and local government officials in China continue to put economic growth above much else, with some often undesirable consequences (notably pollution and a growing issue with local government debt). But the government no longer needs to believe any of its own propaganda. It has already lifted a massive number of people out of poverty and achieved an economic "miracle." The Chinese government is now shifting its emphasis onto quality of growth, not just volume of growth.

The Chinese government is now shifting its emphasis onto quality of growth, not just volume of growth

It understands that both sets of GDP figures (central and provincial) serve different political ends. The GDP figures are targeted centrally for each year, with provincial targets set by central government which have to be at least met, if not exceeded, to maintain political "face" and preserve a position of authority within the Party. Not that statistics manipulation is any kind of route to promotion, especially as cooking the statistical books is technically illegal and increasingly frowned upon in practice. But the Chinese leadership understands full well that GDP is not a good indicator of "social harmony," and that getting a better sense of how things are progressing requires the use of other, perhaps more accurate indicators of economic growth, industrial health and from that social stability. The leadership is also increasingly facing the fact that incentivising its 40 million administrators based on volume growth alone can no longer work, and that it has to incentivise more based on other, better indicators.

Since the start of 2013, the local and central GDP figures have continued to diverge, along with their different political ends. According to the official first quarter 2013 China figures, GDP grew, apparently, by 7.7%. Here are the figures direct from the NBS (see Table 1.2).

But, looking at the data from each provincial statistics bureau for the same quarter, every single province within China grew faster than the national total (see Table 1.3).

This defies logic, and indicates that local government officials are still playing games with economic data to preserve political careers, as the NBS itself is increasingly finding.[2] If the Q1 figures are indicative of how the total year figures will go, based on their proportion to the 2012 data, then at the end of 2013 I expect to see an 11% discrepancy

Table 1.2 China's GDP by sector, Q1 2013

	Absolute value (RMB 100 million)	YoY growth rate (%)
Gross Domestic Products	**118,854.8**	**7.7**
Primary industry	**7,427.0**	**3.4**
-Farming, forestry, animal husbandry, and fishery	7,427.0	3.4
Secondary industry	**54,569.3**	**7.8**
-Industry	48,832.5	7.5
-Construction	5,736.8	9.8
Tertiary industry	**56,858.6**	**8.3**
-Transport, storage and post	6,563.4	7.0
-Wholesale and retail trades	11,913.9	10.5
-Hotel and catering services	2,418.8	4.5
-Financial intermediation	8,098.5	11.5
-Real estate	8,382.9	7.8
-Others	19,481.0	6.8

Source: NBS China Statistical Information Network (www.stats.gov.cn).

CHINA'S FIVE-YEAR PLANS

Since 1953, China has had a series of social and economic development Five-Year Plans. In Soviet-style command economy logic, each plan sets out the economic and social development targets to be met, including GDP growth, job creation, food security, etc.

The plan is passed down to each government ministry, provincial and local governments, and they dutifully fulfil all the requirements of the plan, at least on paper.

Since 2006, the Five-Year Plans have become Five-Year Guidelines, indicating a shift in emphasis, so that rather than claiming to achieve all set targets, whether achieved or not, local officials might aim to get near to the guidelines and report the true results.

Old habits, and official promotional bonus systems, die hard!

between the cumulative total of provincial GDP data and the central NBS total GDP national figure, based on my own calculations.

A change of plan

The latest Chinese leadership plan is driven by an attempt to stamp out corruption among the 40 million or so local government officials, without which economic reform will go nowhere. An immediate effect of government bans on excessive banquets and extravagance by officials was that spending on Chinese New Year banquets reduced in early 2013, causing a strong loss in earnings for many restaurants and retailers and a delay in some big restaurant chains, such as South Beauty, pursuing initial public offerings (IPOs).

But any immediate pain is necessary to decouple the rent-seeking and collusion among officials using public money to invest in companies

Table 1.3 China's GDP growth by province, Q1 2013

Provinces	YoY GDP growth
Anhui	11.2
Beijing	7.9
Chongqing	12.5
Fujian	11.3
Gansu	12.9
Guangdong	8.5
Guangxi	10.5
Guizhou	12.6
Hainan	10.5
Hebei	9.1
Heilongjiang	9.0
Henan	8.8
Hubei	9.7
Hunan	10.1
Inner Mongolia	9.9
Jiangsu	9.7
Jiangxi	10.3
Jilin	10.2
Liaoning	9.0
Ningxia	8.6
Qinghai	10.1
Shaanxi	11.2
Shandong	9.7
Shanghai	7.8
Shanxi	9.5
Sichuan	10.2
Tianjin	12.5
Tibet	12.2
Xinjiang	10.3
Yunnan	12.6
Zhejiang	8.3
Total provinces	9.4
Total China	7.7

Source: NBS China Statistical Information Network (www.stats.gov.cn) and provincial statistics bureaux.

and projects from which they get kick-backs, for the long-term health of the economy. Many officials are keeping their heads low to avoid drawing attention to themselves from the Communist Party of China's (CPC) disciplinary machinery. Many officials have complained of being bugged by political rivals.[3] They know that the CPC cannot physically investigate all 40 million of them to expose their graft, so they are being careful to cover their own tracks, meanwhile making sure they have the dirt on their competitors.

But the latest plan appears to be an earnest push by the new leadership to untangle the webs of vested interest that stifle real growth of efficiency in the economy and lift China up the value-added chain. This reform plan has not necessarily made the numbers any better yet, but it has helped to lift the lid on the corruption that in part causes the distortion in the data.

"Use a proxy!" he suggested

Incoming Chinese premier Li Keqiang was himself quoted, in a controversial US diplomatic cable published by Wikileaks in 2011, as saying that China's GDP figures were "man-made" and therefore only one indicator of the growth and size of China's economy. This quote was apparently made by Li to the US ambassador in a meeting held in 2007, when he was also quoted as saying that focus should be placed on indicators such as electricity consumption, rail cargo and bank loans. GDP figures are all best estimates, whichever country they come from. A small, well-ordered country, like Singapore, is probably able to produce more accurate GDP data than China, which makes sense given Singapore has only 5 million people to China's 1.3 billion (give or take). But even tiny Singapore's data can never be entirely accurate. Human society is just too untidy around the edges and is constantly becoming more complex.

The Chinese leadership is not alone in using proxy indicators to measure more realistic growth for China's economy. Stephen Green, regional head of research for Greater China at Standard Chartered Bank, has for several years used such proxies (among them electricity generation, freight volume, diesel consumption and concrete production) in his "On the Ground – China" series of economic monitoring documents. In mid-February 2013, Green postulated that China's GDP growth in 2012 was only 5.5%, arguing that the index used to deflate nominal GDP to real figures was inadequate, and put forward other proxy indicators to try to map real growth in the Chinese economy. Other countries use proxy indicators of economic progress or regression, including unemployment figures, trade balance, millions of barrels of oil pumped from the ground, etc.

In his February 2013 document, Green focused on steel production, cement production and same-store sales from Yum! Brands' stores in China (mainly KFC and Pizza Hut, but also local cuisine offerings Little Sheep and East Dawning) to work as proxies for manufacturing, construction and consumer expenditure. Green's central argument was that GDP is unlikely to be as high as reported, given the significantly lower growth in these indicators. Those indicators are not as far-fetched as they might seem, nor is the contention that China's GDP growth was as low as 5.5% in 2012. Much more reliable a measure is value added to the economy.

Value added equates to wealth created that goes into consumer incomes and spending. While China retools its economy more towards one reliant on domestic consumption for growth, it is consumer spending data that increasingly become the prime indicator of what is really going on in China's economy now, and, much more importantly, in the future. It is for this reason that the concern about how China's GDP is slowing ignores the story about how China's retail economy seems to continue to power ahead at low double-digit figures. Are 14.4% year-on-year nominal retail sales growth rates really a sign of economic slowdown? Even removing the 3% or so of retail inflation, growth remains above 10%. Few other countries in the world are enjoying such rates of growth in their retail economies.

But the inflation rates are also a bone of contention. In his August 2013 paper, unabashedly titled "*How Badly Flawed is Chinese Economic*

*Data? The Opening Bid is $1 Trillion,"* Christopher Balding, Associate Professor of the HSBC Business School at Peking University, suggests that, because of using incorrect consumer inflation rates, skewed by an 80:20 urban/rural weighting since 2000 (when only a third of the population was urban), and further distorted by China's understated and weirdly uniform unemployment statistics, China's real GDP is overstated by, you guessed it, about US$ 1 trillion. His conclusion: that China's economic statistics require some no small measure of revision.

There is also the argument, which follows the Li Keqiang logic, that GDP is not that useful a data set. Does it really matter if China's GDP is the world's second biggest? It is not as though investors can buy shares in China Incorporated. Indeed, it makes sense that the economy of the world's most populous nation will eventually, given continuing favourable conditions, become the world's biggest economy thanks merely to its demographic size. Because it is such a large and rapidly developing country, its statistics will at best be estimates. More important is what is going on under those top-line figures.

GDP – the fundamental particles

As Andy Rothman at Hong Kong-based investment bank CLSA has often argued, China continues to be the "world's best consumption story." With the world increasingly looking less at China as a cheap factory, and more as a consumer market to sell to, the rate at which domestic consumption rises in significance within the Chinese economy is a more important indicator of China's macroeconomic health.

I explore the consumer economy later in this book, but it is worth looking at the contributing dimensions that make up GDP (including consumption) to better understand their relative and changing significance to China's national wealth. Table 1.4 shows how China's GDP component figures are shifting towards the tertiary industry (domestic consumption and services) end of the spectrum, with secondary industry (manufacturing and construction) continuing a steady decline in significance, between 2006 and 2012.

Table 1.4 Key components of China's GDP, 2006–2012

RMB trillion (current prices)	GDP	Primary industry	Secondary industry	Manufacturing	Construction	Tertiary industry
2006	21.6	2.4	10.4	9.1	1.2	8.9
2007	26.6	2.9	12.6	11.1	1.5	11.1
2008	31.4	3.4	14.9	13.0	1.9	13.1
2009	34.1	3.5	15.8	13.5	2.2	14.8
2010	40.2	4.1	18.7	16.1	2.7	17.4
2011	47.3	4.7	22.0	18.8	3.2	20.5
2012	51.9	5.2	23.5	20.0	3.5	23.2
% of GDP						
2006	100.0	11.1	47.9	42.2	5.7	40.9
2007	100.0	10.8	47.3	41.6	5.8	41.9
2008	100.0	10.7	47.4	41.5	6.0	41.8
2009	100.0	10.3	46.2	39.7	6.6	43.4
2010	100.0	10.1	46.7	40.0	6.6	43.2
2011	100.0	10.0	46.6	39.9	6.8	43.3
2012	100.0	10.1	45.3	38.5	6.8	44.6

Note: Totals may not sum due to rounding.

Source: NBS China Statistical Yearbook 2012, Table 2.1.

Primary (agricultural) industry seems to have halted its decline as a proportion of GDP. Land lease reform has allowed rural Chinese to sell their land leases, in recent years, to large-scale farming cooperatives that bundle adjacent land parcels to be farmed at more efficient scales using better technology and mechanisation, raising land yield and productivity. If agriculture in China can grow by raising its productivity, and there are those who say China[4] can still greatly increase its agricultural yield per hectare, then this would counter the argument that China cannot support a population growth not hemmed in by the One Child Policy. However, despite the potential rise in yield, there remains doubt whether China's agricultural industry can grow fast enough to keep up with the cost of labour and not push food prices too high. More likely, China is going to have to learn to both raise yields whilst also live with rising food costs and greater reliance on international food trade. The old prime objective of the CPC, to remain self-sufficient in food, looks increasingly unsustainable and undesirable.

In 2012, the trend continues, and below we see that the two sectors driving tertiary industry growth the fastest are wholesale and retail trades and financial services (Table 1.5). Rapid urbanisation and economic growth have doubled the average salary in the past ten years, and as urbanisation continues, more new city dwellers will likely enjoy improvement in their average wages, allowing them to become significant consumers. More hinterland cities will grow their economies as "export" manufacturers, not towards far-off countries, but other cities in China where the consumer demand is strongest. Although this data is no more reliable than top-line GDP, it does give an indication of how things are shifting.

GDP – the consumption conundrum

But if we compare tertiary industry added value with the total for rural and urban domestic household expenditure, we find domestic household consumption represents almost all of tertiary industry added value between 2008 and 2010, exceeds it in 2007, and thus must

Table 1.5 Key components within China's GDP, Q1–4, 2012

RMB trillion (current prices)	Absolute value	% of total GDP	YoY growth (%)
Gross Domestic Products	**51.9**	**100.0**	**7.8**
Primary industry	**5.2**	**10.1**	**4.5**
-Farming, forestry, animal husbandry and fishery	5.2	10.1	4.5
Secondary industry	**23.5**	**45.3**	**8.1**
-Industry	20.0	38.5	7.9
-Construction	3.5	6.8	9.3
Tertiary industry	**23.2**	**44.6**	**8.1**
-Transport, storage, and post	2.5	4.8	7.0
-Wholesale and retail trades	5.0	9.7	11.9
-Hotel and catering services	1.0	2.0	7.8
-Financial intermediation	2.9	5.5	9.9
-Real estate	2.9	5.6	3.8
-Others	8.8	17.0	7.3

Notes:

1. Totals may not sum due to rounding.
2. Absolute value is computed at current price, growth rate is computed at constant price.
3. Statistical data in this Table are preliminary accounting results according to the data in 2011.

Source: NBS China Statistical Information Network (www.stats.gov.cn).

be exaggerated. These figures don't include government expenditure, which adds another RMB 5.3 trillion in 2010, rising to RMB 6.4 trillion in 2011. However, they do miss out large chunks of the services sector.

What is also striking in these figures is that in the four years between 2007 and 2010, urban consumer spending grew by almost 50%. While the rest of the world began to suffer financial crisis, China began shifting economic emphasis away from export manufacturing towards domestic consumption. But there is a whiff of exaggeration in this consumption data (Table 1.6).

If GDP is a sum of consumption, investment, government spending and net exports, then public procurement is a major factor in shaping

Table 1.6 China's tertiary industry and rural/urban household expenditure by sector, 2007–2010

RMB trillion (current prices)/% of total	2007		2008		2009		2010	
Tertiary industry value added	**11.1**	**41.9**	**13.1**	**41.8**	**14.8**	**43.4**	**17.4**	**43.2**
Total household expenditure	**11.2**	**100.0**	**12.4**	**100.0**	**14.1**	**100.0**	**16.5**	**100.0**
Rural household	**2.8**	**24.8**	**2.9**	**23.5**	**3.2**	**22.7**	**3.7**	**22.7**
-Food	1.1	10.2	1.1	9.2	1.2	8.7	1.4	8.5
-Clothing	0.2	1.3	0.2	1.3	0.2	1.3	0.2	1.4
-Residence	0.5	4.5	0.5	3.9	0.5	3.6	0.6	3.5
-Household facilities, articles and services	0.1	1.1	0.2	1.3	0.2	1.4	0.3	1.5
-Health care and personal articles	0.2	2.2	0.3	2.5	0.4	2.6	0.5	2.8
-Transportation and communications	0.3	2.3	0.3	2.3	0.3	2.2	0.4	2.2
-Recreation, education and culture articles	0.2	2.0	0.2	1.9	0.2	1.8	0.3	1.6
-Financial service	0.1	0.5	0.0	0.4	0.1	0.5	0.1	0.5
-Insurance service	0.0	0.2	0.0	0.2	0.0	0.2	0.0	0.2
-Others	0.1	0.5	0.1	0.5	0.1	0.5	0.1	0.5
Urban household	**8.4**	**75.2**	**9.5**	**76.5**	**10.9**	**77.3**	**12.8**	**77.3**
-Food	2.6	23.5	2.8	23.0	3.2	22.4	3.7	22.7
-Clothing	0.7	6.4	0.8	6.6	0.9	6.7	1.1	6.9
-Residence	1.4	12.7	1.6	12.9	1.9	13.6	2.2	13.1
-Household facilities, articles and services	0.4	3.8	0.5	4.0	0.6	4.3	0.7	4.3

(continued)

Table 1.6 Continued

RMB trillion (current prices)/% of total	2007		2008		2009		2010	
-Health care and personal articles	0.7	6.6	0.9	7.1	1.0	7.1	1.3	7.6
-Transportation and communications	0.9	7.8	1.1	8.6	1.3	9.3	1.5	8.9
-Recreation, education and culture articles	0.8	7.5	0.9	7.6	1.1	7.6	1.3	7.6
-Financial service	0.2	1.9	0.2	1.6	0.3	2.3	0.4	2.2
-Insurance service	0.2	1.4	0.2	1.3	0.2	1.5	0.3	1.5
-Others	0.4	3.6	0.5	3.8	0.3	2.3	0.4	2.4

Source: NBS China Statistical Yearbook 2012, Table 2.19.

the economy. And extravagant spending by officialdom on the public purse distorts the real size of China's retail market. Since taking office, one of the new leadership's first acts was to ban such extravagances, which often saw local government officials overpaying by as much as four or five times[5] for products like consumer electronics in return for kick-backs from the retailers/brands! The central government stipulates that government procurement prices should be wholesale, and below retail.[6] There was RMB 1.13 trillion in official government procurement in 2012, up by 10% on 2011. However, if other procurements are also included, such as social housing subsidies, education, healthcare and railways, total procurement could have been as high as RMB 8 trillion[7] in 2011. GDP in that year was RMB 47.3 trillion, so government procurement may really represent 17% of GDP.

There have been many scandals surrounding government procurement in the media (notably Liu Zhijun, China's ex-minister of railways, given a suspended death sentence in July 2013), and most have centred on government suppliers promising "commissions" (bribery/kick-backs) on purchases to buyers to win project bids, allowing the buyers to skim commissions into their own pockets. If public procurement scams are as rampant as suggested by the Chinese media, the surprisingly unmoving percentage of consumption GDP attributed to government expenditure looks too small and too stable. This indicates that the official procurement figures are not reliable – a point the central government is doubtless upset about, and working to rectify through punishment of corrupt officials.

Reported under gross capital formation are investments in fixed assets used in production, such as factories, machinery and vehicles. The new government leadership has also been cracking down on private car sales to government officials and company bosses, who, rather than using their own money, use public or company money to buy cars used as their own private vehicles, accounting such purchases as business (production) assets. So the massive growth in gross capital formation not only includes over-charging by suppliers for government procurement – and likewise State Owned Enterprises (SOE) procurement – but also such "investments" in production "assets" that are nothing more than personal purchases made with public money.

This kind of corrupt use of public funds even extends into the People's Liberation Army (PLA), which in early 2013 began an audit of PLA-owned cars due to too many cadres buying luxury cars, including Mercedes-Benz and Porsches, which have nothing to do with public need, are an inflation of public spending and an inflation of real market demand for private cars in China.

The car market has long been subsidised by the government to create demand and build flagship manufacturers. But it has also created pollution and traffic mayhem in China's cities. This has forced a growing number of cities in China to limit the number of cars allowed to be sold, usually by limiting car registration plates. Many smaller cities began following the lead of tier-one cities like Beijing, Shanghai and Guangzhou in 2013, by introducing limits to car sales. Suzhou, Hangzhou and Shenzhen have begun considering such limits, while Guiyang (capital of Guizhou province) introduced vehicle purchase limits in 2011.

Despite this, and the accumulated bad press in the industry due to car recalls for manufacturing faults, the car companies keep ramping up their sales expansion plans. During April 2013's Shanghai Auto Show, Volkswagen announced plans to build seven new plants in China in the near future to reach an output capacity of 4 million cars a year by 2018. They hope to build cars to grow sales in interior and western cities, where car ownership is lower, including cities such as Guiyang, just as they are looking to cap car sales. For its part, in May 2013, Mercedes-Benz announced plans to offer 20 new China-specific car models, and to sell 300,000 units in China by 2015, of which two-thirds would be made locally, and open 75 new dealerships by the end of 2013 in tier-3 and -4 cities. In May 2013, Cadillac announced plans to open a new plant in Shanghai's Pudong district to eventually make 150,000 cars.

Looking at official data on government expenditure by type of expenditure (Table 1.8), we also see that even declared spending within the statistical yearbook section on government accounts is much higher than the declared expenditure within the GDP account in the same yearbook. There is no attempt in the yearbook to explain the different

Table 1.7 China GDP by expenditure approach, 2000–2011

RMB trillion	GDP by expenditure approach	Total final consumption expenditures	Household consumption expenditures	Rural house-hold	Urban house-hold	Government consumption expenditures	Gross capital formation	Net exports
2000	9.9	6.2	4.6	1.5	3.1	1.6	3.5	0.2
2001	10.9	6.7	4.9	1.6	3.4	1.7	4.0	0.2
2002	12.0	7.2	5.3	1.6	3.7	1.9	4.6	0.3
2003	13.7	7.8	5.8	1.6	4.1	2.0	5.6	0.3
2004	16.1	8.8	6.5	1.8	4.8	2.2	6.9	0.4
2005	18.7	9.9	7.3	2.0	5.3	2.6	7.8	1.0
2006	22.3	11.3	8.3	2.2	6.1	3.1	9.3	1.7
2007	26.7	13.2	9.6	2.4	7.2	3.6	11.1	2.3
2008	31.6	15.3	11.2	2.8	8.4	4.2	13.8	2.4
2009	34.9	16.9	12.4	2.9	9.5	4.6	16.4	1.5
2010	40.3	19.4	14.1	3.2	10.9	5.3	19.4	1.5
2011	46.6	22.9	16.5	3.7	12.8	6.4	22.5	1.2
% of GDP								
2000	100.0	62.3	46.4	15.3	31.1	15.9	35.3	2.4
2001	100.0	61.4	45.3	14.5	30.9	16.0	36.5	2.1
2002	100.0	59.6	44.0	13.5	30.5	15.6	37.8	2.6

(continued)

Table 1.7 Continued

RMB trillion	GDP by expenditure approach	Total final consumption expenditures	Household consumption expenditures	Rural house-hold	Urban house-hold	Government consumption expenditures	Gross capital formation	Net exports
2003	100.0	56.9	42.2	11.9	30.3	14.7	41.0	2.2
2004	100.0	54.4	40.5	11.0	29.5	13.9	43.0	2.6
2005	100.0	53.0	38.9	10.6	28.3	14.1	41.5	5.4
2006	100.0	50.8	37.1	9.8	27.3	13.7	41.7	7.5
2007	100.0	49.6	36.1	9.1	27.1	13.5	41.6	8.8
2008	100.0	48.6	35.3	8.8	26.6	13.2	43.8	7.7
2009	100.0	48.5	35.4	8.3	27.1	13.1	47.2	4.3
2010	100.0	48.2	34.9	7.9	27.0	13.2	48.1	3.7
2011	100.0	49.1	35.4	8.0	27.4	13.7	48.3	2.6

Source: NBS China Statistical Yearbooks Tables 2.17, GDP by Expenditure Approach, and Tables 2.18, Components of GDP by Expenditure Approach.

outcomes of two measures of the same thing. The government expenditure total based on the sum of the constituent parts is a much larger figure than in the GDP by expenditure table (Table 1.7) for total consumption expenditure by government in 2011, to the tune of RMB 4.5 trillion. But this does not take into account the government procurement figures cited above, which could be more accurately put at approximately RMB 8 trillion. Clearly, the government expenditure within the economy is not being reflected in official figures.

Retail versus income and savings growth

Retail sales figures are also larger than household consumption expenditure, so must include non-retail sales to government and commercial (business-to-business) consumers. Something is amiss between what are officially classed as retail sales and what the real figures are – a point considered in more detail in the third part of this book.

As seen in Table 1.9, retail sales continue to outpace growth in personal income without a proportional decrease in savings. The logical outcome should be that retail sales reflect some combination of growth in incomes and a proportional decline in savings. So either income growth is understated, or savings growth or retail sales growth is overstated.

It is unlikely that savings rates are overstated, as the data about the value of the deposits they hold is closely controlled and maintained by the state-run banks. Average urban wages are unlikely to be overstated because, if anything, data from an October 2010 report by China by China Reform Foundation deputy director Professor Wang Xiaolu and Wing Thye Woo of the University of California Davis' Economics Department suggests that the incomes surveyed for the purposes of his study[8] among different income groups were significantly higher than those shown in NBS survey data. Using the same income groupings, Wang found that the group with the smallest percentage divergence from the official figures still has a +17% difference of income compared to the NBS survey data. The highest income group was found to have a +276.1% divergence.

Table 1.8 China government expenditure by type and by central/local government spending, 2011

RMB billion	Total govt. expenditure	Central govt.	Local govt.	% central govt.	% local govt.
National government expenditure	10,924.8	1,651.4	9,273.4	15.1	84.9
General public services	1,098.8	90.3	1,008.5	8.2	91.8
Foreign affairs	31.0	30.7	0.3	99.1	0.9
External assistance	15.9	15.9	0.0	99.9	0.1
National defence	602.8	583.0	19.8	96.7	3.3
Public security	630.4	103.7	526.7	16.4	83.6
Armed police	108.2	79.0	29.2	73.0	27.0
Education	1,649.7	99.9	1,549.8	6.1	93.9
Science and technology	382.8	194.2	188.6	50.7	49.3
Culture, sport and media	189.3	18.9	170.5	10.0	90.0
Social safety net and employment effort	1,110.9	50.2	1,060.7	4.5	95.5
Medical and health care	643.0	7.1	635.8	1.1	98.9
Environment protection	264.1	7.4	256.7	2.8	97.2
Urban and rural community affairs	762.1	1.2	760.9	0.2	99.8
Agriculture, forestry and water conservancy	993.8	41.7	952.1	4.2	95.8
Transportation	749.8	33.1	716.7	4.4	95.6
Purchasing vehicles	231.5	7.3	224.1	3.2	96.8
Affairs of exploration, power and information	401.1	46.4	354.7	11.6	88.4
Affairs of commerce and services	142.2	2.7	139.5	1.9	98.1
Affairs of financial supervision	64.9	41.4	23.5	63.8	36.2
Post-earthquake recovery and reconstruction	17.4	0.0	17.4	0.0	100.0

(continued)

Table 1.8 Continued

RMB billion	Total govt. expenditure	Central govt.	Local govt.	% central govt.	% local govt.
Affairs of land and weather	152.1	23.2	129.0	15.2	84.8
Affairs of housing security	382.1	32.9	349.2	8.6	91.4
Affairs of management of grain and oil reserves	127.0	54.0	72.9	42.5	57.5
Interest payment for domestic and foreign debts	238.4	182.0	56.4	76.3	23.7
Other expenditure	291.1	7.5	283.6	2.6	97.4

Source: Government expenditure in 2011, from NBS China Statistical Yearbook Table 8.15 – Main Items of National Government Expenditure of Central and Local Governments (2011).

Table 1.9 Official total retail and wholesale trade, average urban wage, total household savings and net new household savings, 2003–2012

RMB trn	Total retail and wholesale trade	% annual growth	Average urban wage (RMB)	% annual growth	Total household savings	% annual growth	Net new household savings
2003	4.8	13.3	13,969	12.9	10.4	19.2	1.67
2004	6.0	25.0	15,920	14.0	12.0	15.4	1.59
2005	6.7	12.9	18,200	14.3	14.1	18.0	2.15
2006	7.6	13.7	20,856	14.6	16.2	14.6	2.05
2007	8.9	16.8	24,721	18.5	17.3	6.8	1.09
2008	10.8	21.6	28,898	16.9	21.8	26.3	4.54
2009	12.5	15.5	32,244	11.6	26.1	19.7	4.29
2010	15.5	23.3	36,539	13.3	30.3	16.3	4.25
2011	18.1	17.3	41,799	14.4	34.4	13.3	4.03
2012	20.7	14.3	47,183*	12.9	40.1	16.6	5.71

Note: *www.pbc.gov.cn/publish/diaochatongjisi/3172/2013/20130109165552137337875/20130109165552137337875_.html

Sources: From NBS China Statistical Information Network (www.stats.gov.cn) Total Retail Sales of Consumer Goods (社会消费品零售总额) for months 1–12 for each year, average urban wage from NBS yearbooks Tables 4.13 and total investments and YoY increases in total savings from NBS China Statistical Yearbooks Tables 10.3. 2012 average wage based on first three-quarters YoY growth. 2012 household savings deposits based on the People's Bank of China.

So the official income figures are unreliable, most likely because Chinese citizens feel uncomfortable giving real data to official inspectors. The lack of reliability in the official savings, incomes and retail sales figures are considered in more detail later in this book. But for the purposes of this chapter, it is worth noting that the consumer side of the market is not properly represented within GDP data, further challenging the overall accuracy of GDP data.

Summary

With provincial GDP summed coming to 10% more than central GDP reported, government expenditure not likely to be accurate due to under-reporting of procurement, household expenditure likely to be under-reported due to undervaluing real incomes as a result of a high proportion of "grey" income among consumers, and household spending on housing being under-reported due to not factoring-in real property values, the only conclusion is that the GDP figures must be wrong.

How wrong is difficult to say due to the lack of access to the raw data, and because of the effects of misreporting from corruption. It is impossible for the government to obtain completely reliable data when so much distortion is created and covered up by official institutions. A charge could be made that the Chinese government is holding back on real growth data in order to add it to the accounts later (revise upwards) when growth slows, as a way of boosting the accounts. But it is not really in the interests of the central government to do this, as it needs to know as much as anyone what is really going on, how much wealth is really being created, where it is going and where government tax revenue is falling short.

Via state institutions, the government controls the economy. Free-market economics are allowed but constrained by the state-sector, so to describe China as a free-market economy is incorrect. Even the free-market activity within the country is circumscribed by the Chinese government. So such economic metrics only reflect the outcome of political, not market, will.

GDP is prescribed and produced by the party-state. That there may be contradictions in the data is, as Li Keqiang intimated, of little significance to the party-state. It is more concerned with managing the economy through the institutional levers at its disposal to sustain growth in a direction that maintains social harmony, reduces social conflict, increases social wealth and ultimately legitimises CPC rule over China. It may wish to extract itself from such micro-controls, but that could invite even more corruption.

It is the areas of the economy where China's government has less control that causes more concern both to the government and those trying to ascertain the health of the Chinese economy. It is better to look at GDP in terms of how the country's wealth is being used and distributed and the efficiency of those functions, how that is helping to improve people's lives and how much of that wealth is being used inefficiently, squandered, wasted, stolen, illegally transported overseas or lost to tax evasion, to the detriment of those who would otherwise benefit from that wealth.

This is why the reforms being put forward now, especially the cleaning up of corruption within China's economy and the elevation of the rule of law, are so important. In a report published following a recent International Monetary Fund (IMF) mission to China,[9] the IMF acknowledges that the Chinese government is aware of the problems within its social, political, environmental and economic systems, and that the new leadership is trying to address those problems, but urges them to recognise the urgency of tackling these issues before it is too late.

chapter 2

Fiscal Fudging – Tax, Balancing the Government Books and Paying for Social Harmony

Extracting tax

One problem China's government has extracting tax from the layers of government and both domestic and foreign businesses is that China's tax laws are as new to everyone operating under them in China. This is also true of the legal system, where companies need be cautious lest they fall foul of unexpected turns of legal interpretation. Tax is a complicated issue in any country, not least one as large and fast-growing as China. The room for tax-dodging manoeuvres is wide, and many have found ways to do so, putting the public coffers at a disadvantage. Policing new tax laws can be difficult to implement, both because of the newness of the laws and due to the layers of local government that are open to corruption.

Tax is a complicated issue in any country, not least one as large and fast-growing as China

The central government account balance is increasingly in the black, but meanwhile local governments are increasingly running up debts. The central government can bail out the local governments, assuming the local government debt declared is correct, but there are increasing concerns that local governments are hiding the true amount of debts they are running up (see Table 2.1).

Tax avoidance

According to a report submitted in July 2012 to China's State Council by the State Council Research Centre (SCRC) and the National Development and Reform Commission (NDRC), the country had suffered total tax evasion of an estimated RMB 1 trillion[1] (US$159 billion) during 2011, representing about one tenth of total national government revenue received in that year. This compared with about 8 per cent in the US in 2011.[2] The biggest culprits identified in the report were China's state-owned enterprises (SOEs), to the tune of between 26 per cent and 28 per cent of that total tax evasion figure. No wonder the new leadership quickly showed interest in proposing that SOEs should pay more of their profits back as dividends to the government, for it to use to invest in healthcare, education, unemployment benefit and social housing, all of which are much needed.

That tax evasion is rife in China, and has been going on for decades is undisputed. Addressing tax evasion is increasingly urgent as the government strives to shake out the corruption and cronyism that exacerbates the gap between rich and poor, the potential for social catastrophe it could generate, as well as the unfair environment that stifles more profitable and value-adding businesses. Tax evasion in China is aided by the opportunities that arise from the large amounts of bureaucracy, with multiple layers of registrations and certifications for many economic activities, often crossing government ministries.

For example, there have been several cases of companies faking import data by hiding true quantities of goods brought into the country and the unit values, or by mislabelling higher tax rate goods as those of a lower tax rate. The extent of import duty evasion is also hard to gain strong evidence for, but given the number of ports of entry into China, the sheer volume of goods flow, the number of agencies involved and

Table 2.1 China national and local government revenues and expenditure, 2005–2011

RMB bn	National govt. revenue	National govt. expend.	Net budget deficit	National domestic debt	Central govt. revenue	Central govt. expend.	Net budget deficit	Local govt. revenue	Local govt. expend.	Net budget deficit
2005	3,164.9	3,393.0	228.1	3,261.4	1,654.9	877.6	–777.3	1,510.1	2,515.4	1,005.4
2006	3,876.0	4,042.3	166.3	3,501.5	2,045.7	999.1	–1,046.5	1,830.4	3,043.1	1,212.8
2007	5,132.2	4,978.1	–154.0	5,207.5	2,774.9	1,144.2	–1,630.7	2,357.3	3,833.9	1,476.7
2008	6,133.0	6,259.3	126.2	5,327.2	3,268.1	1,334.4	–1,933.6	2,865.0	4,924.8	2,059.9
2009	6,851.8	7,630.0	778.2	6,023.8	3,591.6	1,525.6	–2,066.0	3,260.3	6,104.4	2,844.2
2010	8,310.2	8,987.4	677.3	6,754.8	4,248.8	1,599.0	–2,649.9	4,061.3	7,388.4	3,327.1
2011	10,387.4	10,924.8	537.3	7,204.5	5,132.7	1,651.4	–3,481.3	5,254.7	9,273.4	4,018.7

Source: NBS China Statistical Yearbooks.

the levels of bureaucracy, it is likely to be significant, possibly as much as 10 per cent of accounted trade.

The tip of the iceberg

It is difficult for anyone, even the Chinese government, to assess the full scale of tax evasion within China

It is difficult for anyone, even the Chinese government, to assess the full scale of tax evasion within China. Assessing the size of such problems is made hard because so much is so well hidden. Multiple layers of paperwork to get things done mean multiple layers at which corrupt officials can skim off bribes unseen. There is also the issue of "ghost employees"[3] in lower-level local government bureaux, whose positions are not only utilised to rubber stamp fake transactions, but even to create salary accounts through which illegal transactions can be pushed. Such ghost employees are also often created to provide jobs for officials' relatives, which they never fulfil.

One interesting case was that of Wenzhou businessman Lin Chunping,[4] who was charged in early 2013 with fabricating value-added tax (VAT) invoices for over 300 companies between July 2011 and May 2012. Lin had allegedly engaged some of his employees to set-up a shell company in Liaoning to fake VAT bills for his own companies, allowing him to evade RMB 7.22 million in tax. Lin also used five companies, that did not actually do any active business, to make profits by charging fees to 315 other companies to help them evade about another RMB 76 million in taxes. Not satisfied with that, Lin also allegedly bought fake Chinese customs tax receipts which provided him with a further RMB 115 million in tax deductions. Lin came to the authorities' attention because he began making grandiose claims about having bought a US bank (the mythical Greater Atlantic Bank of Delaware).

VAT, business tax and corporate income tax avoidance by any scale is a very big problem for China's government, given that these taxes represent the biggest sources of fiscal revenue. Combined, in 2011 these three taxes represented 60.9 per cent of total government income (see Table 2.2). If companies in China are routinely avoiding tax or are

Table 2.2 The importance of the relevant taxes to government revenues, 2000–2011

RMB bn	Total	Domestic value-added tax	Domestic consumption tax	Business tax	Corporate income tax	Individual income tax	Tariffs
2000	1,258.2	455.3	85.8	186.9	100.0	66.0	75.0
2001	1,530.1	535.7	93.0	206.4	263.1	99.5	84.1
2002	1,763.6	617.8	104.6	245.0	308.3	121.2	70.4
2003	2,001.7	723.7	118.2	284.4	292.0	141.8	92.3
2004	2,416.6	901.8	150.2	358.2	395.7	173.7	104.4
2005	2,877.9	1,079.2	163.4	423.2	534.4	209.5	106.6
2006	3,480.4	1,278.5	188.6	512.9	704.0	245.4	114.2
2007	4,562.2	1,547.0	220.7	658.2	877.9	318.6	143.3
2008	5,422.4	1,799.7	256.8	762.6	1,117.6	372.2	177.0
2009	5,952.2	1,848.1	476.1	901.4	1,153.7	394.9	148.4
2010	7,321.1	2,109.3	607.2	1,115.8	1,284.4	483.7	202.8
2011	8,973.8	2,426.7	693.6	1,367.9	1,677.0	605.4	255.9

%	Total	Domestic value-added tax	Domestic consumption tax	Business tax	Corporate income tax	Individual income tax	Tariffs
2000	100.0	36.2	6.8	14.9	7.9	5.2	6.0
2001	100.0	35.0	6.1	13.5	17.2	6.5	5.5
2002	100.0	35.0	5.9	13.9	17.5	6.9	4.0
2003	100.0	36.2	5.9	14.2	14.6	7.1	4.6
2004	100.0	37.3	6.2	14.8	16.4	7.2	4.3
2005	100.0	37.5	5.7	14.7	18.6	7.3	3.7
2006	100.0	36.7	5.4	14.7	20.2	7.1	3.3
2007	100.0	33.9	4.8	14.4	19.2	7.0	3.1
2008	100.0	33.2	4.7	14.1	20.6	6.9	3.3
2009	100.0	31.0	8.0	15.1	19.4	6.6	2.5
2010	100.0	28.8	8.3	15.2	17.5	6.6	2.8
2011	100.0	27.0	7.7	15.2	18.7	6.7	2.9

Source: NBS China Statistical Yearbooks.

involved in financial scams, then the Chinese government faces a huge task in properly deriving the tax it needs to implement its social policy target spending requirements. This is not just about enforcing laws to punish significant fraud cases, but also needing to change Chinese people's perceptions about the need to contribute tax to improve the lot of their fellow countrymen, given that petty tax avoidance is also rife.

The crime of buying fake papers is not even done under the counter, but is often quite brazen, with "companies" faxing out adverts claiming to sell "legitimate" government and corporate receipts so that people and companies can make claims against unmade transactions, thus helping reduce their tax burden. Buying receipts is done not just by individuals, but companies[5] too, and even though most amounts evaded tend to be small, it is the commonplace occurrence of the use of fake receipts that means this kind of tax avoidance accumulates into large amounts when spread across a large number of people.

Among companies, this kind of fake receipt culture leads to the need for multiple bookkeeping, combining the real accounts, the set of accounts that are shown to the government tax authorities and the set shown to business partners. One set to keep the real business running, one to diminish tax liability and one to boost accounts to dupe partner businesses into believing the company is doing better than it really is.

According to the July 2012 report from the SCRC and the NDRC, if the state-owned corporate sector is responsible for 26–28 per cent of evaded taxes, then the other 72–74 per cent must come largely from the private sector – from people like Lin Chunping.

Despite the State Council cracking down on tax evasion, and threatening provincial and local officials in regions where serious tax evasion problems persist with being made accountable, it is hard to see how changing a corporate culture that has tax evasion etched into its genetics will fundamentally be changed easily or quickly. Changing such practices takes much more rigorous policing, but that policing comes under the control of the local authorities in each region, the very officials that can be in collusion with the companies evading tax. The only way to break such cartels with strong vested interests is to purge the Party, and clearly delimit and police relationships between industry and government. But that is a mammoth task, given the sheer numbers of local authorities and companies in China.

In the meantime, the government account is haemorrhaging significant amounts of cash. To really understand where the highest degree of tax avoidance is, the authorities needed to be able to better understand in which sectors of the economy companies routinely report lower profit margins than would be anticipated for those sectors. This is an endeavour the State Administration of Taxation (SAT) has already undertaken. By looking in more detail at different business sectors and their financial structures, they are learning what the realistic profit rates should be in those sectors. SAT has initially been looking at service sectors such as retailing, real estate and shipping, these being particular havens for receipt-faking and inventory-hiding.

SAT is also putting more scrutiny into associated equity between company enterprises and intangibles, as well as more traditional types of trading. But as China's economy is growing and its sectors changing and developing so fast, standard business models in different sectors are not easy to come by. For example, the retail sector is undergoing huge changes now due to the rise of online retailing which is forcing radical changes as business structures adapt to the online challenge whilst sustaining bricks-and-mortar retail businesses.

If the Party is successful in cracking down on corruption generally and specifically reducing corruption within the official ranks, this will weaken the cosy vested interests between officialdom and corporate China that create the opening for corporate fraud and tax avoidance. However, breaking up those vested interests will not be easy, given how deep-rooted they are, and how much those vested interests stand to lose, not just in terms of money, but also in paying for crimes committed. Even if China has reduced the list of capital offences, many of those caught out will face very long sentences, and for many that means a life behind bars.

The benefits to China of an even slightly more honest and accountable corporate sector would be immense. If the tax avoidance estimates of

RMB 1 trillion per year were recouped, that could allow at least some increase in spending on social services that benefit a wider majority of people, rather than a select few – if spent wisely.

Spending on social welfare to create its "harmonious society"

Where the government is spending more of the money it does manage to collect in taxes tells a lot about its economic and social priorities, and which issues are the biggest "vote winners."

Spending on transportation is largely directed at infrastructure: building roads, railways and transport hubs that help improve the efficiency of distribution of people and goods across the economy to help it grow. In the short-term this provides jobs for many migrant workers in the construction of these projects. China has sometimes been accused of spending on infrastructure simply to keep unemployment figures down, but China does need new infrastructure. Without that infrastructure investment, the country's economy will continue to face logistics bottlenecks that stymie growth, especially in less-developed regions.

It is also important that the government continues to spend more on basic social security. Without a better social security system, Chinese people will continue to save a significant (even if overreported) portion of their incomes to provide for their own health care, children's education, pensions and a pot of "rainy day" cash. In Table 2.3, we can see that people are still adding significantly to household savings, at growth rates ahead of both declared income and spending. Such self-taxation keeps significant amounts of cash tied-up in savings accounts that bear little interest, and can actually lose money for savers – "financial repression," as it is termed. These "frozen" liquid assets suppress economic dynamism, and the lack of spending by people hinders China's consumer economy growth potential.

Government social welfare spending is therefore a necessary part of driving economic growth. The first task tackled has been reform of the health care system, and medical and health care spending has been

Table 2.3 The growth of total retail and wholesale trade, average urban income and household savings, 2000–2012

RMB trn	Total retail and wholesale trade	% annual growth	Average Urban wage (Yuan)	% annual growth	Household savings	% annual growth
2000	3.4		9,333		6.4	
2001	3.8	10.1	10,834	16.1	7.4	14.7
2002	4.2	11.8	12,373	14.2	8.7	17.8
2003	4.8	13.3	13,969	12.9	10.4	19.2
2004	6.0	25.0	15,920	14.0	12.0	15.4
2005	6.7	12.9	18,200	14.3	14.1	18.0
2006	7.6	13.7	20,856	14.6	16.2	14.6
2007	8.9	16.8	24,721	18.5	17.3	6.8
2008	10.8	21.6	28,898	16.9	21.8	26.3
2009	12.5	15.5	32,244	11.6	26.1	19.7
2010	15.5	23.3	36,539	13.3	30.3	16.3
2011	18.1	17.3	41,799	14.4	34.4	13.3
2012	20.7	14.3	47,183	12.9	40.1	16.6

Source: NBS China Statistical Yearbooks.

a key growth area of government spending as we can see from the growth figures in Table 2.4.

Government health care spending

For most people in China, getting ill means spending their own money on getting better. Part of the reason is that hospitals and health care centres, although required to provide medical services for the benefit of the Chinese public, are actually run as profit centres, earning income from selling drugs to patients – the more expensive and greater volume of drugs sold, the better the institution's income. This has led to doctors working with drugs sales agents to promote certain (more expensive) drugs over others, and overprescribing, all to ensure the commercial viability of the institution concerned.

Table 2.4 Government budgetary and non-budgetary expenditure by type, 2007–2011

Government expenditure by type						
RMB bn	2007	2008	2009	2010	2011	% period growth, 2007–2011
Transportation	113	144	358	400	717	532.5
Medical and health care	196	271	393	473	636	225.1
Agriculture, forestry and water conservancy	309	424	640	774	952	208.0
National defence	7	8	13	16	20	173.2
Environment protection	96	139	190	237	257	167.0
Total budgetary expenditure	**3,834**	**4,925**	**6,104**	**7,388**	**9,273**	**141.9**
Urban and rural community affairs	324	419	510	598	761	135.0
Education	673	852	987	1,183	1,550	130.4
Culture, sport and media	77	96	124	139	170	121.0
Science and technology	86	105	131	159	189	119.7
Social safety net and employment effort	510	646	785	868	1,061	107.8
Public security	288	341	390	464	527	83.0
General public services	635	745	808	850	1,008	58.7
Extra-budgetary expenditure by type						
RMB bn						% period growth, 2007–2010
Other expenditure	130	136	146	174	na	33.8
Education	220	233	237	248	na	13.0
Total non-budgetary expenditure	**611**	**635**	**623**	**575**	**na**	**–5.9**
Urban and rural community affairs	77	81	65	61	na	–20.5
Social safety net and employment effort	26	22	17	18	na	–28.0
General public services	61	57	54	38	na	–38.1
Transport	98	107	105	36	na	–63.5

Note: 2011 extra-budgetary spending not given in the 2012 China Statistical NBS Yearbook.

Source: NBS China Statistical Yearbooks.

So instead of being funded as a public service, according to Wang Hufeng and Wei Ouyang, writing for the Centre for Strategic and International Studies Freeman Chair in Chinese Studies report "Implementing Health Care Reform Policies in China" in December 2011, public hospitals have been *"put at the mercy of market forces,"* and *"Public hospitals began to rely more and more on mark-up income to maintain daily operations. Such a 'drugs serving to nourish doctors' mechanism contributes to the for-profit tendency of public hospitals, leading to the overuse of prescriptions and expensive drugs."*

To justify the term "public," public health care institutions are supposed to be funded through service charges and government subsidies, as well as drugs charges, to cover operational costs. However, many such institutions make up for funding shortfalls, or find additional development funds, from drugs sales. This system shifts the burden of cost onto patients and their families, requiring cash-on-the-barrel payment before treatment delivery, and before costs can be reclaimed. And the sick and needy tend not to argue too hard against the professional advice of doctors, even if those doctors are routinely courted by drug company sales agents, both of whom have bottom-line sales targets to meet. And they are big bottom lines, as the GlaxoSmithKline scandal of the summer of 2013 illustrated.

As well as increasing spending on health care, in 2009 the Chinese government launched its "New Health Care Reform Plan" with the aim of reforming health care system funding to provide universal health care by 2020. Part of this plan is to make public sector health care largely publicly funded, removing the profit motive from health care institutions, and decoupling the profit relationship between doctors and drugs companies. This is a prime reason behind the recent hike in health care spending, with the government share of health care spending doubling since 2001 to help cut out-of-pocket spending by patients in half.

But the government has (quite rightly) focused on the neediest in society, raising basic health care provision for China's poorest people: raising breadth of cover rather than depth. For those on higher incomes and in cities, spending on health care will remain cash-on-the-barrel for some years to come. However, the new plan is specific in its aim of "promoting the separation of medical services and pharmaceuticals sales," to which end some of the new funding is being directed into gradually reforming or rescinding the drug margin policy. But the key words here are "promoting" and "gradually" – meaning that the public health care sector is being encouraged to give up drugs sale profit margins over time, rather than being ordered to cease such activities quickly.

Table 2.5 shows how fast growth in government health care spending has been, having accelerated faster than either social health care spending or out-of-pocket spending. According to the NBS China Statistical Yearbook definitions, government health expenditure is government expenditure at all levels (central down to local) on medical and healthcare services, health administration and health insurance management and undertakings of family planning; social health expenditure is all inputs of society except the government in public health, including expenditure on social medical security and commercial health insurance, private expenditure on operations of medical and

Table 2.5 Ten-year growth in health care expenditure in China, by expenditure source, 2002 and 2011

RMB bn	2002	2011	% growth
Government health expenditure	90.85	737.90	712.20
Social health expenditure	153.94	842.46	447.27
Out-of-pocket health expenditure	334.21	846.53	153.29
Total	**579.00**	**2,426.88**	**319.15**
% of total			**% pt. diff.**
Government health expenditure	15.69	30.40	14.71
Social health expenditure	26.59	34.70	8.11
Out-of-pocket health expenditure	57.72	34.90	-22.82
Total	**100.00**	**100.00**	–

Source: National Bureau of Statistics (NBS) China Statistical Yearbooks and other Chinese government sources.

health care, social donations and contributions and income from administrative fees; while out-of-pocket health expenditure is cash expenditure on various health services by rural and urban residents, including self-payments of residents within the system of multi-medical insurance. There is also the hard-to-quantify issue of red envelope "*hongbao*" payments by patients to doctors to queue-jump waiting lists – a common practice.

The government contribution to overall healthcare spending should continue to increase in share of total health care expenditure to halve the out-of-pocket share again (see Table 2.6). But this will take time, given that many health care institutions and drug companies find it very profitable to maintain the status quo. According to data published on patient spending in China's hospitals by the National Health and Family Planning Commission,[6] the average outpatient service cost per patient was RMB 192.50 in 2012 (of which 50.3% was prescription fees), up by 7.1 per cent compared to the 2011 average, with the average cost of in-patient treatment hospital stays rising 5.3 per cent compared with 2011 to RMB 6,980.40 (RMB 697.60 per day, 41.1% of

Table 2.6 Forecast growth in health care expenditure in China, by expenditure source, 2012 and 2020

RMB bn	2012	2020	% growth
Government health expenditure	885.58	2,258.85	155.07
Social health expenditure	954.76	2,187.13	129.08 129.08
Out-of-pocket health expenditure	792.25	480.39	−39.36
Total	**2,632.59**	**4,926.37**	**87.13**
% of total			**% pt. diff.**
Government health expenditure	33.64	45.85	12.21
Social health expenditure	36.27	44.40	8.13
Out-of-pocket health expenditure	30.09	9.75	−20.34
Total	**100.00**	**100.00**	–

Adapted from source: Author's own forecast based on NBS China Statistical Yearbooks and other Chinese government sources.

which was prescription fees). Both cost increases were well above the inflation rate.

Capping of drugs prices

Another tactic China's government uses to suppress health care costs for poorer people is drugs price-capping. Since 1998, it has persisted in capping the prices of thousands of drugs available in China. Since 2001, it has capped all drugs prices in the market. However, the price-capping policy squeezes retail pharmacies rather than drugs manufacturers, because manufacturers control pricing down to the pharmacies. The drugs companies are also able to request price increases from the government, something pharmacies cannot. And drugs companies have often been accused of grossly inflating retail drug prices to absorb the cost of price-capping, with investigations quoted in the *China Daily USA*[7] in November 2011 (following more price caps by the government) showing retail prices for some drugs are inflated by up to 60 times the production cost.

While a key reason for capping prices was to curb profiteering by drugs sales agents, who stand accused by the government of manoeuvring prices up to increase profits, price-capping has effectively strengthened the cartel between drugs sales agents and health care institutions. To rectify this, the Chinese government, as part of ongoing health care reforms, is attempting to increase state funding of public health care institutions.

Health care coverage

The Chinese government is trying to build a fairer health care system by addressing the direct cost of health care borne by individual people by introducing universal health care insurance. Such insurance is meant to provide government cost subsidies for prescription drugs to consumers through insurance cover, thus reducing the out-of-pocket amount people need to pay. This both reduces the burden of cost for the relatively poor and reduces health care spending requirements (eventually) for wealthier consumers, who can then spend more money on discretionary items, such as Gucci bags, iPhones, BMWs, etc.

Since introducing wider health care insurance, the Chinese government now claims to have achieved near universal health insurance coverage, in urban areas rising from just over half the population in 2003 to more than 90 per cent by 2011, and only a fifth of the rural population in 2003 to near universality in 2011 (see Table 2.7). Certainly, the government has achieved much in increasing the breadth of coverage, but in the depth of coverage the statistics look a lot less convincing.

In juxtaposition to the universal coverage claims (see Table 2.8), the Chinese government's own Ministry of Health data for 2008 showed that some 36 per cent of rural and 48 per cent of urban people failed to seek medical treatment for many ailments. The reason was cost, because although health insurance cover is near universal, to reach that universality the depth of coverage is still very shallow, allowing only for basic costs. This leaves people with more complicated and expensive ailments to either pay for their own treatment, do without, or seek cheaper alternatives such as traditional Chinese medicines. Others succumb to the massive supply of fake drugs from back-street clinics.

The government has also invested in building many more new medical service facilities to raise service penetration. This has made medical assistance more accessible to many more people, reducing travelling

Table 2.7 Health insurance coverage in China according to the National Health Services Survey, by location, 2003, 2008 and 2011

% of population surveyed	2003	2008	2011
Urban health insurance coverage	55.2	73.5	90.9
Rural health insurance coverage	21.0	93.0	97.4
Overall health insurance coverage	29.7	87.9	95.7

Note: Survey sample: 2003 – 193,689; 2008 – 177,501; 2011 – 59,835.

Source: National Health Services Survey in 2003, 2008 and 2011, as quoted in *The Lancet*.

Table 2.8 Health insurance coverage in China, by region, 2003, 2008 and 2011

% of population surveyed	2003	2008	2011
East	38.9	90.0	95.7
Central	22.9	82.2	94.4
West	27.3	90.3	96.6
Overall health insurance coverage	29.7	87.9	95.7

Source: National Health Services Survey in 2003, 2008 and 2011, as quoted in *The Lancet*.

distance, especially for rural people. According to Liu Yuanli,[8] a senior lecturer on international health at the Harvard School of Public Health, this has meant health care services utilisation rates among rural Chinese almost doubled within five years.

But while lauding the investment in new health care facilities, Liu also claims that insurance cover remains insufficient for needs, and the average reimbursement rate of inpatient expenses is only 48 per cent among urban and 44 per cent among rural residents. This view is supported by Professor Liu Guo'en,[9] director of the China Centre for Health Economic Research at Guanghua School of Management at Peking University, who stated that "based on his findings, the New Rural Cooperative Medical Scheme today can only cover 40–50 per cent of rural patients' medical costs, far lower than the 70 per cent claimed by the authorities." This further demonstrates that government health insurance coverage rates are still rather cosmetic. There are also regional inequalities in coverage offered under different local insurance plans, each run by different local governments according to local budget conditions.

How does health insurance work in China?

The biggest problem with China's social security system is its complexity. Not only are there three different schemes in place, according to whether people are rural or urban, but different locations within China run their own health care insurance cover, with varying ranges of costs, drugs and treatments paid for.

TYPES OF HEALTH CARE COVER IN CHINA

The three main categories of health insurance cover areas as follows:

The New-Rural Cooperative Medical Scheme (NCMS)

Launched in 2003, the NCMS is a voluntary insurance programme that raised rural insurance provision from 21 per cent in 2003 to 93 per cent by 2008. When it began, average annual premiums were RMB 30 per person, rising to RMB 120 by 2010 (this figure is split RMB 50 each from central and local governments, with the other RMB 20 contributed by individuals), then rising to RMB 200 by 2011. However, different county governments provide different cover, depending on how rich or poor each county government is.

The Urban Employee Basic Medical Insurance (UE-BMI)

The UE-BMI was launched in 1994. By 2003, 30.4 per cent of urban residents were covered under this programme. As with rural health insurance, each city government can select its package of benefits according to the economic situation in each city, meaning benefits provided often vary significantly by location. The minimum annual premium rate in the scheme is fixed at 8 per cent of salary, with employers contributing 6 per cent and employees contributing 2 per cent.

The Urban Residents' Basic Medical Insurance programme (UR-BMI)

The UR-BMI is a non-mandatory scheme, established in 2007, designed to provide cover for non-working urban residents, including children, students, the elderly and disabled – people otherwise not covered by government health care insurance programmes since the 1980s. By 2008, 308 cities were signed up to the scheme, and this has of course significantly improved the health care coverage across the urban population. The average premium across the pilot cities in 2007 was RMB 245, with local governments contributing to premiums from between RMB 40 to RMB 80. Again, the level of premiums and cover depends on the local economic situation.

There are also a few companies in China providing private health care insurance to the wealthy, but this represents a tiny part of the picture.

Because richer cities and counties are able to pay for better levels of cover than poorer ones, the idea that near universal coverage reduces the out-of-pocket spending on health care for all is erroneous. Even the National Health Services Surveys results show that despite greater insurance coverage, health spending continues to increase as a proportion of total household expenditure (see Table 2.9). So consumers continue to save (self-tax) more of their salaries to cover future health care costs for themselves and their families.

Much of that health care cost comes later in life. Based upon research done by the US National Center for Biotechnology Information (NCBI), total average per capita lifetime health care spending of US citizens is about US$ 316,600. The research also found that because women live longer, their average spending is about one-third higher than for men, with about 40 per cent of that difference being directly due to living longer. This is because as people get older, they are more prone to illness. The NCBI found that about one-third of the total average lifetime health care spending came during middle age, but nearly half during old age. For those living to 85 or older, more than one-third of all cost comes in their last years.

Table 2.9 Health spending as a share of total household expenditure in China according to the National Health Services Surveys, by location and region, 2003, 2008 and 2011

% of population surveyed	2003	2008	2011
Urban	9.3	10.6	11.9
Rural	12.1	12.6	13.3
East	10.9	11.2	12.4
Central	11.0	11.8	13.2
West	11.9	13.0	13.1
All respondents	11.3	12.0	12.9

Source: National Health Services Surveys in 2003, 2008 and 2011, as quoted in *The Lancet*.

We can assume Chinese people face similar kinds of increased health care issues as they age as their American counterparts, seeing increasing out-of-pocket spending from their pensions, needing to draw on their life savings, or sell homes to pay for more expensive treatments for chronic illnesses less likely to be covered by current health care insurance benefits provision. This also increasingly makes them a financial burden upon their families.

Old age financial security is a key concern for Chinese people. It is why they prefer to have sons, who traditionally took over running the family farm and looked after elderly parents – a cornerstone of the Confucian ethic that shaped Chinese social structures from the agrarian embers of Chinese civilisation. But the rising costs of living, and of getting older, mean the burden of cover cannot be borne by children of aging retirees alone (the declining fertility and One Child Policy exacerbate this problem), and while the government has increased the breadth of health care cover, it still faces further investment needs to improve depth of cover.

Pensions reform – will China get old before it gets rich?

The Chinese government, since ditching Maoism following the chaos of the Great Leap Forward and the Great Proletarian Cultural Revolution (neither of which was particularly great), has massively improved the health care, nutrition and life expectancy of its people. It also introduced the One Child Policy to reduce population growth. China's population is therefore aging, with average life expectancy now at 73.5 years. Between 2000 and 2011, the population of China aged 60+ grew from 10.7 per cent of total population to 16.9 per cent. Moreover, the Chinese population aged 60+ is forecast to reach about 390 million by 2035, meaning China will only have two people of working age to every retired person.

It's little wonder that the Chinese government, faced with the prospect of spiralling pensions costs concurrent with a declining workforce, is considering pushing-back China's retirement age, and that China now faces having a pensions funding deficit. Some reports[10] put the pensions system funding shortage as having reached US$ 2.6 trillion (RMB 20.6 trillion) by 2010, which would take a significant chunk out of China's foreign exchange reserves of US$ 3.31 trillion. But forecasts have speculated that this cost will increase to US$ 10.8 trillion in the next 20 years as China's population ages.

Before going too deeply into the values, it is worth looking at how the pensions system in China works. Like health care, it is complicated and consists of three schemes, called "pillars:"

CHINA'S PENSIONS SYSTEM

First pillar

A mandatory scheme split into two tiers. Tier A is a pay-as-you-go (PAYG) scheme. Contributions should not exceed 20 per cent of wages. Tier B requires the employee's contributions equal to 8 per cent of covered wages into funded individual accounts. The collective target replacement rate against local salary is 58.5 per cent – 20 per cent from Tier A, the social pool of the first pillar, and 38.5 per cent from Tier B, the individual account of the first pillar (based on a 35-year accumulation). This pillar covers both urban and rural workers.

Second pillar

A voluntary occupational pensions plan in the form of enterprise annuities (EAs). These are fully-funded, defined contribution accounts, referred to outside China as occupational pensions. Plans take contributions from both employers and employees, but only large, profitable companies sponsor them. Being linked to enterprises, this pillar covers only urban workers. Ping'An Annuity, from Ping'An Insurance, is China's largest EA service provider, with in excess of RMB 33 billion in trustee investments, and RMB 49 billion in investment assets by mid-2011.

Third pillar
Also voluntary, this includes complementary private savings and individual depository pension schemes (effectively primitive private pensions). This sector of the pensions market has not grown very large yet, although there are already over 50 companies offering these plans, with more becoming available. Group plans have not really taken off due to a lack of tax advantages. This pillar requires significant surplus discretionary income to invest, and so is largely restricted to the middle classes and the rich.

The pension market is therefore dominated by the mandatory first pillar, followed by the voluntary second pillar, while the third pillar is still small. Urban Chinese are probably more likely to put money into life insurance rather than a discretionary pension.

According to China's official statistics (see Table 2.10), pension coverage expanded rapidly in recent years, especially among China's rural poor, increasing rural worker coverage by in excess of 40 per cent growth in both 2009 and 2010, with a massive 216 per cent increase in 2011. Urban pension cover increased by over 9 per cent and 10 per cent in 2010 and 2011 respectively – an acceleration in growth over previous years. This is a great achievement, but there are still nearly as many people again without any kind of pension. There will continue to be a rapid spread of pension coverage, but the increasing worry is where the government plans to get the money from.

Although pension system coverage appeared to have reached two-thirds of the population by 2011, basic pension provision at retirement varies greatly depending on local government finances in each location. Rural residents who choose to work in cities as migrant workers are in principle allowed to move their own contributions and 60 per cent of employers' contributions with them, but in practice much of this money gets lost (either stolen, diverted or unaccounted for). According to Albert Park of Hong Kong University of Science and Technology,[11]

Table 2.10 Urban employees' basic pension insurance coverage, 2006–2011

Million people	2006	2007	2008	2009	2010	2011
URBAN						
Employees covered	141.3	151.8	165.9	177.4	194.0	215.7
Retirees covered	46.4	49.5	53.0	58.1	63.1	68.3
Total	187.7	201.4	218.9	235.5	257.1	283.9
Total % annual growth	7.3	7.3	8.7	7.6	9.2	10.4
Total urban population	571.9	589.6	603.5	619.9	665.8	693.1
% urban coverage	32.8	34.2	36.3	38.0	38.6	41.0
RURAL						
Contributors	53.7	51.7	56.0	72.8	102.8	326.4
Retired participants	4.6	3.1	8.2	20.2	28.6	89.2
Total	58.3	54.8	64.1	92.9	131.4	415.7
Total % annual growth	9.5	-6.1	17.1	44.9	41.4	216.3
Total rural population	724.4	715.8	711.0	703.8	666.9	647.3
% rural coverage	8.0	7.7	9.0	13.2	19.7	64.2
Total people covered	246.0	256.2	283.0	328.4	388.5	699.6
% total population coverage	19.0	19.6	21.5	24.8	29.2	52.2

Source: NBS China Statistical Yearbooks.

only a quarter of migrant workers in cities were covered by pensions in 2010, compared with four-fifths of locals.

An even bigger problem for China's pension system is that while pensioners are supposed to receive a pension of 60 per cent of their final salary, contributions do not increase in line with salary growth, and money in pension funds simply sits in current accounts or government bonds where interest rates are below inflation. They are not invested in growth funds, and significant quantities of pension assets are channelled by local governments into infrastructure developments or investments into state-owned companies. This leaves certain accounts low on cash, and as Zheng Bingwen of the Centre for International Social Security Studies at the Chinese Academy of Social Sciences (CASS)[12] has estimated, despite RMB 2.5 trillion having been paid into

individual pension accounts, actual assets held were worth only RMB 270 billion by end of 2011. The majority of the remaining funds are used to pay pensions to existing retirees, but the funds to pay future retirees are therefore being lost.

Effectively this means pension pots are in deficit, and as the Chinese population gets older and more people retire, more stress will be placed on pension pots and local authorities to replenish them. But given the worsening debt situation among local authorities (described below), that replenishment will increasingly have to come from further borrowing.

Also according to CASS estimates[13] published in December 2012, across 14 Chinese provinces employer contributions into pension funds were short by RMB 67.9 billion, up RMB 25 billion compared with the 2011 deficit. CASS also found 15 provinces and municipalities had a RMB 133.6 billion pension pot surplus. The CASS figures highlighted Liaoning and Heilongjiang as both having over RMB 10 billion in pension deficits, while Tianjin and Jilin had deficits of between RMB 5 and 10 billion. The central government has stepped in with subsidies to plug the gaps, but it cannot carry on being a fall-back for local government budget imbalances, and doing so skirts the fundamental problem that poorer provinces have worse pension provisions than richer ones, creating an unfair class system among pension contributors.

The unfairness of the system is partly due to the pension system reform having only been recent, so the issues between poor provinces lacking funds and rich ones being in surplus are symptoms of the system's immaturity. To address the imbalance, SCRC chairman Guo Shuqing suggested that pension funds should be invested into equities to feed the stock markets and that stocks feed the pensions with better investment returns. Former head of the central bank, and then National Council for Social Security Fund (NCSSF) president Dai Xianglong also expressed interest in this idea, and went further by suggesting state-owned companies allocate more of their corporate shares to social security funds. The central government already requires state-owned companies listed on the stock market since 2005 to put 10 per cent of shares into pension funds.

Dai Xianglong was replaced by former finance minister Xie Xuren as head of the NCSSF in March 2013, at the same time the national pension fund reported a 7 per cent investment return in 2012[14] compared with below 1 per cent growth in 2011. This was its best performance in three years, investment income reaching RMB 64.5 billion in 2012, and assets surpassing RMB 1 trillion. So the NCSSF, which represents a reserve fund to supplement local pension pots, would seem to be managing its investments more wisely. However, it was also helped by a central government capital injection of RMB 52.6 billion and NCSSF taking over management of Guangdong province's pension fund, worth RMB 100 billion. But investing pensions in stock markets is risky, given that China's A-share market dropped 14.3 per cent in 2010 and 21.7 per cent in 2011, and only regained 3.2 per cent in 2012. Public and expert opinion is now veering away from stock market investment[15] for pension funds due to the high potential risks on long-term earnings.

The NCSSF is doing what it can to improve efficiency and positive investment results in how it manages pension funds, but reserve funds remain tiny compared with likely future pension needs. According to Bank of China International's chief economist, Cao Yuanzheng,[16] the pension fund deficit of RMB 16.5 trillion in 2010 could grow to as much as RMB 68.2 trillion by 2033. Such precise dates and numbers might sound suspicious, but it's unlikely such a senior economist would make those claims public without a defensible case and methodology. If true, then China's pension funds need to start accruing value much faster than they are now, and with stock market sentiment so poor, equities seem unlikely to provide a simple answer to the problem.

To put the low rate of investment return into perspective, investments made using China's local pension funds[17] yielded below 2 per cent returns over the past 10 years, and only 2 per cent of revenue for basic pension funds came from interest. Local pension funds have only been allowed to operate bank deposit accounts and buy treasury bills that have yields below the rate of inflation. According to the Social Security Ministry,[18] 84 per cent of China's RMB 4 trillion in social insurance assets, including pension funds, sit in local government fiscal accounts in banks (earning 3.25 per cent interest for one-year deposits) rather than being invested in higher-return options. While the NCSSF can invest in whatever financial vehicles it sees fit (including the Chinese stock market), the public pension pots cannot, and as Zheng Bingwen of CASS has argued, it would be better if those local pension pots were pooled into larger funds jointly invested at a better rate of return – at least enough to remain ahead of the inflation rate.

According to Yin Chengji, spokesman for the Ministry of Human Resources and Social Security[19] in April 2013, while some of China's pension funds will be invested in the local stock market, the government is also considering other investment channels to provide more stable investment returns. According to Li Daxiao, director of the research institute with Shenzhen-based Yingda Securities, the government investing pension funds in the stock market would send "a positive signal to the stock market, and will help boost market sentiment." However, given that the government is also looking at other "investment channels that can bring stable returns," to quote Yin Chengji, this doesn't show much confidence in the stock market by the Chinese government. Furthermore, Dong Dengxin,[20] a finance professor at Wuhan University of Science and Technology, said the "authorities should be prudent, given the number of problems in the market" and invest pension funds "in low-risk financial products such as national, financial and large corporate bonds." All well and good, until we look more closely at the health of the corporate debt situation.

Whatever the investment structure for pension funds, they need to grow faster. Not only is China's population aging, there is also growing resentment among pensioners and workers over unfair pay-outs across the dual-track pensions system. In May 2013, a Sina[21] news article highlighted how unfair it is that the pension system for officials pays out so much more to government workers than others, stating that while the fixed retirement income given to rural retirees is RMB 55 per month, for government officials it is RMB 6,000 per month. Many workers in the private sector are also very unhappy with the dual-track system, creating increasing social tension.

Government education spending

Another area where government funding has certainly grown strongly, but remains in "catch-up" mode, is education. Although education spending has grown rapidly, as a proportion of gross domestic product (GDP) total education funding is still small at only about 3.3 per cent in 2002, compared to 7.2 per cent in the USA in the same year, and the 6 per cent recommended by the United Nations. By 2011, total government spending (including extra-budgetary) was still only 3.9 per cent of GDP (see Table 2.11). Adding in non-governmental education funding in 2011, total funding reached 5.2 per cent of GDP, still a significant way off the recommended 6 per cent. To reach the UN-recommended education spending level, China would have needed to commit over RMB 3.1 trillion since 2012.

What is also interesting is that although growth in governmental funding of education has overtaken growth in funding from non-governmental sources, non-governmental funding remains a

Table 2.11 Education spending in China as a percentage of GDP, 2007–2011

RMB bn	2007	2008	2009	2010	2011*
GDP	27,584.4	30,067.0	33,535.3	40,151.3	47,156.4
Government budgetary education spending	672.7	851.9	987.0	1,182.9	1,549.8
Government extra-budgetary education spending	219.7	232.6	236.5	248.2	275.3*
Total government education spending	892.4	1,084.5	1,223.5	1,431.1	1,825.1
Total educational funding from all sources	1,214.8	1,450.1	1,650.3	1,956.2	2,468.0*
Total government education spending % GDP	3.2	3.6	3.6	3.6	3.9
Total educational funding from all sources % GDP	4.4	4.8	4.9	4.9	5.2

*Note**: Author's own estimates for 2011, based on proportional growth trends.

Adapted from source: NBS China Statistical Yearbooks.

significant slice of the pie. Funding from tuition and other fees still grew in excess of 300 per cent between 2001 and 2010, and still represented over 10 per cent of education funding in China, meaning self-funding by families of students remains very significant. However, things have steadily improved (see Table 2.12).

Without proper education funding, China will find it hard to encourage industrial innovation to create added-value, and that will hurt long-term economic growth if not addressed. Government education funding has gradually improved, but there remains a shortfall which has to be met by either non-statutory organisations or parents' own pockets – mostly the latter. This means parents need to plan financially (and make significant savings) to cope with funding education for their child. Another virtual self-taxation towards covering the shortfall in social spending, and more of consumers' income locked into savings and not spent shopping.

Table 2.12 Education funding by source, 2001–2010

	2001 RMB bn	2010 RMB bn	2001 %	2010 %	% change 2001–2010
Government appropriation for education	305.7	1,467.0	65.9	75.0	379.9
– of which budgetary	258.2	1,349.0	55.7	69.0	422.4
Funds from private schools	12.8	10.5	2.8	0.5	-17.7
Donations and fund-raising for running schools	11.3	10.8	2.4	0.6	-4.4
Income from teaching research and auxiliary activities	115.8	410.6	25.0	21.0	254.7
Tuition and miscellaneous fees	74.6	301.6	16.1	15.4	304.4
Other educational funds	18.2	57.2	3.9	2.9	214.2
TOTAL	463.8	1,956.2	100.0	100.0	321.8

Note: In 2007, certain indicators of educational funds had been revised. "Funds from private schools" from 1992 to 2006 is equal to funds from social organisations and citizens for running schools, but that of 2007 is equal to funds from runners of private schools.

Source: NBS China Statistical Yearbooks.

To rectify the situation and help reduce household contributions towards education costs, the Chinese government needs to increase corporate taxation and improve tax collection. Education funding will only become more expensive, due to rising costs of property, utilities, staff salaries, etc. But part of the problem with improving education spending is also that two-thirds of it relies upon local government spending budgets (see Table 2.13), and as I explore below, local governments are struggling to balance their books. This means that education spending is being hit by the stark financial choices of local governments, meaning education funding goes short in many local jurisdictions, especially the poorer ones.

In January 2009, Han Qinglin, an expert in strategic issue studies who participated in designing the programme outlines for, and was an inspector of, the Education Department of Hebei Province, was interviewed by the *People's Daily*[22] on China's then recently launched public opinion gathering exercise on education policy plans entitled the "Outline for National Mid-Term and Long-Term Educational Reform and Development Planning." Han argued that the Chinese government needed to step up its education funding, and identified the lack of education funding as being critical to economic and social development

Table 2.13 The significance of local government spending to education funding, 2010

RMB bn	2010 total	2010 central govt.	2010 local govt.	% central govt.	% local govt.
Government appropriation for education	1,467.0	149.2	1,317.8	7.6	67.4
– of which budgetary	1,349.0	140.4	1,208.6	7.2	61.8
Funds from private schools	10.5	0.0	10.5	0.0	0.5
Donations and fund-raising for running schools	10.8	1.5	9.3	0.1	0.5
Income from teaching research and other auxiliary activities	410.6	53.5	357.1	2.7	18.3
Tuition and miscellaneous fees	301.6	26.0	275.6	1.3	14.1
Other educational funds	57.2	11.6	45.6	0.6	2.3
Total	1,956.2	215.8	1,740.4	11.0	89.0

Source: NBS China Statistical Yearbooks.

in China, especially in raising the quality of education. Han felt that at the time both the central and local governments were not providing enough opportunities for education and that many students could not afford to continue with education past the compulsory nine years. Han also pointed to the growing problem of graduate unemployment.

Another incentive for parents to save more on future education provision for their (most likely) only child, is competition for places at "good" schools which begins at primary level (or even pre-school in some cities), and that competition intensifies as children grow through the education system, up to college or university. This puts huge pressure on children to perform well in exams that allow them to move up to the next educational stage, and places a huge financial burden on parents to pay for that education.

But even all the hard work and money children and parents put into their education cannot guarantee a job. Each year China produces six million new graduates, and the continued stock of graduates is creating a glut of skilled labour that artificially suppresses wages for those who get jobs, leaving large numbers struggling to find employment that reflects their qualification. According to Texas A&M economist Gan Li, quoted in the *Wall Street Journal*[23] in March 2013, the unemployment rate for 21–25-year-olds with a university degree was 16.4 per cent by the end of 2011.

According to Yao Yuqun, a professor at Renmin University's School of Labour Relations and Human Resources, unemployed college graduates are not counted in China's official 4.1 per cent unemployment rate. No longer required to be allocated a job, graduates are increasingly choosy about their desired career, but many end up working in restaurants, bars or as office juniors, just to make some money while they continue to look for a "real" job to suit their qualifications. Many more simply stay at home unemployed and living off their parents.

Many graduates also now opt to take postgraduate degrees to raise their level of qualification and employability. This adds further to the parental cost of education. There has also been a notable rise in Chinese students going overseas to study, with many not coming back due to the lack of job prospects, even with a foreign degree and life experience under their belts. However, the return rate has increased in recent years.

In 2006, the Ministry of Education began limiting the number of new university undergraduate places, with higher education institutions being allowed only up to 5 per cent more students than the previous year. But this only served to make competition for university places tougher, increasing pressure on secondary school students to achieve better, and thus raising the cost of supplementary education through private cram schools for the average family. It also means children take fewer risks in their choice of academic qualifications, and are less likely to gain a more rounded education outside of pure academia.

Education costs rise with inflation anyway, but pressure to drive children to succeed more and more also adds to the cost, inevitably through the usually uncounted costs of private tuition (see Table 2.14). The result is that children in China are spending increasing amounts of time studying, and less time playing and with their families in leisure activities. When children reach higher education, the burden of tuition and fees increases dramatically, as the proportion of cost rests much more on parents finding the tuition fees compared to government funding. The costs may be manageable for middle-class families, but combined fees can represent as much as, if not more than, half the average annual income[24] of many poor families.

The pressure to achieve also often adds the uncounted cost of stress on families and children, something it appears the Chinese government now wishes to alleviate. According to a post on China Central Television's blog,[25] China's Ministry of Education has drafted new policies aimed at reducing education stress, forbidding homework for children in grades 1–6, reducing the number of mandatory exams and stopping testing of children in grades 1–3. Yet, even if these regulations are brought in, they are unlikely to reduce the competitive element in China's education system for a long time, nor the financial cost that comes with it.

So, while parents increasingly stress about the cost of education, children increasingly stress about attaining academic grades. They spend less time playing and trying out non-academic activities, and

Table 2.14 Proportion of higher education funds by different resources, 1996–2010

	Government appropriation (%)	Tuition and fees (%)
1996	80.3	13.7
1997	78.3	14.8
1998	65.0	13.3
1999	62.5	17.0
2000	58.2	21.1
2001	54.2	24.2
2002	50.6	26.3
2003	47.9	28.8
2004	45.5	30.4
2005	42.8	31.1
2006	42.9	29.2
2007	44.0	33.7
2008	47.6	33.7
2009	48.7	32.2
2010	52.7	30.6

Source: NBS China Statistical Yearbooks.

spend more time sitting studying. They also spend less time involved with sports because they are tired after so much studying. A side-effect of this has been spiralling obesity rates among China's desk-bound children. Yet all of this cost still does not guarantee employment at the end of the education system.

Summary

China's 40 million administrators are assessed and their career progress is based on achieving different targets. Failure to maintain social order or enforce the One Child Policy can mean being fined, demoted or even sacked, while creating economic growth, investment and raising fiscal revenues (more often than not from creating the former two) can lead to promotion and pay bonuses (not to forget opportunities to make friends in industry that can lead to serious money in kick-backs). Making improvements to education, health care and pensions can earn points but is not likely to lead to promotions or pay bonuses. They are therefore incentivised to create economic growth above all else, and that means they are likely to neglect issues such as health care, education and pensions in favour of seeking a plug for gaps in fiscal revenue by driving investment and economic growth to raise taxes, rather than pursuing tax dodgers to raise tax efficiency within the existing economy.

Creating a "harmonious society" for more Chinese people, however, is no longer just about putting money in their pockets and giving them a home to fill with consumer goods. Once basic needs are fulfilled, the next step is improving quality of life by making the places people live in comfortable, clean and safe. Chinese people are increasingly vocal in their concerns and in their protests. But improving the situation requires understanding the extent of how bad the environmental problems are, the size of the pension deficit, and how far short of needs is education spending. All important questions for China's administration to be asking, but completely impossible to answer or act upon unless credible data measuring the extent of the problems exists.

Also, while government spending needs will increase significantly, it has to ensure that tax income growth can match growth in spending needs. These social welfare spending needs are must haves, but it is hard to know how much tax needs to be raised if you don't know how much of that you need to spend. If the government cannot raise more tax, it will need to borrow more to meet those needs and enforce tax contributions from those who currently avoid paying. But China's local governments have already racked up huge debts that they struggle to pay. Raising corporate taxes to pay for more contributions towards social welfare funding will be needed, but this will drive up costs for business and consumer prices.

Understanding the data on these issues, what they really represent and how they affect people's spending is therefore directly relevant to companies looking to do business in China. Lack of health care, pension and education cover means big chunks of consumer income get saved away to cover costs normally covered by government, reducing overall spending power.

chapter 3

Red Ink on the Red Carpet – China's Barely Hidden Debt

Government debt worries

In a *Financial Times*[1] article on 16 April 2013, it was reported that a senior auditor in China, Zhang Ke of accounting company ShineWing and vice-chairman of China's accounting association, had stopped allowing bond sales by local governments in China because their debt was *"out of control"* and could cause a financial crisis bigger than the US housing market crash. He had audited a sample of local government bond issues and found them to be *"very dangerous."* According to Zhang, the situation is already at crisis point, but the Chinese government is delaying payments against these debts, estimated to be between RMB 10 and 20 trillion.

While local governments in China cannot issue debt, they can issue bonds through local government-owned investment companies involved in funding infrastructure projects. But the central government has become spooked by this, and in December 2012, the Finance Ministry prevented local governments from using public assets (such as government buildings, hospitals, schools, etc.) to raise cash for the special purpose vehicles local governments use to sell bonds.

According to estimates attributed to leading Chinese securities broker Huatai Securities,[2] local government debt in China reached RMB 16.3 trillion by the end of 2012, representing about 29 per cent of the declared GDP figure – up from 28 per cent in 2011. This estimate took into account all loans taken out by local government financing platforms, urban investment bonds and local government debts issued by China's Ministry of Finance (MoF). Of this figure, at the end of 2012, RMB 9.1 trillion was represented by outstanding loans held by local government financing platforms (a figure put at RMB 9.3 trillion by the China Banking Regulatory Commission); RMB 2.5 trillion was in urban investment bonds, leaving between RMB 4.5 and 4.7 trillion attributed to MoF-issued local government debts. In a note entitled "*China: Explaining 'Augmented' Government Debt and Deficit*," the IMF estimated that augmented government debt in China rose to nearly 50 per cent of GDP in 2012.

The IMF estimated that augmented government debt in China rose to nearly 50 per cent of GDP in 2012

But the Chinese government cannot keep rolling over local government debt forever. On 24 April 2013, an article in *China Business News* quoted Shang Fulin, chief of the China Banking Regulatory Commission, as saying that local government debt had reached an estimated RMB 9.3 trillion in 2012, representing 1.5 times the cumulative fiscal revenue of China's local governments, and that almost RMB 3.5 trillion of local government debt in China would become due within the subsequent three years, putting a massive amount of pressure on local government finances. In June 2012, the National Audit Office[3] stated that direct liabilities, guaranteed debt and indirect liabilities for 36 local authorities in China had reached RMB 3.8 trillion, an increase of 13 per cent over two years, and that some provincial cities were so in debt they were taking out new loans to repay over a fifth of existing debts.

According to a People's Bank of China estimate in 2011,[4] local governments had raised funds for infrastructure products by establishing over 10,000 financing companies. And these companies, according to a statement made by former finance minister Xiang Huaicheng,[5] mean that China's local governments could have run up over RMB 20 trillion in debts, more than double the amount claimed by Shang Fulin.

Whether Shang Fulin, Xiang Huaicheng or Zhang Ke has the correct figure is debatable, but the key issue here is that such eminently positioned people, who should be as well placed as anyone to have a measure of the issue's scale, have such varying estimates of the problem. The numbers not only show China's local governments to be looking increasingly insolvent, and that corruption within local government is likely distorting the real picture downwards, but that without clarity in the data it is hard for the central government to budget for the shortfall when it comes to paying off or writing off those debts. These numbers also show that administrative reform of the way China's 40 million officials run local accounts has become an imperative. China cannot carry on running the country based on the existing system, and has to reform its administration root-and-branch, which it appears to now be doing.

Paying-off the debt

It seems unlikely that the Chinese government will simply write off those debts, as it will mean those who have invested in the bonds issued by local governments will lose their money – and that will hurt a lot of people and companies. It also seems impossible it would sell off its holding of US government bonds: valued at US$ 1.202 trillion by the end of 2012, about RMB 7.5 trillion at end-2012 exchange rates. Selling off all that holding would be impossible all at once, and would trigger a devaluation of the US$, so the unsold bonds would lose value and would push the US economy into recession again, triggering another global economic funk that would further ail China's export economy.

China does have foreign exchange reserves of US$ 3.31 trillion, which would give it RMB 20.6 trillion to cover the costs of the local government, but not also the likely cost of its pension system at the same time.

Companies, individuals and other countries buy China's local government bonds. For example, on 24 April 2013, the Reserve Bank of Australia,[6] the country's central bank, announced it would invest almost A$ 2 billion in Chinese government debt, a move it claimed would "*dramatically strengthen ties with our biggest trading partner.*" Previous to this, in March 2012, Japan[7] achieved approval to buy up to US$ 10.3 billion of Chinese sovereign debt bonds.

Is the local government debt issue really as bad as commentators are saying? Certainly the scale seems to be of increasing concern, whatever the real scale is. What is perhaps more worrying is that not only are the figures lacking in transparency, but the policy of how to handle the issue also remains unclear. Adding to the problem is the difficulty that the central government will have in reigning in the tendency of local Chinese officials to maintain political policy focus on economic growth and investment over balancing accounts.

Chinese local governments rely on taxes gained from land sales and property transactions for a hefty chunk (40%[8] of local government income according to a *Financial Times* report in 2011) of their revenues. According to Li Shenming,[9] a member of the legislature's Standing Committee, and referring to the situation, "*It's getting so bad that if* [local governments] *don't sell land, they can't even pay salaries.*" The need for local governments to sell land for infrastructure, commercial and housing projects often leads to the creation of projects not fit for real local economic needs – building unused roads, uninhabited neighbourhoods, vacant shopping malls and undersubscribed office buildings. Meanwhile, all of this construction is being carried out following forced evictions of the people who used to live where the new construction begins, creating growing amounts of social unrest and resentment, especially at poor compensation payments and bulldozer crews' heavy-handed approaches to evictions.

May 2013 saw the publishing of a report[10] produced by think tank The China Finance 40 Forum, comprised of 40 leading local financial and academic luminaries. It recommends that the government should consider three options for reform of land sales by local governments to generate revenues. The first suggestion is to scrap the auction system in favour of providing land at either low cost or for free. The second is to take land sales out of local government hands and place all sales revenue in the hands of the central government, as in Hong

Kong. The last suggestion is a complete exit from the land market by the government. The report argues that each of these options would direct local governments away from heavy reliance on land sales for income, reduce corruption and profiteering, and lead to more efficient use and pricing of commercial land. It could also slow the supply of land to the market, push up prices, and lead to better investments and more efficient land use.

Don't burst my bubble!

It is increasingly apparent that this local government debt-fuelled land grab and construction investment binge is creating bubbles in local property markets, skewing the local economic growth figures. These figures help cadres to rise up the ranks, based on their political "achievements," but they also create shaky ground economically that is accumulating towards bubbles bursting. What is also worrying is the unknown potential for a bubble to burst in one city (or groups of cities at similar times) that could set off real problems for property markets, the finances in several local administrations and the investment vehicles that have bought up local government debt.

China's banks are growing worried about local government loans, and in March 2013,[11] China allowed banks to securitise local governments' financing vehicles loans under a pilot scheme into newly formed special purpose vehicles (SPVs), which are special purpose trusts and other financial institutions (including insurance companies, mutual funds and social security funds) approved by the China Banking Regulatory Commission (CBRC). SPVs are meant to use proceeds from assets to pay returns on the securities. By doing this, the banks are basically taking these debts off their books to free up liquidity and pass on risk to outside investors. To reduce risks attached to the securitised loans, they have to be rated by two credit rating agencies, those ratings being submitted to financial regulators (China Securities Regulatory Commission), and the originator of the debt must retain certain portions of the lowest class of asset-backed securities, to a minimum of 5 per cent for the debt duration, while institutions investing in securitised debt can only hold up to 40 per cent in any individual security. SPV trustees must also submit periodical public health reports' asset performance, which must remain simple in structure.

Although, also in March 2013,[12] Chinese onshore private equity companies were initially given the go-ahead to invest in public funds or trade in public securities by the China Securities Regulatory Commission (CSRC), the National Development and Reform Commission (NDRC) prohibited such private equity involvement. Clearly the CSRC wants private equity to trade up these debts, but the NDRC fears creating too much risk for public finances.

In 2013, the Finance Ministry announced plans to issue RMB 350 billion worth of bonds[13] for all local governments, representing a 40 per cent increase on 2012, and that local governments were likely to also increase their issuance. In Jiangsu, the provincial government is targeting RMB 5.1 billion in funds it raises at building transport infrastructure, and RMB 400 million on subsidised housing.

In June 2013, the National Audit Office[14] revealed that local government debt was continuing to grow. The report covered 223 local government finance vehicles, 1,249 local government-funded institutions, 903 government agencies and over 22,000 projects across 15 provinces and provincial capitals as well as Shanghai, Tianjin and Chongqing municipalities. It found that 36 governments had debt totalling RMB 3.85 trillion by the end of 2012, up 12.9 per cent since the end of 2010 when the previous audit was conducted. While 24 governments had reduced their debt levels, nine provincial capitals had debts exceeding their total fiscal resources, with one city having debts of 190 per cent of fiscal revenues, rising to 220 per cent when guarantees of debts to other institutions were taken into account. In 13 out of the 15 sample provincial capitals, the interest on principal loans needing repayment by the end of 2012 was equivalent to 20 per cent of fiscal resources, reaching nearly 68 per cent for one unnamed city.

Also of concern is that local governments are using new debt to pay off old debt, including taking on new additional debt. While the Jiangsu government is putting RMB 5.1 billion into infrastructure and housing, in 2013 it also has to pay off RMB 6.2 billion in debts due. Other provinces and municipalities are perhaps not as leveraged, but all are running worryingly high credit tabs. While the Chinese banking sector (state-owned and therefore extensions of the central policy bank) and the central government will keep propping up the local governments' finances, it would make more sense for the central government to simply centralise certain taxes and fund provinces directly, forcing local authorities to justify spending plans.

There is a rather all-too-cosy relationship between local government and businesses that generate many avenues for corruption and misappropriation of both funds, equipment and other assets. If severe enough, this leads to local government debt being used to buy infrastructure assets at inflated costs, meaning assets become worth less than the cash invested, and the associated debt is unserviceable. The opacity of local government funding, coupled with the opacity of corporate accounts and layers of crony corruption, masks graft and tax avoidance that jeopardise the proper working of economies and create unfair market competition. The scale of the local government debt is therefore indicative of the scale of market distortions.

Corporate debt

According to the *Wall Street Journal*[15] in December 2012, mutual funds accounted for some 50 per cent of the demand for the most common type of corporate bond in 2012, up from 45 per cent in 2011 and 18 per cent in 2010. China's state-owned banks and insurance companies traditionally have been its big bond buyers, while foreign investors account for only a small fraction of bond purchases. But there are increasing concerns that the corporate bond market is reaching bubble proportions.

Tightening of corporate bond rules[16] in late 2012 may have come rather late to fix the bubble. According to Goldman Sachs' frequently asked questions (FAQ) document on China's bond market, the combined public and private bond market in China at the end of December 2012 reached a value of RMB 21.73 trillion, making China's the fourth largest bond market globally, of which enterprise and corporate bonds represented about RMB 2.5 trillion. But according to economic–political blog ZeroHedge,[17] as reported in Caijing Online in November 2012, corporate debt as a percentage of GDP was estimated to be 151 per cent, making China the largest credit bubble in the world. Also, it's expanding fast, from 96 per cent of GDP in 2008 to 130 per cent of GDP in 2011.

Late in 2012 and into the first quarter of 2013, many commentators began to display serious concern that China's corporate debt was ballooning out of control. According to Beijing-based economics consultancy and publisher of the *China Economic Quarterly*, GK Dragonomics, quoted in *Businessweek*[18] in November 2012, because many of the most heavily indebted companies are state-owned, and the banks they are indebted to are also state-owned, the corporate debt situation is one that the government ultimately has to deal with if defaults occur, meaning the government is obliged to bail out 49 per cent of government debt. Also according to Dragonomics, if you add up corporate, public and household debt in China, you reach a figure that is about 205 per cent of GDP, which is a lot compared to other emerging markets![19] This figure was corroborated in May 2013 by Credit Lyonnais Securities Asia's (CLSA's) China research division managing director Zhang Yaochang, who went on to say that in the past four years China's domestic debt grew to 2.9 times GDP.[20] In June 2013, an editorial in *China Securities Journal*,[21] an official mouthpiece publication under the Ministry of Finance, suggested total debt in the financial system in China had already reached 221 per cent.

This leads to concerns that a major state-owned corporate in China might default on its debts and go bankrupt, triggering a call on the government's underwriting obligations. This kind of economic problem is hard to predict, but there are indicators that can test how bad the situation has become. One such is total amount of accounts receivable within industry, representing money owed by recipients to companies that have sold goods to them. By the end of March 2013, total accounts receivable in China reached RMB 8.29 trillion according to the National Bureau of Statistics (NBS), an increase of 14.9 per cent year-on-year, dwarfing industrial profits for companies over the statistical threshold, which grew to RMB 1.17 trillion, up by 12.1 per cent.

If company profits take a hit, then paying for goods received is often delayed, hurting suppliers down the line and leading to the problem known as triangular debt, where a company is not paid for its goods sold, in turn failing to pay its suppliers, and so on.

Triangular debt – the perfect storm

Anne Stevenson-Yang, co-founder of J Capital Research, a Beijing-based equities analysis firm, warned of a scenario where capital flows grind to a halt as debt begets debt, and companies begin folding under pressure of accounts not received coupled with continuing and increasing operating costs in markets where competitive oversupply compounds narrow margins. A few companies at the bottom end of the triangular debt line seeking legal recourse to recover money owed can be dealt with by the courts, but if triangular debt builds up through a supply chain, and more companies end up owing more money to each other, then this creates the spectre of masses of claimants going to court to recover money from companies that cannot pay – leading to mass bankruptcies. Not that anyone really expects the Chinese courts to help them get their money back, as there is usually no enforcement of repayment of debts, and debts are routinely written off.

Examples of mounting debt problems among companies in China are increasing. One is that of a logistics company subsidiary of Ma'anshan Iron and Steel, which filed 23 lawsuits against companies owing it money in September 2012. By early October 2012, the logistics company went bankrupt. Concurrently, an article from the state Xinhua News Agency warned that the kind of triangular debt China suffered in the 1990s, when large-scale industrial restructuring caused a mass of company closures, was again becoming a very real risk.

According to Helen Lau,[22] senior analyst at Singaporean securities company UOB Kay Hian, debt as a percentage of equity at China's leading four steel companies had risen to an average of 80 per cent, where 50 per cent is considered very high. Lau attributes the problem to overcapacity, estimating that China's steel industry output of 900 million tons is about 200 million tons too high for real demand, despite revitalisation in the construction industry.

What is most troubling is that most big companies in China, such as steel makers, are running their businesses based on loans from China's banks. Bank lending is artificially sustaining companies to keep them churning out goods into markets where overcapacity and oversupply are growing issues. This increases the likelihood that some of that lending will reach a point where companies, unable to shift stock, begin defaulting on loans to suppliers and failing to pay bank loans, creating a pool of nonperforming loans on bank books.

Non-performing loans

In early March 2013, China's Banking Regulatory Commission announced that bad loans increased by RMB 64.7 billion to reach RMB 492.9 billion by the end of 2012, but the nonperforming loan ratio remained at 0.95 per cent. In January 2013, China's banks extended RMB 1.07 trillion worth of lending, the highest monthly total in three years. If loan defaults continue to increase, coupled with reduced loan profitability because of higher reserve requirements on the banks, this could present a very serious problem for China's banking system. Standard & Poor's[23] has made the prediction that the percentage of nonperforming loans could increase to as much as 5 per cent of total bank lending by the end of 2013.

But the problem is not just that of short-term liquidity. The problem seems to stem from oversupply and overcapacity in many of China's industrial sectors. Throwing good money after bad companies in sectors with oversupply and competition is a recipe for financial disaster. What is needed is more efficiency and competitiveness, but many sectors remain dominated, if not monopolised, by large state-owned enterprises (SOEs). The government until recently remained loath to trim the sails of these behemoths lest they shed too many jobs and lose control over key "strategic" sectors, while SOEs are equally loath to relinquish the control of the sectors they dominate.

The state-owned sector sucks up 80 per cent of bank lending, but (as noted below)[24] it is the private sector, starved of mainstream lending and investment, that represents 99 per cent of the companies in China, 60 per cent of total GDP, 70 per cent of jobs and 65 per cent of new patents filed in China each year. This creates distortions in market and corruption that inflates the scale of the local government debt situation. The debt situation therefore directly influences industrial market and sector competition, to varying degrees according to the type of sector.

Cleaning-up

The debt–corruption nexus is now a big issue, with Chinese authorities detaining protestors[25] demanding that government officials declare their asset holdings. The new leadership's central plank of fighting corruption at all levels of the government, which Xi Jinping has vowed will investigate both "tigers and flies" (both minor and very senior cadres), faces huge vested interests among corrupt officials who will do whatever they can to protect themselves.

In a May 2013 editorial, the *Global Times*[26] reported that the Communist Party of China (CPC) Central Commission for Discipline would begin random checks on asset declarations made by officials and that information previously held in confidential files would be scrutinised, looking at income, property holdings, and the occupations, employers and business holdings of immediate family members. Shanghai and Guangzhou were the cities to first implement such spot-checks, and those who file false information could face severe punishments.

As well as the political corruption issue, the mounting corporate debt is leading to concerns[27] that China could be facing the kind of financial crisis that Japan and Korea faced in the mid-1990s,[28] and that Chinese banks will find it increasingly hard to deal with both mounting corporate and local government debt all at once. If corporate debt as a percentage of GDP in China really is 151 per cent, then even with its huge capital reserves, the Chinese government will find it difficult to plug the gap, especially if those debts daisy-chain down to thousands of supplier companies as their creditors go belly-up, leaving them to stand in line behind the banks in reclaiming debts. The direct risks of significant debt default will likely be mostly contained within China's borders,[29] but the side-effects could significantly impact upon China's economy, and that could badly hit the economies of its trading partners.

The Chinese government could privatise some state-owned assets and land holdings, but with debt being so prevalent across the industrial sector, and financial institutions already holding so much local government debt, it is hard to see who they would sell those assets to within China, and I sincerely doubt that the Chinese government will be at ease selling off such assets to foreign entities. It could raise taxes on small- and medium-sized enterprises (SMEs) – the private sector companies that contribute most to the economy – but this could severely impede economic growth and competition, pushing even more of the competitive advantage over to the SOEs. The government could tax more from China's consumers, but this would inhibit growth in the domestic consumption component of GDP, lead to some serious wage hike demands, and seriously piss off a very vocal and economically significant part of the population: perhaps enough to create some significant social problems.

If Zhang Ke's (founder of accounting company ShineWing and vice-chairman of China's accounting association) worries about the debt situation in China are correct, then the situation's best way out, selling off state-owned assets, could prove problematic because so much of the assets that could be sold off are potentially well below the value of the debt accrued in their construction. According to Michael Pettis, professor of finance at Peking University, much of those worrying debts have been accrued to invest in "*empty real estate, empty highways, empty airports, unnecessary manufacturing capacity, etc.*"[30] So not only have debts mounted faster than the ability of the financial system in China to pay them off, but the assets that could become available to sell off to service those debts could simply fail to generate the value needed to pay off the cost of their construction. This is because they were so poorly devised in the first place – being created to gild local official achievement targets (and promotion prospects) and support corrupt crony relationships between local officials and SOEs. There is the argument that China's massive urbanisation will ensure that these so-called ghost developments will eventually fill up with people, but even if true, that is cold comfort to anyone who has lost money investing in them.

The new Chinese leadership, in its November 2013 Third Plenum document, indicated gradual privatisation of SOEs through allowing private investment to come into the state sector. What this means is that private shareholders could begin to force changes in management at SOEs to improve their efficiency, and reduce their reliance on government investment. This could allow SOEs to become more competitive, sustainable, profitable businesses that could be sold off as viable assets, in non-strategic sectors. The continued corruption crackdown is also shaking out many of the vested interests that would otherwise stand in the way of SOE reform. These reforms will help, but not in all sectors, and they will take time to implement and for private investors to be convinced about the potential for a positive return on their investments. Meanwhile the debt continues to mount.

Personal debt and the rise of credit cards

In China, all bank cards are issued by commercial banks and provide consumption credit, fund transfers, cash deposits and withdrawals. Issued cards include debit cards and credit cards, of which debit cards represent about 90 per cent of all cards. Credit cards have maximum interest-free repayment periods of 60 days. Credit card holders can apply for supplementary cards. Spending using bank cards, excluding real estate, automobile sales and wholesale transactions, accounted for 42.7 per cent of total official retail sales data by mid-2012.

The total number of cards in circulation grew by nearly 125 per cent between 2007 and 2012, while the value of total bank card transactions grew by 631 per cent. The total number of cards held per capita grew by 125.9 per cent, with average spending per capita growing by 608 per cent to reach over RMB 5,894. While corporate and local government debts are nothing new to China, personal debt is. Chinese consumers were traditionally debt-averse, but increasingly they are getting used to it, if not embracing it wholesale. They are encouraged by a government that knows that if consumption is to be spurred among a population who habitually save, then getting the banks to hand out credit cards is a great way to get that kick-started.

The surge in China's bank card use has been helped by growth in online retailing. But could more credit card use be leading to a debt crisis? Many of China's credit card users are new to their use, and less attuned to the risks of running up uncontrolled card debts as those in more developed countries. By the end of September 2009,[31] at which point China's banks had issued 175 million credit cards, new card issuance had grown by a staggering 33.3 per cent increase from the same time in 2008, leading the PBoC to begin sounding alarm bells about the amount of overdue credit card debt.[32] At that time, accounts overdue by six months or more represented 3.4 per cent of total credit card debt outstanding in China.

Another warning came from PBoC,[33] in November 2010, after the amount of money owed 180 days past due date again rose in the third quarter (Q3) of that year, to reach RMB 7.92 billion, having increased 8.5 per cent over the second quarter (Q2) that year to reach 2.1 per cent of total credit card debt. This was down on the level seen in 2009, but still worrying the central bank. By the end of 2011, the balance of credit card payments overdue by six months or more reached RMB 11.03 billion, up 43.5 per cent since the end of 2010, according to PBoC,[34] with accounts overdue by six months or more representing 1.4 per cent of total outstanding credit card debt. By the end of the final quarter (Q4) of 2012,[35] the total value of overdue credit with an outstanding term of over six months was RMB 14.66 billion.

Clearly this unpaid debt is getting bigger. It is also a growing concern that many Chinese people, new to the use of credit cards[36] and with little experience of managing the amount of debt they run up using them, can quickly lose track of how much they are spending and how much they owe. Also worrying is the ease with which people in China can apply for and obtain yet more credit cards, even young students. That concern became manifest when the CBRC in August 2012 issued new regulations on the credit card businesses of commercial banks. They included a ban on cards being issued to minors (unless guaranteed by an adult), those without a regular source of income and/or lacking the "*capacity for civil conduct.*"[37] Banks became required to bring credit card lending controls within their internal risk control and management systems, and bank staff were not allowed to be incentivised with rewards for issuing volumes of cards.

These new rules show how Chinese banks have been dishing out credit cards to anyone able to stand on two legs, and that they have been paying scant attention to controlling the amount of debts that any passing bipedal life form might manage to run up with their per capita three credit cards. The banks have been binging on credit card transaction fees ranging from nil for public institutions to about 1.25 per cent. Banks also make money from credit card holders rolling over their credit card debts. According to Richard Huang of Boston Consulting,[38] somewhere between 3 per cent and 8 per cent of Chinese credit card users roll over their debts each month. This is quite low, given that the figure is closer to 40 per cent in the US, so banks are still encouraged to keep pushing out more cards to make more money. If you take the number of credit cards, as shown in Table 3.1, issued between 2007 and 2012, put them into a spreadsheet and project forward, you get 1 billion credit cards by 2026. This nearly matches a 2010 MasterCard prediction of the total number of credit cards in China.

But the worry is not the sheer number of credit cards, as much as how they are being used. Searching online for news on credit cards in China, what is most surprising is the number of stories of young students[39] who apply for multiple credit cards, lured by discounts linked to everything from cosmetics, cinema tickets, to restaurant vouchers and Starbucks coffee. They perceive they can save money and improve their lifestyles,

Table 3.1 Number of credit and debit cards in circulation and value of transactions, 2007–2012

Million cards	2007	2008	2009	2010	2011	2012
Debit cards	1,410	1,658	1,880	2,185	2,664	3,169
Credit cards	90	142	186	230	285	331
Total cards	1,500	1,800	2,066	2,415	2,949	3,500
Value of transactions (RMB bn)	1,074.0	1,933.2	3,079.8	4,682.5	7,318.8	7,854.9*
Total retail sales	7,504.0	9,119.9	10,541.3	13,691.8	16,068.3	18,388.4
Value of transactions % of total retail sales	14.3	21.2	29.2	34.2	45.5	42.7
Population (mn)	1,290.0	1,296.3	1,305.4	1,314.5	1,323.7	1,332.7
Per capita cards	1.16	1.39	1.58	1.84	2.23	2.63
Per capita transaction value (RMB)	832.6	1,491.3	2,359.3	3,562.2	5,529.1	5,894.0

Notes: * Based on first half of 2012.

Source: People's Bank of China (PBoC) (www.pbc.gov.cn).

paying little attention to the amount of debt they accumulate. China's cities are littered with stalls pushing credit cards marketed with enticing special offers and promising greater freedom to consume, but offering scant (if any) warnings about the consequences of running up debts.

One story[40] in early 2013 described how a student in Chongqing ran up debts to buy an iPhone and, finding himself unable to keep up with payments, was forced to work for eight days on a building site doing manual labour to earn the money to pay off those debts. What was outstanding in that example was his determination to work his way out of debt, but many young Chinese are simply getting further and further into debts they cannot repay. Rapid recent growth of online retailing, combined with online payments, makes it even easier for people to spend on the never-never and lose track of how much debt they are amassing. The debt is not yet too big for the banks to control, but the growth in debt is still concerning enough for the central bank to take intervening steps.

Credit card fraud is also on the rise. According to Shanghai's High Court, quoted in an article in the *Global Times*[41] in March 2013, in Shanghai credit card fraud, mainly among people deliberately running up debts they cannot pay, represented 88 per cent of financial crime in the city in 2012. A similar picture of rising credit card fraud was also emerging in Beijing, and highlighted in an article in the *China Daily*[42] in April 2013. The situation has been allowed to worsen due to banks largely ignoring the need to verify people's identities or their claimed income, dishing out cards with impunity, especially those that have lower credit limits. The problem is, of course, once someone uses a false identity to get one card, they will likely be emboldened to get more cards, so that they can increase their overall credit amount.

The PBoC's concerns about credit card debt surfaced with a warning[43] back in November 2010. That it has been somewhat slow to act on this means that the authorities are less concerned about credit card debt than keeping the consumer market growing. But a consumer market grown on debt, rather than dipping into savings, is hardly a healthy model for long-term consumer market economy growth.

Summary

Mounting debt among China's local governments, companies and citizenry is a worrying trend that is beginning to look all too familiar to those in the West who have witnessed the consequences of mounting debt on their economies. At the end of August 2013, Morgan Stanley[44] was of the view that China's bank non-performing loan rate had reached 9.7 per cent of total loans. It seems that many assume that, if all else fails, the central government can step in with its huge foreign exchange reserves, state-owned assets and land sale potential and wipe clean the slate. But the government's money should be meant for investment in social services and social security, not underwriting wasteful consumption among officials, companies or individual consumers.

The new leadership's anti-corruption campaign and its attempts to clean up the banking system are to be applauded, but can they stem the growth of debt, and the debt culture that has already manifested itself? My own view is that, despite the resistance it faces, the new leadership has already proven resolute in pursing those who distort the system, but sustained progress can only be achieved through a fundamental overhaul of the system itself. It is clear that lending and borrowing is not being controlled properly, as the figures show.

Steering the Chinese economy away from debt calamity will, if the Chinese government pulls it off, and it is confident it can,[45] be a huge achievement. Failing to do so could leave China stuck in the kind of economic funk that Japan found itself in the 1990s, only Japan was already rich by then with a highly developed and comprehensive welfare state and high rates of personal and corporate tax collection with low tax avoidance, whereas China's per capita GDP remains quite low, with only basic social welfare coverage for the very poorest and widespread tax avoidance.

> Steering the Chinese economy away from debt calamity will, if the Chinese government pulls it off ... be a huge achievement

One crucial factor makes China different – that its banking sector is state-owned and the country has low need for overseas lending. Given an undertaking to reduce debt across the state, corporate and private sectors now, the Chinese government could avert significant build-up of problems in the future. It will be worth keeping an eye on the continued intensity of corruption clamp-downs to see how committed the government is to reducing the cronyism that helps sustain profligate spending on dubious investments, and concurrently raise the efficiency of investment and reduce the amount of bad debt.

chapter 4

Monetary Policy

Controlling inflation reigns supreme

Because political stability is what keeps the Communist Party of China (CPC) in power, and to keep political stability the government needs to keep currency stability, keeping inflation in check is a prime political objective. In democracies, governments get voted out if they lose control of inflation, but where voting isn't an option, people take more direct action. If inflation gets out of control, then prices get out of reach and poor people get hungry, and there's no more socially destabilising a demographic group than hungry people. Indeed, the People's Bank of China (PBoC) is tasked with keeping inflation in check as its primary objective, and it performs control over the flow of money through China's economy through state-owned banks. The government can therefore turn on the cash taps to inject money into the economy, or close off those taps to cool things down, a direct means of control over the economy few other governments have.

there's no more socially destabilising a demographic group than hungry people

Banks rule the command financial market

For example, China's economy has certain high-tide points where more cash is needed in the economy than other times, such as Chinese New Year (CNY), when the whole of China goes on a retail spending binge. The retail binge requires more cash in the economy, and each year, depending on when CNY falls, the PBoC injects more cash into the economy. Then, once CNY is over, the PBoC drains out any excess cash in the economy to keep things calm. One thing that made 2013 slightly unusual was that the PBoC (and by extension, the government) appeared to be concerned about the potential for overheating, and in February, after CNY, it drained off RMB 910 billion of liquidity[1] out of the banking system, a not unusual move except that the amount was much larger than the RMB 662 billion put into the banks before CNY 2013. With a large balance of payments surplus and inflows of foreign capital, there had been an oversupply of liquidity in the domestic economy that could further push up inflationary pressure and that the banks needed to keep in check.

China's banks have been instrumental in helping the government to control lending in the real estate sector, and avert overheating in the property sector. They have also been used to keep lending prices down by maintaining low interest rates, which has made investment capital cheap and has arguably made it easier to waste capital investment in big development projects that are not given due commercial diligence or economic stress-testing.

Reform needed to drive better monetary controls

Keeping a lid on rash local government spending, controlling bank lending both on-the-books and through shadow banking mechanisms, and curtailing the advantage that state-owned enterprises (SOEs) have in access to financing are all key points that the government needs to address in reforming monetary policy, and were points brought up by the International Monetary Fund (IMF) task force[2] that visited China in May 2013 and met with the new Chinese leadership. Chief among the IMF recommendations was reform of the financial sector and fiscal control to improve financial discipline, warning against any liberalisation of the financial markets. The IMF also indicated it would like to see more interest rate liberalisation to make money prices follow market demand, forcing borrowers to better plan their investments and ability to repay to help reduce wasted capital.

As might be expected, the IMF also had concerns that should economic growth slow more sharply than anticipated, then to sustain growth in the domestic consumer market the government will need to ramp up social security spending to help consumer households to continue consuming rather than stashing cash in savings. The need for better social security spending means the central government needs to take over spending allocation and therefore fiscal income, centralising taxation to take fiscal accounts out of local authorities and bring them under tighter central government control. This will also help to bring mounting local government debt under control, by centralising spending and reducing the amount of capital local governments need to raise from land sales to obtain cash to fulfil spending commitments.

Lack of transparency at China's banks

Despite their roles as economic levers in the domestic economy, China's banks publish surprisingly little information[3] about their financial situations compared to foreign banks. This is perhaps not so surprising though since Chinese companies generally rank low in terms of financial transparency,[4] and anti-corruption watchdog Transparency International found that of 24 international financial companies surveyed for their latest report, the three least transparent were Chinese banks. This is an issue not just for investors holding shares in those banks, but also the Chinese government and public at large, as it is they who cannot get a clear picture of the kind of shadowy dealings that Chinese banks are involved in. The lack of transparency and rising incidence of corporate book-cooking hardly helps the case for Shanghai becoming an international financial centre to replace Hong Kong. The emergence of private lending, trust loans and credit through off-balance sheet[5] bank investments in wealth management products also sparks concern.

There is also the issue of how banks lending more favourably to large SOEs is creating a significant lack of competitive lending to private enterprises, stifling private competitiveness in favour of large, monopolistic SOEs which are hogging both industrial sectors and access to credit from banks. The financial system in China favours state-owned interests, including control of foreign exchange, and that creates distortions both in industrial sectors and the financial system, where strong vested interests emerge between banks and SOEs which lean towards cronyism and mutual protectionism. According to statistics compiled by brokerage Credit Lyonnais Securities Asia (CLSA),[6] the amount of shady, off-book lending done by banks via trusts and wealth management products tripled between 2009 and 2012 to a figure equivalent to 25 per cent of gross domestic product (GDP), or about RMB 13.5 trillion.

When the central banking regulator, the China Banking Regulatory Commission (CBRC), introduced new regulations to curtail the involvement of banks in wealth management products in late March 2013, many commercial bank stocks tumbled[7] as investors sold interest in these banks, knowing full well that such regulations would hit bank profits. Not that this really worries the banks, although a few cadres might lose the promotions they were expecting at year-end, the banks all being underpinned by central government. Investing in shares in Chinese banks was always going to be risky so long as they remain levers to control money flow in the economy and therefore are likely to face lean years.

But the main commercial banks are not the only organs of financial and monetary control or supply in China, nor the only source of monetary malpractice. It is also important to understand the role played by rural credit cooperatives, acting as local banks across China, as well as the shadow banking industry. While the state-owned banks may control much of China's money, they do not control all of it. Much of China's markets and consumption is funded through channels over which the Chinese government has far less control.

China Development Bank

There is one banking institution with a lot of influence on China's industrial growth. China Development Bank (CDB) is one of China's three policy banks, the other two being the Agricultural Development Bank of China and the Export–Import Bank of China. The CDB is tasked with raising funds for large infrastructure and economic development projects within China, which it does by issuing bank bonds bought by insurance companies and other banks. For instance, it is responsible for bank-rolling the development of Tianjin's Yujiapu financial district, and helping Chinese companies invest overseas. As it is run directly by the State Council, it extends its influence across the state-owned corporate sector, helping SOEs to maintain their dominant role in their respective sectors, both in China and increasingly as they look outside China for investment opportunities.

In effect, it is a government department that raises capital by issuing bonds to fund commercial controls in key sectors, and is therefore very much an instrument of the command economy. While the CDB might be a force for good in concentrating funds towards development of logistics in some of China's more remote regions, thus bringing them into more developed status, it could also be argued it provides continued and further unfair advantages to large SOEs at the expense of private enterprises, thus distorting real market demand. For example, does Tianjin really need a huge new financial district that will compete with Beijing, Shanghai, Shenzhen and Hong Kong?

Again, the need for reform in terms of how capital is utilised in China is becoming more pressing, as more of China's wealth becomes used in inefficient and grandiose projects of dubious commercial use. That would also mean a review of what role the CDB should undertake, and what it should be barred from involvement in, to allow markets to develop and money to flow where there is real demand, rather than as political edict appoints.

Without market discipline, China's stock markets will continue to perform badly, its SOEs continue to provide poorer profits than private companies and its banks get embroiled in subbing local governments yet more debts. In such a situation, it is also not surprising that rich Chinese have little faith in investment vehicles inside China and often look offshore to store and invest their substantial cash.

Capital flight – cash illegally moved overseas

In October 2012, in an article in the *Wall Street Journal*,[8] professor of finance at Peking University Michael Pettis suggested that there were significant amounts of capital flight out of China among the country's business leaders. The article used China's trade and foreign exchange reserves data between September 2011 and September 2012 to show that over those 12 months some US$ 225 billion flowed out of China (both legally and illegally), representing about 3 per cent of GDP.

Officially, China restricts individuals to a US$ 50,000 limit to the amount of cash they can take out of the country, but it is likely that many are able to shift much more offshore through their companies. What the *Wall Street Journal* calculations suggest is that there is now a significant enough amount of capital flight to have caused China's foreign exchange reserves to have declined slightly. Given that China has vast foreign reserves, this is not going to be a nationally significant issue yet, but it does indicate a lack of confidence among China's rich in keeping money inside China.

According to a 2011 survey jointly commissioned by China Merchants Bank and Bain & Co.,[9] of the more than 500,000 Chinese who have assets of over RMB 10 million, 60 per cent are considering or actively pursuing emigration from China. While the deteriorating environmental situation might be reason enough for rich Chinese to leave, most are probably doing so to help their children get an education overseas. However, there are also likely to be concerns among China's rich about financial stability in China. While they will continue to work and run businesses in China, they are hedging their bets in case things turn sour.

China's rich are also hoarding gold. According to Hong Kong Census and Statistics Department[10] data, in March 2013, net gold trade into China from Hong Kong grew to 136 tonnes, up from nearly 60 tonnes in February and 114 tonnes in December 2012. The total trade in gold from Hong Kong to China for 2012 was 557.5 tonnes. Total gold trade into China via Hong Kong in the 15 months up to March 2013 was 1,206 tonnes. This could mean that rich Chinese are investing in gold because other forms of investment inside China are so poor, but it also raises the possibility that gold is one way to smuggle wealth out of China.

It could be argued that the rich in China are always likely to be potential targets of legal problems. Even those who are as clean as they can be in China know that to get anything done you have to bend the rules, work the connections in government and resort to some kind of basic corruption, even if it sticks in the craw a bit, because otherwise nothing would get done.

Only when economic development does not require corruption, as is often the case now, and people can make money cleanly without resorting to bending the rules, will those who make it rich in China feel completely comfortable staying in China, and keeping their cash there. The data on capital flight raises the issue further of distortions in the workings of China's domestic industries and markets. It also shows that while people keep funnelling income offshore, keeping reliable data on incomes becomes even harder.

Only when economic development does not require corruption, will [the] rich in China feel completely comfortable keeping their cash there.

The exchange rates issue

Also of significant influence to China's monetary situation is the influx of foreign exchange into the country and the value of the Renminbi (RMB) against foreign currencies. This has been a hot political potato for China in relation to its trading partners, especially the US,[11] and the valuation of the RMB continues to be a highly contentious issue. The argument goes that the low value of the RMB means China's exports have an unfair advantage in export markets. However, China is in the midst of a full-blown retooling of its economy towards more of a domestic consumption model, while its consumers are both increasingly better paid and demanding of better-quality (higher-value) products and services.

While the government does its best to keep inflation down, the cost of living will undoubtedly drive upwards. If the RMB's value increases more strongly now, China's exporters would become less profitable at a time when their export markets are shrinking due to the poor global financial situation, forcing them to either face bankruptcy or move into offshoring production into lower-wage countries, and that would mean job losses in China, as has already been seen in its shoe manufacturing industry. It would also mean that China would face a situation where imported goods became strongly competitive against domestic goods (because the increased value of the RMB would increase the value of consumer incomes in China), raising competition from imports for local companies and reducing the trade balance. Already China has become expensive for foreign tourists, with inbound tourism numbers trailing off recently, while more Chinese find they can afford to go overseas to travel.

China would get an increased share of GDP from domestic consumption at the expense of domestic companies and jobs, and that would not help create an orderly rebalancing of the economy towards domestic consumption because China's population is still relatively poor, on average. China would face a growing population of migrant workers without jobs or forced to take lower-paid jobs, and many Chinese would see their real incomes decline even though the value of their currency increased. There would be a lot of angry people out of work, or demanding higher wage rises that affect job creation. Not a situation that the Chinese government is going to allow.

If the Chinese government were to allow the RMB to appreciate faster, it could reduce interest rates to force a credit expansion, but that would further hit manufacturers of goods and put more money into the investment sector. That could just lead to more cheap credit-fuelled investment by local government officials, pouring more of China's money in the form of concrete into the already bubbly property market. Keeping the appreciation in the value of the RMB to a pace that allows China's domestic consumer market to develop healthily is not only good for the Chinese economy, but also those manufacturing markets that increasingly hope that China's consumers will develop into a sizeable market for their goods – including, arguably, US manufacturers. So China allowing the RMB to rise in value faster could potentially be more damaging to US jobs than allowing it to appreciate more sedately.

The domestic monetary situation continues to face the problem of increasing inflows of foreign exchange even without an appreciation of the RMB, which would make it even cheaper to buy foreign currency. In mid-May 2013,[12] it was revealed that China's banks bought in RMB 294 billion more foreign exchange than they sold out in April 2013. This meant M2 money supply (a category within the money supply including M1 plus all time-related deposits, savings deposits and non-institutional money-market funds) within China had grown by 16.1 per cent over the same period in 2012 when the government had set a target of only 13 per cent growth, creating a surge in the money supply in China and a rise in the RMB's value against the US dollar. The State Administration of Foreign Exchange (SAFE)[13] was then forced to issue tighter foreign exchange trading rules to curb the amount of "hot" money coming into China and stop capital flows that are not linked to real goods trades. The problem of some companies creating fake goods trades,[14] especially in Hong Kong and Shenzhen, to trade on the differences in exchange rates between the two cities, obviously became severe enough for SAFE to implement much more stringent surveillance against this kind of fake trading. This is a situation that new offshore RMB trading was supposed to avert. SAFE has also taken steps to apply tougher foreign exchange rules[15] on banks and trading companies to curb hot money inflows.

Letting the RMB gradually rise in value should help to weed out much of the low-end export manufacturing that has passed its usefulness, and improve the environment for higher-end, more technically advanced industries that can supply jobs for a better-educated, higher-earning workforce. The high flow of hot money into China might be concerning, but inflation has not gone too high (if you believe the inflation figures), so now would be a good time to let interest rates loose to force better investment, while still allowing them to be adjusted (by the central government through the state-owned banks) to accommodate short-term hiccups.

Summary

The myth about China's monetary control is that China's government is somehow trying to build its domestic economy, banks and companies so that they can have some kind of unfair competitive edge in the global economy. The exchange rate peg is there to stop wages and prices rising too fast at home, and allow time for China's domestic companies to adapt to the demands of the domestic market. In truth, China's government is really trying to protect its economy, rapidly growing and as strong as it may seem, from its inherent fragility.

It is fragile because it is so new and its institutions are still learning to manage such fast-paced growth and to protect that growth from inflation, from overheating and from being drawn into the same kind of debt accumulation and rampant corruption that the government knows it can so easily drift into. It is also fragile because the control systems over the economy and monetary shifts are not as complete as might be assumed, nor is the data entirely reliable given the problems noted above about macroeconomic data, income data and capital flight.

Another myth that does not square, given the apparent super-nationalism of the Chinese, is why there already appears to be so much capital flight. Grass-roots (non-rich) nationalists, students and workers, go onto Weibo to argue that the government must protect the nation's borders against the territorial claims of its neighbours in the region. Meanwhile, others who also espouse being staunch nationalists, yet are very rich, are often making plans to park their money, if not themselves, in pastures new, basically hedging against their own country.

There is waste in the financial system, which props up the least efficient and most wasteful parts of the economy and suppresses China's entrepreneurial people and enterprises. The waste is also dangerous because it is only a matter of time before Chinese people wake up to the fact that the money being wasted in the financial system is theirs.

Part II
Industry and Companies

chapter 5

Manufacturing Measures

"Made in China" – possibly the most quoted phrase in the English language

At a macroeconomic level, the manufacturing output data coming from China appears quite accurate. Many external economic analysts, typically stationed in foreign investment banks, use a raft of proxy indicators to cross-check growth data for the total manufacturing sector growth data. Such proxy indicators include changes in total electricity output and consumption, coal consumption, freight traffic, etc. An example, in March 2013, was The Federal Reserve Bank of San Francisco, which issued a paper entitled "*On the Reliability of Chinese Output Figures*,"[1] authored by John Fernald, Israel Malkin and Mark Spiegel, that independently found that China's industrial output figures, based on their own proxy indicator analysis, do tend to reflect the official data.

But a macro view of measuring inputs and outflows can be misleading in a communist, partially command economy, like in China. The logic of such proxies is that the manufacturing output has somewhere to go – to a buyer who is waiting to pay for the goods. But while China's is a colossal manufacturing force, many sectors are

But while China's is a colossal manufacturing force, many sectors are grossly inefficient

grossly inefficient. Scrutiny at a micro level relies upon measuring the production and sales figures of the leading companies in each of the sectors, which often hide the reality because of false accounting. Also, because most sectors of the Chinese industrial landscape are highly fragmented, with many small competitors, undercutting between companies can leave many with much unsold inventory.

In short, there is a lot of oversupply and unsold goods, which the headline data does not fully include or deduct. In the 1950s and 60s, the command economy propaganda lauded so many thousand tractors made, or dams built. But what they did not report was how many of those tractors sat and rusted in the factory lot they were left in, or how many dams simply burst or silted up. The situation is not as bad now, but there is still a huge deal of inefficiency in China's industry that the figures do not reflect.

Fragmentation

To underline just how fragmented China's markets are, it is worth looking at a couple of examples:

- Restaurants: Over 4 million full-service and fast-food restaurant outlets in 2012, of which about half are fast-food outlets, but even the largest chain in China, KFC, with about 4,000 outlets by the end of 2012, only has about a 10 per cent share of the fast-food market. These figures don't include the mass of smaller, less-formal restaurants across China.
- In the manufactured snacks market, the top five companies combined only represented 8 per cent of the total market value in 2011, the biggest having less than 3 per cent.

As a general rule-of-thumb, any market in China that was largely introduced by foreign companies will tend to be less fragmented, while indigenous markets tend to be more so.

According to the China Chain Store and Franchise Association[2] (CCFA), the top 100 chain store retailers in China combined had a total turnover of RMB 1,866.5 billion in 2012, representing just 10.1 per cent of the total official retail sales figure. The total of the top 100 fast-moving consumer goods retailers' combined turnovers was, again according to the CCFA, RMB 835.8 billion in 2012, or 4.5 per cent of total official retail sales, and only 11 per cent of total retail food sales. China Resources Enterprise, the leading supermarket chain in China in 2012, according to the CCFA, with over 4,400 stores across the country, still only held a 1.3 per cent share of the total food retail market. Massive Chinese electronics and appliances retailer Suning, with RMB 124 billion in sales in 2012, according to the CCFA, represented only 1.2 per cent of total official non-food retail sales. According to my own total retail sales values for China, which are approximately half the value of the official figures, that means that these percentage shares only roughly double in size, which still represents a hugely fragmented retail industry.

According to Wang Yijiang,[3] professor of economics and human resource management at Cheung Kong Graduate School of Business in Beijing, small companies represent 99 per cent of the companies in China, 60 per cent of total economic output (gross domestic product), provide jobs to 70 per cent of the total workforce and are the source of 65 per cent of new patents filed in China each year, but receive less than 20 per cent of available investment resources.

Fragmented markets mean lots of small companies with poor economies of scale, remaining low-cost, low-quality manufacturers more likely to cut corners (worker safety, low wages, poor technology, poor hygiene, poor ingredients, etc.), and therefore unable to increase added-value. Even for big companies with better economies of scale, high degrees of fragmentation in markets makes growth difficult and means a drag on potential profitability. Big companies with deep pockets and a long-term view, with investors being happy to not see a return on investment for several years, can succeed in such environments of attrition, but there are many risks attached.

High fragmentation means sizing the market based on players' shares is prone to inaccuracy. Market share claims are also difficult to verify because different companies define their markets differently to other companies in the same sectors, often because they have subsidiary or side interests in sectors completely outside their core markets. For example, most of Yunnan's leading tobacco companies derive much of their income from non-tobacco activities, including selling cars, running hotels, investing in commercial property, growing and selling crops other than tobacco, etc. Many of China's sugar companies make more money from making and selling paper products made from the pressed "waste" sugar cane fibres than they do from the actual sugar they extract.

Private companies and private finance (and more debt!)

Finding it hard to compete against state-owned enterprises (SOEs) for resources or get loans from Chinese banks, private small- and medium-sized enterprises (SMEs) must often rely on non-bank lending. This private, shadow banking system is financed by private individuals who prefer to invest their spare cash in companies because the deposit rates at state-owned banks are so low – while things remain good, investing in a company set up by an entrepreneur with drive and dreams is likely to be a more efficient investment of spare capital than putting it in a bank account. So pools of private money have accumulated through brokers, and according to estimates from UBS,[4] that pool of cash is pretty significant, standing at about US$ 3.4 trillion (about RMB 21 trillion), which I estimate to be about 40 per cent of total gross domestic product (GDP) in 2012, although *Business Week* put the percentage at 45 per cent.

According to a People's Bank of China (PBoC) survey in 2011, in the city of Wenzhou (a city historically a hive of shadow banking, being both rich and traditionally inclined to be much more independently entrepreneurial than other parts of China), about 90 per cent of families and 60 per cent of companies are involved in shadow banking loans in some way or other. But as the economy has slowed, businesses have not been growing at expected rates, and money borrowed for business development has not come to fruition as quickly as hoped. Debts are beginning to be defaulted. According to the Zhejiang provincial Supreme Court, as reported in *Business Week*,[5] in Wenzhou alone in 2012 there were 25,900 lawsuits over RMB 46.2 billion in debt defaults, six times the amount in the preceding year.

Just as getting capital loans from banks has remained hard for private SMEs in China, the harder times are leading loan brokering agencies to raise their lending rates to even more punitive heights and to demand collateral on the loans, which many SMEs simply don't have. In this kind of climate, any attempts to regulate shadow lending are likely only to founder unless SMEs can provide more flexible terms than the banks or loan brokers. Already there is a growing micro-financing industry which provides smaller loans with smaller repayments, and with increments in lending based on the rate of success in the return on existing investment, thus reducing the risk on both sides.

The state-owned banks are not geared for that kind of role, and the "official" financial sector views such private, micro-financing as somewhat dubious. But the growth of shadow banking is not the problem in itself, because private financers will generally be very careful with their money, who they lend it to and under what terms. Rather, the fast-growing shadow banking industry stands as a symptom of the failures of the "official" financial industry. As Joe Zhang points out in his book *Inside China's Shadow Banking: The Next Subprime Crisis* (Enrich Professional Publishing, 2013), it is not the shadow banking industry that is lowering its lending criteria to keep giving money to local governments already highly in debt, it is the mainstream banks.

The role of private equity (PE) in China

The slowdown in the economy is also generating some critical stress on the relationship between investors and the directors/founders of the companies receiving investment, showing that many Chinese companies are now being forced to learn how to live with and respond to the rights and demands of the investors whose money they are spending. The sometimes adversarial relationship[6] between corporates and private investors also creates an incentive for companies to fudge their accounts to hide financial problems, while investors get creative with their lawyers to try to get companies to sign up to unfair legal terms. There is also the traditional despisal of "money lenders" in China, which goes back centuries, to contend with. And PE stands in stark political contrast with the core founding values of the Communist Party. The newness of PE in China also means that it has to operate in an environment where government legislation is weak and legislating motives are often inconsistent with those of capital investors, while legal grey areas create problems for those operating in the PE sector.

That aside, China needs not only the cash of PE investors but also, one can argue, the market discipline and scrutiny. Allowing private capital to flow where investors feel growth potential is strongest (rather than necessarily fastest) and away from where there is inefficiency, PE can present China with the potential to reform its industrial and corporate sectors through the discipline of cash alongside government attempts to improve legislation. According to China First Capital, there was probably already about US$ 50 billion of PE capital invested in private companies in China, with about the same again being raised for future investments. An increased role of PE within China's economy could not only help improve market discipline but also market data, with PE investors being more likely to scrutinise financial details thoroughly to protect their investments, and less likely to accept data at face value.

Oversupply and the waste of investment capital

In many of China's manufacturing sectors the landscape is of hundreds, in some cases thousands of small, localised companies all making very similar products to each other, and all selling to as many people as they can by undercutting each other. This piecemeal market development landscape means many companies' long-term businesses are unsustainable, facing rising costs of labour, energy, distribution, raw materials, etc. To survive they cut corners, and cutting corners leads to the kind of bad practices that resulted in the melamine in milk and other food scandals. In an attempt to sort out the dairy sector, in early 2010 the government stepped in to close down half of the 1,000+ companies involved in the industry, forcing them to re-apply for their operating licences – many did not bother. Despite this move, systemic problems still persist in the dairy sector.

A good example of oversupply in the China market was marked by the end of the Beijing Olympics in 2008, when the sportswear sector in China found itself awash with unsold stock. The sector had been growing well in the run-up to the 2008 Beijing Olympic Games, and in 2008 itself grew by 14 per cent, a two percentage point improvement on 2007. But there was an incorrect assumption in the industry that sportswear sales had something to do with sports participation. They did not. It was just a fashion trend, and like any other fashion it came with the inevitability of going out of fashion. Yet sportswear chains expanded fast and filled lots of new stores with sports shoes and clothing.

But after the Olympics, China's consumers grew tired of sportswear and the market shrank back down to 8 per cent growth in 2009, while China's shoppers went off looking for the next big fashion thing, cancelling gym memberships and selling off equally redundant exercise equipment. Instead, they turned their attention to buying outdoor wear, dreaming of trekking through far-off wildernesses far removed from their urban reality.

The sportswear market and its many competing brands found themselves sitting on huge piles of unsold stock, with inevitable effects on the balance sheets of many brands. For example, in April 2012, the Hongkong and Shanghai Banking Corporation (HSBC) estimated that domestic sportswear brand poster-boy Li Ning was sitting on excess inventory valued at around RMB 1.65 billion, which would require a year to clear. For Li Ning, the excess inventory led to a 65 per cent decline in profits during 2011, and a further 85 per cent drop in the first half of 2012. Not alone in this predicament, another domestic sportswear brand, Anta, found itself sitting on RMB 3.12 billion worth of excess inventory, and another brand, Peak, issued a profit warning[7] in January 2012, stating that orders for its apparel had declined by "the mid-20s" in percentage terms compared with 2011. Li Ning has been closing stores and restructuring its business since 2008, and only stopped closing stores, and reached its de-stocking target, at the end of May 2013.

The car sector in China is one that has long been considered a flagship industrial development within China, but one that has brought with it huge social and planning problems – not least my own particular gripe that China's cities were simply not designed for either the movement or the storage of cars (with most residential property still being poorly served by parking places). Despite continued ebullience among car makers in China, the picture is actually a lot less pretty than the industry paints, with the inventory index for the car industry (based on inventories divided by sales) by June 2012 reaching 1.98, according to industry data[8] published at the time. This meant that for every car sold, there were two more sitting in a holding lot somewhere, waiting for a buyer. An index of 1.5 is, apparently, worryingly high.

These are just a few of the many examples. The situation can only improve when oversupplied industries clear those inventories, but that means dropping prices, and therefore making losses on rising production costs. This oversupply is all down to bad planning, and that is caused by bad market data and understanding of the real dynamics in many sectors by the many companies involved. In my own view, one of the reasons that online retail in China has really taken off since 2008, is not only to do with security improvements to online payment methods, as well as a growing delivery infrastructure, but also because online retailers have been great at clearing discounted stock. The online retailers compete on the basis of shifting large volumes of competitively priced goods to wider population pools than is achievable through physical stores.

Online retail – a cheap clearing house?

Shifting large amounts of cheap goods should make profit earnings, except when the market keeps filling-up with new competitors, each slicing the pie more thinly than before, and profits in many of the online retail sectors in China remain very thin indeed. Off-price shifting of slow-moving stock, particularly seasonal products like fashion, where last season's must-have quickly becomes old-hat, is common online. No surprise then that clothing and footwear represent the biggest sector of China's online retail market, but even given the scale of sales in this sector, leading guns like Vancl continue to struggle to make a profit – in 2011 Vancl was reported to have made losses[9] of US$ 95 million.

China's online retail market is also increasingly fragmented, especially in the online apparel retail sector, which sees new players entering the market month-on-month. As more enter the market, many also depart, unable to sustain their operational losses. The lack of profitability also makes investors nervous. Vancl failed to do an initial public offering (IPO) in the US in 2011 due to weak investor confidence in the Chinese online retail market, and in H1 2012, private equity and venture capital investment in online retail in China dropped by 57 per cent year-on-year, according to the July 2012 report "*Online Retailing in China*" by Li & Fung Research Centre. Even though China's online retail market is growing fast, it is not growing great profit returns – yet.

According to a report entitled "*Click by click: How consumers are changing China's e-commerce landscape*", published by McKinsey & Company in July 2012, even one of China's largest online retailers, 360Buy.com, continued to lose money in 2011, and did not expect to make a profit for several more years due to its need to continue to invest in expanding its business. This requires not only the development of IT for online retail sites, but also building back-of-office delivery logistics. It is this rather less glamorous side of the industry that is the real development bottleneck for online retail in China.

To remain competitive, online retailers resort to damaging price wars and deep discounting, a war of attrition that relies on burning investment cash to keep operations going in the hope that those competitors less able to access investment cash will eventually crash, leaving the way to make profits in the future. But more new entrants mean the market continues to be diluted, and all the while Chinese consumers get used to, and come to expect, continued low prices from their online retailers, making it hard for them to switch tactic in the future.

Many online retailers are also chain store operators, such as Chinese appliances and electronics giants Suning and Gome. The problem for these companies is balancing sales between online retail sites and their own physical stores to avoid the danger of undercutting or cannibalising their own customers. Suning is now shifting its business model more towards one of an online-first retailer. China's hypercompetitive markets are no haven for SMEs and entrepreneurs, who often end up undercutting each other just to survive because of massive fragmentation.

Significant amounts of distribution spoilage

Logistics has always been a big headache for companies active in the China market. For one thing, China is just such a big country, with many mountainous regions and large rivers. For a long time its logistics industry was highly fragmented, with goods having to pass through different transport and warehouse companies at each stage of distribution, leading to gross price mark-ups, inefficiency and significant amounts of spoilage. China has invested vast amounts of money in improving its road, rail and air transport systems, and the entry of modern retail chains has drawn in investment by retailers in modern warehousing and logistics infrastructure.

But there is still a long way to go. Part of this is further consolidation of the logistics industry, where according to the 2012 *China Cold Chain Yearbook*,[10] there are more than 20,000 cold chain companies in China operating more than 30,000 cold warehouses and distribution centres, with a total storage capacity of 15 million tons. This still represents only a fraction of the capacity needed, and there remain huge gaps between the consumption demands of a country with a population of over 1.3 billion and supply chain coverage. For instance, *Yearbook* data shows only 15 per cent of the fresh and frozen food being handled by cold chain transportation, and up to 90 per cent of meat and 80 per cent of seafood being transported or distributed without proper cold chain environments.

The result is an estimated 20–30 per cent damage rate for food products because of them not being transported properly. It is a target of the Chinese government that by 2015 a number of cross-region cold storage distribution centres be established with proper cold chain transportation equipment and facilities to reduce the damage rate by 10–15 per cent. But this means that much of China's precious food resources will still be wasted, and many of its production and sales figures still count products not actually sold to end consumers.

Clearly this presents a challenge and an opportunity for new thinking and investment, especially with the recent growth in online retailing, including online food sales. This is an area where the competition from efficient, organised retail food chains, such as the supermarket and hypermarket chains, can have a positive impact on improving supply chain efficiency, and reducing waste. As China shifts more towards a domestic consumption-driven economy, and consumers' demand for better-quality produce in their stores increases, it will be the companies that can deliver goods in good order – be it food, pharmaceuticals or anything else – that will succeed in the future in China.

The bloated state-sector monopolies

A competitive market like China demands that more profitable, well-run, innovative and healthy companies should rise to dominance, but they still face a sea of low-quality competitors diluting markets, propped up by local governments worried about unemployment caused by company closures. There is also the problem of SOEs having unfair competitive advantages in monopolising credit from state-owned banks and political patronage through tax breaks and preferential treatment when investing in new property (factories and offices), etc. SOEs continue to gain advantages, including being bailed out when facing bankruptcy[11] and being allowed to run at a continual loss, propped up by government money. This situation suppresses growth in the private sector and means China's economy and industry are less able to improve efficiency and added-value. If it is to rise above being a cheap manufacturing base, China must break the stranglehold on resources and investment held by the SOEs.

Looking at the data in Table 5.1, we can see clearly that SOEs, on a productivity per employee basis, are more productive only on a gross industrial output and revenue basis than private enterprises, mainly due to economies of scale from their generally larger sizes. But in terms of profitability per employee, private enterprises are much more productive, despite SOEs owning much more significant assets per employee. This indicates how much less efficient SOEs are in their use of assets and profit generation. It is also worth noting that SOEs created less average gross industrial output than principle revenue, while private companies created more.

The list of industries in China, ranked on volume output growth rate, are also those with significant private company involvement (Table 5.2). For instance, China's leading computer maker is Lenovo,[12] a publicly listed company in Hong Kong, predominantly owned by private shareholders, a third by Legend Holdings. The most successful mobile phone handset makers are either foreign or privately owned, such as Huawei. Geely is the leading private Chinese automotives maker, and it now owns Volvo.

If China's industry and companies cannot add value to what they do, then many foreign and Chinese companies will find it increasingly hard to justify producing in China when other countries in the region are more cost-effective – such as Vietnam, the Philippines, Indonesia or India. US companies, for example, might find that "near-shoring"[13] their manufacturing to Mexico, or even back into the US, could soon work out more cost-effective than staying in China. Unless the monopoly held by SOEs in many sectors is broken, and private companies are allowed to thrive and innovate, China could face losing its manufacturing cost advantage.

China's new Monopolies and Mergers Commission has been flexing its muscles over foreign companies, with its rulings in the cases of the proposed purchase of juice maker Huiyuan by Coca-Cola and InBev/AB's shareholding in Tsingtao Beer being the most notable early cases. It is likely these were not only legitimate cases of protecting consumers against monopolies forming, but were also a political warning flag from the Chinese government to tell companies (both foreign and domestic) that it is serious about breaking damaging monopolies.

Table 5.1 Number of state-owned and private enterprises over the National Bureau of Statistics (NBS) statistical threshold, and key financial indicators, 2011

	Number of enterprises over the NBS statistical threshold	Gross industrial output value (current prices)	Total assets	Revenue from principle business	Total profits	Average annual number of employees
	(RMB bn)	**(RMB bn)**	**(RMB bn)**	**(RMB bn)**	**(RMB bn)**	**(thousands)**
State-owned enterprises	6,707	6,667.3	8,875.4	6,903.0	356.7	5,906.8
Private enterprises	180,612	25,232.6	12,775.0	24,727.8	1,815.6	29,564.1
Average per enterprise	–	**(RMB mn)**	**(RMB mn)**	**(RMB mn)**	**(RMB mn)**	**(Average employees)**
State-owned enterprises	–	994.1	1,323.3	1,029.2	53.2	880.7
Private enterprises	–	139.7	70.7	136.9	10.1	163.7
Productivity per employee	–	**(RMB '000)**	**(RMB '000)**	**(RMB '000)**		**(RMB '000)**
State-owned enterprises	–	1,128.7	1,502.6	1,168.7	60.4	–
Private enterprises	–	853.5	432.1	836.4	61.4	–

Source: NBS China Statistical Yearbook 2012.

Table 5.2 Volume output growth by industrial sector, 2002–2011

	2002	2011	% period growth
Microcomputer equipment (1,000 units)	146.4	3,203.7	2,089.0
Mobile telephones (1,000 units)	1,214.6	11,325.8	832.4
Cars (1,000 units)	10.9	101.3	827.4
Large and medium-sized tractors (1,000 units)	0.5	4.0	785.2
Integrated circuit (billion units)	9.6	72.0	647.1
Cigarettes (billion pieces)	346.7	2,447.4	605.9
Motor vehicles (1,000 units)	32.5	184.2	466.5
Household refrigerators (1,000 units)	159.9	869.9	444.1
Rolled steel (1,000 tons)	1,925.2	8,862.0	360.3
Air conditioners (1,000 units)	313.5	1,391.3	343.8
Household washing machines (1,000 units)	159.6	671.6	320.9
Crude steel (1,000 tons)	1,823.7	6,852.8	275.8
Pig iron (1,000 tons)	1,708.5	6,405.1	274.9
Primary plastic (1,000 tons)	145.6	499.2	243.0
Chemical fibre (1,000 tons)	99.1	339.0	242.0
Yarn (1,000 tons)	8,500.0	28,701.7	237.7
Plate glass (1,000 weight cases)	2,344.6	7,910.8	237.4
Natural gas (billion cu.m)	32.7	102.7	214.4
Coke (1,000 tons)	1,428.0	4,327.1	203.0
Cement (1,000 tons)	7,250.0	20,992.6	189.6
Metal-cutting machine tools (1,000 units)	3.1	8.9	187.4
Electricity (billion kwh)	1,654.0	4,713.0	184.9
Caustic soda (1,000 tons)	87.8	247.4	181.7
Ethylene (1,000 tons)	54.3	152.8	181.3
Cloth (billion metres)	32.2	81.4	152.5
Chemical pesticide (1,000 tons)	9.3	23.0	147.6
Sulphuric acid (1,000 tons)	305.0	748.3	145.3
Hydropower (billion kwh)	288.0	698.9	142.7
Colour television sets (1,000 units)	515.5	1,223.1	137.3
Machine-made paper and paperboards (1,000 tons)	466.7	1,101.1	135.9

(*continued*)

Table 5.2 Continued

	2002	2011	% period growth
Soda ash (1,000 tons)	103.3	229.4	122.0
Beer (1,000 kilolitre)	24,027.0	48,345.0	101.2
Salt (1,000 tons)	36,024.3	67,421.6	87.2
Chemical fertilizer (1,000 tons)	379.1	621.3	63.9
Refined sugar (1,000 tons)	9,260.0	11,874.3	28.2
Crude oil (1,000 tons)	167,000.0	202,875.5	21.5

Source: NBS China Statistical Yearbooks 2003 and 2012.

Breaking state-sector monopolies

The Chinese government has been pushing for SOEs to become more efficient and market driven in recent years, but many SOEs have continued to be protected by vested interests that hamper their real improvement. However, there are signs that the government is beginning to implement measures to force SOEs to abide by the rules. For example, leading Chinese liquor companies Kweichow Moutai and Wuliangye Group were dealt out fines totalling RMB 449 million by the National Development and Reform Commission (NDRC) for monopoly practices in which they colluded with each other to force sales agents to fix prices when the Baijiu (Chinese grain spirit) market began to decline in late 2012 on the back of the government push for Party officials to reign in their profligate spending on banquets and expensive alcoholic drinks. What was interesting also was that neither company issued an apology for this law-breaking, and one of Moutai Group's directors even went as far as telling the local press that "*companies that have made mistakes should be allowed opportunities for correction*."[14] Hardly appropriate contrition, and indicative of the arrogance such companies have in their sense of entitlement to run their industries as they please.

Also, the government continues to tinker with groupings of large state-sector companies. Shanghai's massive Bailian Group was constructed by agglomerating Shanghai's leading department stores and supermarket groups into one, colossal company meant to stand as a bastion of

Chinese retail might in the face of growing foreign competition. What happened was that this over-diverse company failed to run its disparate department store and supermarket chains efficiently, which allowed foreign department store and supermarket groups to develop stronger competitive markets in China. The department store division has since been spun off. Bailian continued to run low-cost supermarket chains supported by government patronage, but the chain began to look tired and low-grade compared with its competitors, which quickly rose to being on a par with the best chains around the world with strong innovation and quick expansion. More recently, Lianhua supermarket chain has cut store numbers, taken a hit on sales and is now attempting to improve efficiency.

Summary

Some SOEs in China have improved their efficiencies and attempted to improve their real business competitiveness, especially as many have begun to look outside China for markets to expand into. However, China's SOEs remain less profitable than the country's private companies.[15] SOEs still receive preferential treatment by the government that allows them to survive in their markets despite their competitive frailty. This amounts to government money, via state-owned banks, being unwisely invested in companies that are not run efficiently thanks to their privileged positions, resulting in capital being wasted.

Such wasted capital, takes away from more competitive and innovative private companies that create more jobs and innovative and competitive vibrancy in the market and adds overcapacity that dilutes markets. This creates a growing drag on the economy that will become greatly amplified by the slowdown in both industry and consumption.

The new Chinese leadership has pledged to reform SOEs.[16] Along with toppling corrupt bankers, ministers and cadres, the new leadership is having to shake down the very large vested interests of the SOEs. But breaking up some of the state sector (and perhaps privatising it) cannot be done without creating significant job losses, and possibly airing some questionable accounting.

SOEs have become a key draw for the many unemployed graduates that China produces, eager to enjoy the safe jobs and good salaries that SOEs provide. The government is already calling for SOEs to put more of their profits into the state budget so as to create new money that can be directed into social welfare spending, but the temptation to recycle that money back into the SOE sector remains strong. The government is also trying to lower average salaries in SOEs to rebalance the income inequality between state and private sector, the inequality driving more of China's graduates to look for jobs in SOEs, rather than in the more vibrant and innovative (but less well-paid) private sector.

Xi Jinping appears to be very open about the issues that need to be tackled, and also appears to have the political strength to take on the entrenched vested interests which would stand in the way of economic and industrial reform. I hope that the promising beginning of his leadership will gain momentum and the opportunity not be lost. But I remain very concerned that the concept of "too big to fail" pervades and bounds the SOEs in a layer of government protection that will not let go SOEs deemed "too important" to go bankrupt, despite remaining a financial and innovative drag on the markets they overshadow.

It is their sheer size, on paper, that raises the myth of the success and durability of China's SOEs

It is their sheer size, on paper, that raises the myth of the success and durability of China's SOEs. However, look into the financials closely enough, and a much less glowing financial picture emerges.

chapter 6

Cooking the Corporate Books

Stir-fried statistics

One of the biggest problems facing the Chinese government in reforming China's economy towards more efficient use of capital, and providing better-quality, innovative and desirable products to consumers to drive growth in the domestic consumer market, is that it must force domestic companies to stick to the rules, running proper corruption-free accounts.

Many companies hide their true accounts, often running double or triple accounts

Opaque accounting is rife among China's companies. Many companies hide their true accounts, often running double or triple accounts – one for official eyes, one for investors and then the real books. They often present the accounts of a shell or holding company, rather than the core business, to hide true business value. And this is not just small companies, but also large ones, including listed companies, among whom accounting creativity appears commonplace. This deception seems to be catching out the accounting firms paid to do company audits, and the lack of thoroughness by these accountants results in costly losses.

Examples emerge all the time, including big, high-profile ones. The scale of accounts irregularities differs in each case, from minor massaging to complete fabrication of accounts and even the existence of fake companies. Paul Gillis,[1] an accounting specialist based in Beijing, laid out some actually quite simple techniques that Chinese companies apply to mislead those who might scrutinise their accounts, and these can be summarised as: fake sales revenue; fake cash/assets; fake customers; fake employees; and fake companies.

One of the biggest recent fake sales scandals to emerge affected Swedish car maker Volvo,[2] which found that to win cash incentives, some of its car dealers in China were inflating their sales figures. Sales of Volvo's cars in China had not been great, not helped by a recall[3] in 2012 of some 12,000 imported cars due to improper installation of wire seat harnesses and possible oil leaks due to friction damage to oil pipes. But in 2011, according to the company, some 7,000 of the 47,140 car sales made in that year were fake – that's nearly 15 per cent of unit sales. Apparently this fakery continued into 2012.

State-owned companies are just as prone to faking their business numbers. In June 2012, China's National Audit Office[4] found that several of China's largest companies had been massaging their figures to avoid tax, the Office finding that the China National Petroleum Corporation (CNPC) and Sinopec – China's two largest oil companies – had together underreported about RMB 2.8 billion in profits. Also found to be using irregular accounting practices were China Southern Power Grid and Sinosteel. Implicated in many of these scandals have been the so-called "big four" accounting firms – KPMG, Ernst & Young, PricewaterhouseCoopers and Deloitte Touche Tohmatsu. The National Audit Office also found financial and operational problems at one of China's largest telecoms companies, China Mobile,[5] which the Office felt had been guilty of misconduct in bidding, contract management and customer information protection between 2009 and 2011.

In February 2011, China's minister of railways was removed from office (and then expelled from the Communist Party) to face investigation for corruption. He was officially charged with corruption in April 2013, and convicted in July to spend the rest of his life in prison. Since the new leadership came into power, this powerful ministry (which was effectively one of the biggest state-owned companies in China) has been disbanded.

There is a history of underreporting to avoid tax, as in the case of the SOEs above, as well as overreporting to secure best price at listing or when selling to another company. One of the biggest recent cases affected one of the world's leading construction equipment manufacturers, Caterpillar. In January 2013, Caterpillar revealed that the Siwei division of ERA Mining Machinery, a company that Caterpillar had paid US$ 654 million to buy in 2012, had deliberately lied about its inventory, inflated its profits and recorded fake costs and revenue. The result was that Caterpillar had to write off most of the money it paid for the company.

The lack of thorough, forensic auditing prior to purchase has caused severe losses for the company. Looking through the paperwork and the numbers provided by Chinese companies is clearly a necessary part of the auditing process. However, in the same way that there is no better way to do market research than to actually go and see what is selling in shops, speak to companies and to consumers, so in auditing there should be no excuse for not getting out of the office and going to the company in question to look at what is actually in their warehouse, what machines are actually running, what nasty chemicals are actually coming out of the drains, making sure that all the employees they claim to have actually exist, etc. It pays, in the long-term, to use a more rigorous due diligence process that assumes guilt, and actively looks for all likely forms of corporate crime. If potential business partners get angry about being treated in this way, then it is probably not worth pursuing the deal anyway.

Bribery in China is a significant force to be reckoned with. You cannot trust the word on paper of bankers, accountants, managers, company customers, etc. It is quite easy for companies to pay off people in a position of influence to say what is necessary to complete a deception. In Transparency International's 2011 "bribe takers index,"[6] China ranks 27 out of 28 countries surveyed, out-corrupted only by Russia. Even Mexico, where rule of law is consistently challenged by violence from drugs cartels, is ranked less corrupt in terms of bribery than China. Many foreign companies have found themselves in hot water due to bribery being uncovered at their China operations: IBM, Pfizer, Wal-Mart and Avon,[7] to name a few. And then came the news about GlaxoSmithKline!

Cooking stocks

The accounting irregularities issue has really come to a head since "short-seller" research companies such as Muddy Waters and Citron Research began investigating Chinese companies listed on North American exchanges. They investigate inconsistencies in stories among listed company suppliers, clients and previous staff and locate the financial records that supply evidence of accounting malpractice. They then borrow and immediately sell shares in those companies at the same time as publishing their research findings for free, so that other shareholders can then sell off their holdings, to make a profit. These companies make a living by using their knowledge of corporate accounting malfeasance.

For its part, Muddy Waters has highlighted wrongdoing at Chinese companies such as Orient Paper, RINO International,[8] China Media Express and Sino-Forest, to name some of the more high-profile cases. Back in April 2011, the Securities and Exchange Commission (SEC) in the US suspended trading of RINO International over public filing inaccuracies and for failing to report the resignation of the company's chairman, board directors and the accountants hired to investigate fraud allegations. Toronto-listed Sino-Forest's[9] directors were alleged by the Ontario Securities Commission to have engaged in fraud that could mean they face about C$ 84 million in penalties.

Chinese companies have become listed on foreign stock exchanges, notably in the US and Canada, by either committing to the normal formal application process, or by using a method known as reverse merger, which entails a private company buying a non-operational public shell company already listed on an exchange, then selling the listed shares using the approvals already given to the still-listed company back to the private company. This allows the company to avoid the kind of scrutiny involved in normal formal application processes.

An exemplar of how this can lead to toxic shares being listed is in the case of Longtop Financial Technologies, which was charged by the SEC of failing to file current and accurate financial reports, with the SEC[10] advising that the financial statements provided by Longtop in 2008 to 2010 could no longer be relied upon to be accurate. Meanwhile, Longtop's auditors, Deloitte Touche Tohmatsu, which had resigned as auditors for the company due to becoming aware that some of the reports it had produced included false information, were also subpoenaed by the SEC to give evidence.

The China Securities Regulatory Commission (CSRC) has also begun investigating all companies coming up for initial public offering (IPO) due to the increasing amount of evidence that many listed companies within China have been filing inaccurate financial data. One example in 2012 was for Xindadi Biotechnology[11] in Guangdong, which came under suspicion of having falsified its IPO prospectus. In Hong Kong, locally listed CCIC Consulting[12] came under scrutiny, and its shares were suspended, following reports that it had falsified research data used in the listing prospectuses of several mainland listed companies' IPOs, falsifying data and using students and family members to create false survey responses for consumer research to verify claims made for companies. Then there is the case of meat-processing company Yurun, buying up various meat-processing plants at below market value, in an accounting move known as "negative goodwill." Such "good luck" can mean either that the assets were undervalued, or that the company can then account for a gain in the value of the acquisition in its accounts.

One of the biggest fraud cases involving a Chinese company in recent years has been that of Suntech.[13] The company quickly became the world's largest manufacturer of solar panels, making its founder, Shi Zhengrong, one of China's richest people. But the company (and Mr Shi) had fraudulently hidden mounting debts by creating false demand for the company's products from a separate investment vehicle called Global Solar Fund. Suntech was forced into bankruptcy in March 2013, but had been in trouble since 2009, when buyers backed by the "Fund" began to be unable to pay their bills, while Suntech simply gave them more time to pay. Eventually, the company succumbed to the weight of its mounting fraud and debt.[14]

Rooting out the problem

The problem of false accounting among so many listed Chinese companies has now come to a head. The CSRC, which for a long time did not allow financial documents for Chinese companies to be scrutinised by US investigators, citing them as "state secrets" at some points, has relented to US pressure, and in May 2013 the two countries agreed[15] to allow auditor access to scrutinise and improve disclosure among Chinese companies listed in the US following a series of accounting scandals. And since December 2012, the SEC is also going after five global accounting companies[16] (KPMG, Ernst & Young, PricewaterhouseCoopers, Deloitte Touche Tohmatsu and BDO) for failing to provide it with documents relating to ongoing investigations into accounting fraud allegations directed at nine Chinese companies.

It is not just foreign auditors who are facing the wrath of regulators over fraudulent companies. Ping'An Securities,[17] the underwriting division of Ping'an Insurance, was recently ordered by the CSRC to pay back RMB 25.5 million, this being the fee it earned from underwriting fraudulent company Wanfu Biotechnology Hunan Agricultural Development Co. Ltd.'s IPO, plus twice that as a fine. It also lost its underwriting licence for three months from May 2013. Furthermore, two of Ping'An's employees were fined RMB 300,000 each and banned for life from securities underwriting. The company set up a RMB 300 million fund to compensate investors.

Summary

What Chinese companies say on paper cannot be relied upon in many cases. Those investing in companies in China need to be very wary of trusting company accounts and their accountants, even the seemingly most reputable. This is not to say that all are institutionally faking their accounts, but that certainly many suffer from significant numbers of employees cooking the books, at all levels.

Even listed companies have ways, sometimes quite legal, of presenting accounts that give the impression that their core business is sound, when in fact their income is supplemented from non-core means, or only the accounts of the listed part of the business are published, hiding areas of concern that might be spotted about the mother company.

> *Even listed companies have ways ... of presenting accounts that give the impression that their core business is sound*

Company financial accounts need to be taken in context of their wider competitive market, and all data scrutinised having first asked the question "does this make sense?"

chapter 7

Red Chips

Why has China's stock market performed so poorly?

Talking of putting company finances in context, that the stock markets in China have not been performing very well for a number of years needs close attention. In one of the world's fastest-growing economies, you would expect share prices to be rocketing through the roof, but China's domestic stock exchanges are possibly the worst performing in the world. That does not make sense.

One key factor is that company earnings have been poor due to the economic slowdown. But this does not explain why the value of stocks in China are now worse than they were in 2010, at the start of the global economic crisis. According to Anthony Neoh,[1] who helped build the China Securities Regulatory Commission's (CSRC) Qualified Foreign Institutional Investor programme as its chief adviser between 1999 and 2004, China's equity market is "dysfunctional." Part of this is due to lack of scrutiny of company accounts prior to listing, opaque accounting practices, poor investor protection and market manipulation. The CSRC brought in new reforms to tackle these issues and to try to repair the market – and the practices of the companies listed on the markets – in 2011. The aim was to improve the way the CSRC vets initial public offering (IPO) applications and the process for delisting companies that have underperformed.

All IPO applications were put on ice in December 2012, so bad was the situation in the markets, the CSRC saying it was concerned any new listings would drain liquidity from existing listed company shares, making their plight even worse. The effect was that the value of the Shanghai Composite Index stopped free-falling, and from December 2012 onwards began to climb, but then began to decline again during February and March 2013. At the beginning of 2013, the CSRC ordered all IPO candidate companies and their underwriters to re-examine their financial records and re-submit their 2012 financial data by the end of March 2013.

In mid-April 2013, the CSRC then introduced further regulatory stringency, announcing it would send 15 teams of auditors in to inspect the accounts of companies seeking to list on China's stock markets. Among the 612 firms that had completed their self-examination prior to April 2013, the CSRC chose 30 to undergo spot-checks of their reports, choosing which companies to audit by drawing lots. Of this 30, 15 were already considered to be financially "clean," while the other 15 were known by the CSRC to have had their accounts verified by an underwriter or auditor known to have violated regulations in the past. The CSRC audit teams not only check the accounts of applicants, but also visit their suppliers to cross-check accounts claims.

The result was that of the 841 companies awaiting listing approval for both the Shanghai and Shenzhen Stock Exchanges prior to this announcement, 124 companies withdrew their applications, even though some were granted an extension past the end of March 2013 deadline for re-submission of financial data.

Many of these companies had to drop their IPO hopes due to faltering business growth. For example, South Beauty, a restaurant chain, had seen its sales drop significantly due to the market slowdown and the government banning officials from spending public money on lavish banquets to celebrate Chinese New Year, or for corporate entertaining. But many companies have baulked at re-submitting their financial reports to further scrutiny because those accounts were likely to be found less than satisfactory, and many were probably also keen to keep deliberate accounting irregularities away from prying official eyes.

Among the practices the CSRC is now looking out for are indicators that companies are hiding costs or inflating profits, especially in related-party transactions (across subsidiaries, for example), unusually low staff wages, unduly late or irregular reporting of profit and loss statements, and the like. Other common tactics are for business owners to fake their company profits using their own cash to buy company supplies, delaying accounting of operating costs to boost apparent revenue figures, using borrowed money from banks to fake revenues, etc.

Many companies where cash transactions are a significant part of the business model will also come under greater scrutiny, such as catering companies like South Beauty, due to the difficulty in verifying payments made by cash. Chain store operations are also likely to be more deeply scrutinised to check that related-party transactions, such as the sale of goods to local distributors or franchisees, actually account for goods sold (and so business revenue), and not just shifting of goods that actually end up sitting unsold in a warehouse.

While CRSC is still fighting fires with fraudulent IPOs in its large-scale company sector, China is still pushing ahead the development of a new, third (over-the-counter) exchange board to raise funds aimed at investment for small- and medium-sized enterprises (SMEs),[2] which had nearly 140 companies involved by September 2012. The third board is meant to provide financing to companies too small for listing on either the Shanghai or Shenzhen exchanges. This is all well and good, but if regulation of the main boards has been so poor, what is the likelihood that there won't be a rash of bad accounts floated on the SME board? Buyers beware!

Red chips are red to the core

If you scrutinise the ownership structure of most listed companies in China, unless they are companies founded by private individuals or built up to a point where they are able to list on one of China's main exchanges, they tend to be majority-owned by local governments, local banks, securities companies and state-owned companies – all

THE FOUR MAIN TYPES OF CONTROLLING SHAREHOLDERS IN LISTED COMPANIES IN CHINA

These are:

1. State asset management bureaux (SAMB), companies established to manage state-owned assets in most provincial cities;
2. State-owned enterprises (SOEs) that are affiliated to the central government, which are the 157 large and strategically significant corporations in various industries considered "flagship" companies or which control significant shares of key industrial sectors, such as oil and gas, banking, metals, etc.;
3. SOEs affiliated to local governments, which are profit-making companies that can invest in "state" and "legal person" entity shares, with such shareholders being the most numerous among China's listed companies;
4. Private investors, comprised both of private individuals and companies.

of which are ultimately owned by the government, either at local or central level, and are monitored by the government. The managers of SAMBs and SOEs tend to be government-appointed. SAMB managers are appointed officials who tend not to be experienced in the (often wide-ranging) relevant industry or sector of the companies in which the state holds shares, and are in place to manage state asset controls, being incentivised not by return on investment but by implementation of government policy. This contrasts with SOEs, which have industry experience and more of a profit motive, but SOEs also have a policy motive, being state-owned, that dilutes their focus on the profit motive.

This means many listed companies in China have significant proportions of shareholders with either little or only partial input into company management in terms of driving the growth of the company to become more competitive. Their motives are driven either wholly or partially by political performance rather than, or as well as, commercial performance. While listed companies in China are there to create profit, this is counterbalanced by them also serving a political end, namely maintaining the state's interest in and often control of many sectors of the economy. This split-personality (between commerce and politics) in majority share ownership in many listed companies is one of the key reasons why SOEs tend to be less profitable and productive (or efficient) than private companies, and why stock markets in China have not been performing as well as might be expected, given the strong growth in the economy.

The Bailian example

An example is Lianhua Supermarket Holdings Co., Ltd., which at the end of 2012 was China's largest supermarket and hypermarket retail group by number of stores, and third largest by sales value. Lianhua was established in 1991, but is ultimately owned by the Bailian Group. Bailian was formally established in April 2003 through the merger of four state-owned retailers, namely Shanghai No.1 Department Store (Group), Hualian Group, Shanghai Friendship Group and Shanghai Materials (Group) Co. Bailian is China's largest retailer (often dubbed the "Great Wal-Mart of China"), and remains the country's leading department store, supermarket and convenience store group. The Group also includes shopping mall management, pharmaceuticals distribution (Number One Pharmacy), materials trading (Shanghai Material Trading Corporation) and retail and other property portfolios.

Hugely diverse within the retail sector, the company was created to be a "flagship" company for China's retail sector in the face of the growing competition from foreign modern grocery retail chains, including Walmart (US), Carrefour (France), Auchan (France), RT-Mart (Taiwan), China Resources Enterprises (Hong Kong), etc. Under Bailian are four listed companies: Lianhua Supermarket Holdings Co., Ltd. (Hong Kong SE 0980), Shanghai Friendship Group (Shanghai SE 600827), Shanghai

Material Trading Corporation (Shanghai SE 600822) and Number One Pharmacy (Shanghai SE 600833). Bailian used to be listed itself (Shanghai SE 600631), but is now not traded as an entity in its own right. Its assets were restructured by Shanghai State-owned Assets Supervision and Administration Commission (Shanghai SASAC) in 2009 to strengthen the competitiveness of the state-owned strategic retailers based in Shanghai, including Bailian.

Lianhua was greatly aided in maintaining a high position in the rankings among China's leading supermarket and hypermarket chains when, in 2009, Bailian merged its Shanghai Hualian and Lianhua (easily confused) into one supermarkets and hypermarkets group under the Lianhua banner. This was very much a political move to create retailers that were of sufficient critical mass to be able to compete with the foreign interlopers, or so the logic went. But size alone is not enough in a market that needs efficiency to be competitive. Indeed, Lianhua has had to undergo significant scaling-back of its store numbers since 2010 to focus more on larger-scale hypermarkets, closing many smaller, low-price stores.

The political fiat that created Bailian saw only the logic of consolidation and sheer scale of size, but each of the listed companies under the Bailian umbrella are now facing stiff competition in their respective sectors because they need to be operated as individual units within their respective sectors (department stores, supermarkets, pharmacy, trading, etc.). The scale of Bailian and its political role as "flagship" impedes it from improving efficiency and competitive effectiveness in each of the relevant sectors – or has done until recently. State ownership in this sense has not helped the Group's various companies become more profitable, and therefore more attractive, to investors.

Arguably, each of the four listed companies were in such diverse sectors (apart from the department store companies) that it would make sense to break them off into separate entities and force them to operate more efficiently alone, becoming better at what they do and better at facing the competition in their respective sectors. The counter-argument to this is that under the Bailian umbrella they are each supported by the financial might of this large, key, strategic SOE. But such a safety net for these companies does not breed a culture of hunger for profitability and competitiveness among their managers, but rather a complacency born from knowing that they have that safety net.

Lianhua is now being reorganised to become more competitive, but this is more a political reaction in response to and borrowing from foreign competition rather than internal innovation and commercial drive. This highlights where the problem of SOEs is most acute, both for the state and shareholders. Without reform of the SOE sector, which forces companies to become more competitive and innovative by cutting the apron strings that preserve their monopolies, businesses will not be forced to become more commercially driven and profitable, and therefore the returns on investment to the state and shareholders will remain weaker than they could be – hence the poor share values on China's stock exchanges.

A call to account

Many listed Chinese companies do have a political role and influence, not just through shareholding but also via a variety of other institutional influences, particularly through the Communist Party of China (CPC) and its relationship with China's business leaders and their access to capital, land, operating licences, listing rights, etc. Holding shares in SOEs in China may at times be lucrative, but the shareholder rights you might expect to exert anywhere else face the dominant influence of the state, and its prerogatives. To understand the strength of the state's share of influence in any particular listed company, investors therefore must look very closely at the share-owning structure of their company of interest to really understand the potential of their investment and the political risk.

Many listed Chinese companies do have a political role and influence

The CSRC's moratorium on new IPOs has given it the time to figure out the best way to shake down the quality of existing and new listings, to winnow out the sub-prime corporate chaff that gets listed in China and tighten up the regulations on accounts and audits to force an improvement in the quality of companies seeking to list or remain listed. As well as making sure that audits of company accounts are much more thorough and forensic in nature, IPO prospectus claims about company shares of market, and operating market sizes also need closer scrutiny.

Ying Yuming, the MD of China Eagle Asset Management in Hong Kong, was quoted in *The Wall Street Journal*[3] as saying that many Chinese companies embellish their financial records prior to IPO, and that his company will not usually buy new stocks until two or three years post-listing because their share prices often drop significantly once trading commences, and the real state of their businesses presumably comes to light, often dropping in value by as much as 50 per cent or more.

For the long-term health of the Chinese stock markets, the CSRC must ensure that the listing regulations improve the quality of the companies that get to list, rather than simply adding to the overall size of the market for the sake of short-term results. This would give investors much more confidence in the companies listed on China's exchanges and make them feel more comfortable that those companies have been properly screened for financial irregularities and creative assertions about the health of their operating sectors and their prospects within them. This means not only better accounts audits, but also more thorough analysis of those sectors, forcing listing candidate companies to use a wider variety of independent market opinion and market research from companies that have also been thoroughly vetted for compliance with market research quality standards. This is an area still needing a great deal of improvement, as my own experience in conducting market research in China has proven.

Better clarity in accounts and market data would also help improve the quality of investors, and would attract more large-scale investors to take the Chinese stock markets seriously, providing more long-term and stable investment rather than short-term investment by those with vested interests (particularly the state-owned companies and asset management companies). To this end it is likely that the CSRC will no longer give state-sector companies preferential places in the queue to list on the local stock markets, but will make commercial rigour and vitality the main listing determinants.

If, as it appears, the CSRC is taking reform of the stock listings in China seriously, and now that the CSRC and Ministry of Finance have agreed with the US Securities and Exchange Commission[4] to allow foreign auditors access to do on-the-ground inspections of the financial reports of Chinese companies, the situation should be sufficiently improved so that foreign investors will become more confident that listing companies have been properly audited, reducing the likelihood of fraudulent accounting damaging stock value and investors' money. However, there remains, in my view, a need to keep pushing for better investigative forensic auditing not just of corporate accounts but also claims made about industrial market performance taken from market research reports and the companies that publish them.

Private companies fed fat on government subsidies

Whether listed or not, private or state-owned, those looking to invest in China need to understand the real financial health of companies they may be looking to invest in or partner with in China to better understand their real competitive strength. This means not only looking at the usual financial indicators, such as sales growth and profitability, but also looking at the credentials of the people running those companies and their claims of experience and expertise, as well as looking more closely at the reputations of those people in the press and among peers, their ethical standpoints, their closeness to or distance from the political establishment, etc. The area of political links is often a difficult one to quantify, unless you have information about whether senior management are all card-carrying members of the CPC, but even that is no real indicator of political leanings as many senior executives use Party membership to open doors that might otherwise remain closed, or would at least require more circuitous routes to achieve the same ends.

More indicative of political influence, and patronage, is the amount of state subsidies private companies receive. And, it is surprising just how much some private companies in China get in terms of government subsidy compared to others. The significance of the subsidies issue was highlighted in an article "Sponging a Living," written for the second quarter 2013 edition of the *China Economic Quarterly* by Matthew Forney, the president of due-diligence research company Fathom China. The article was based on a sample of 50 US- and Hong Kong-listed private Chinese company accounts analysed by Fathom China. The research found that 17 of the 50 companies received over 5 per cent of their net profit in the form of government subsidy, while seven companies received over 10 per cent.

it is surprising just how much some private companies in China get in terms of government subsidy

These are surprising results, and show that some companies are significantly less profitable than their figures show (again illustrating why close scrutiny of financial data is so important). And despite their private status they still have considerable state-sector interest in their companies. Such subsidies are often included as "other income" within gross profit, with little description of where that "other income" comes from. Some companies claim such subsidies come from local governments eager to help companies build operations in their jurisdictions. Forney argues that a significant amount of these subsidies actually comes from central government. He also points out that some companies appear to be more likely to receive such largesse than others, and that this kind of subsidy is a form of political favouritism aimed at giving a leg-up to "key flagship" brands the government wants to see provide a banner-wielding lead to the rest of China's corporate world.

The Fathom China research also suggests that, rather than shrinking its influence in the private sector through subsidy, the government has actually been increasing its subsidy investment in private listed companies. Although this might be looked upon as a healthy dash of government money helping out the private sector, rather than just the SOEs, thus rebalancing the playing field, to my mind this only preserves companies that might otherwise have been struggling, artificially distorting markets and allowing inefficient and badly run companies to persist at the expense of those more efficient and well-managed ones.

For example, Forney's article mentions that sportswear brand Li Ning gets twice as much in subsidies than the next highest recipient in that sector. Li Ning has been struggling with unsold stock since the 2008 Beijing Olympics, a problem arguably created by bad management and a lack of understanding of the real dynamics of its market. Rather than the company being allowed to take a hit and forced to tighten up its management and business model, the subsidies have most likely kept Li Ning from making necessary cuts to its business sooner. This has the effect of preserving both bad management and a bad business model, but it also means that Li Ning was able to continue being a stronger competitive threat to its rivals than it should have been. Whatever the reasoning behind the subsidies (preserving jobs, protecting the banner brand of the Beijing Olympics, etc.), it is fundamentally political reasoning, not commercial, and not the markets'.

Summary

The poor performances of China's stock markets are not helped by subsidy, which distorts the market value. Companies need to survive by their own merit, and markets should reflect that merit, not be a lens that inflates the value of companies. China's stock markets will continue to struggle until the real merit and value is found. Ownership and outside influence also need to be made more apparent if outside investors are going to believe the financials of listed companies in China, and better understand their real relative competitive positioning in their respective markets.

chapter 8

Trade Measures

Measuring domestic trade

How many cigarettes are made in China? Because the tobacco industry in China has always been state-controlled, that should be an easy figure to quote. The official figure for total output of cigarettes in China in 2011 was 2,447.4 billion cigarettes, and the tobacco industry supplies an estimated 8 per cent of government tax revenues. But it has also been estimated that there are about 400 billion counterfeit cigarettes[1] produced in China each year, mainly centred on the city of Yunxiao in Fujian, with much of this output finding its way not just into the local market, but also overseas.

I discuss the market for counterfeit products in China in more detail later, but mention it here as an indicator as to why production figures for different industries in China need circumspection. It is not just claims about output in each sector, but also how much of what is produced is actually sold, given that many companies massage sales figures and inventory size. There is oversupply in many sectors, further distorting output and sales data. And there is also the command-economy problem of local governments making vastly over-inflated claims about industrial output on their patch, such as the case seen in Henglan County,[2] Guangdong province, where local officials were discovered – by the National Bureau of Statistics (NBS) – to have inflated industrial output figures for 71 companies, from a real figure of RMB 2.2 billion to a whopping RMB 8.5 billion!

Given the high likelihood of incorrect output recording and sales figures across a wide field, better measures of industrial activity can be taken from industrial consumption: the purchasing managers' index (PMI), electricity and coal consumption, metals and other commodity consumption data, etc. Absolute size data on market sales, imports, exports, industrial production and apparent consumption in China being indicative at best, it is better to use proxies of industrial inputs to measure economic growth in industrial sectors, not just for volume of output, but by tracking prices of key inputs, the value and cost of production, and from that the value-added.

It should be noted here that there are two main competing PMI indices in circulation. Other than the official NBS index, there is also the Hongkong and Shanghai Banking Corporation (HSBC) index. According to Dong Tao,[3] chief economist of Credit Suisse Asia, the difference between the two is in methodology, with the generally more pessimistic HSBC PMI giving more weight to small- and medium-sized enterprises (SMEs) than the NBS index, which weighs more heavily to the state-owned enterprises (SOEs). SMEs tend to include more of the export-oriented companies that have struggled since the global financial crisis, hence their purchasing has been down in recent years as export markets contracted, reducing numbers of orders to be fulfilled, and therefore input they need to buy.

As already mention in regard to gross domestic product (GDP) earlier in this book, these are not only measures thought more reliable by market analysts, but also by the premier, Li Keqiang, himself. But even these measures are open to interpretation. A great example of the breadth of interpretation came with the May 2013 economic results from the NBS. Reactions ranged from perennial China-bear Gordon Chang saying that "China's May numbers disappoint, no remedies in sight,"[4] to Stephen Green of Standard Chartered saying there was "no pick-up, but no reason to panic"[5] and Andy Rothman at Credit Lyonnais Securities Asia (CLSA) taking the view that the economic situation was "stabilising."[6]

Others say China's economy is running out of steam. For example, Langi Chiang and Jonathan Standing, writing in a Reuters[7] article on 9 June 2013, saw there being a risk that China's economic growth was going to "slide further" based on weaker-than-expected economic data in May. Ken Rapoza writing for Forbes[8] even went as far as saying China's economy was "firing blanks." Xin Zhou and Paul Panckhurst writing for Bloomberg[9] were of the opinion that the Chinese leadership had been overly optimistic about economic growth, too fixated on controlling inflation and needed to rethink their economic strategy. As it turned out, the China-bears were wrong again.

As it turned out, the China-bears were wrong again

I tended to agree most with Andy Rothman, that the weak output and trade data could be explained by weakness in the light manufacturing sector and the government's crackdown on the illegal fake trading of invoices[10] to take advantage of the difference in the cross-border RMB exchange rates between Hong Kong and the Mainland. Export manufacturing represents a fairly big part of the "light industrial" sector that saw the weakest growth in May 2013 compared to previous months and the previous year. This is a symptom of the retooling of China's economy more towards a greater share of GDP coming from domestic consumption.

But along with the more bearish interpretations of the figures, the slowdown does highlight some key indicators to keep an eye on.

KEY TRADE INDICATORS

- Weakening/strengthening imports
- Accelerating/decelerating deflation/inflation
- Weaker/stronger lending
- Producer price index (PPI)
- Consumer price index (CPI)
- HSBC/NBS purchasing managers' indices (PMIs)

The hope is that Chinese consumers keep driving growth in sectors where there should be strong growth, for products and services *they* need, rather than the cheap export Christmas trees and stocking fillers of yore. Growth in domestic sectors should, assuming demand remains strong enough, take up the slack from the decline in export manufacturing and so the money (investment, jobs, power consumption, commodities consumption, value-added) will follow. Chinese companies are pretty adaptable, and will likely be quick to follow the money.

The rising costs of making and buying

One of the issues dogging China's manufacturing sector is that of increasing costs. While the rising costs of industrial inputs[11] in China are beginning to alarm some people, as are the rising costs of wages,[12] these are not unexpected. Recent trends in input costs have not really been that alarming, with the purchasing price index for industrial products actually falling in May 2013. But, as China shifts from low-cost export manufacturing to higher value-added production aimed at increasingly choosy local consumers, so the cost of inputs is bound to rise and wages with them. Wages will tend to keep going up all the time, not least because of government-enforced hikes of minimum wages. Indeed, as the value of the Renminbi (RMB) rises, so prices of imported raw materials decrease, and so the purchasing power of companies and individual wages should increase. All part of the shift from volume-added to value-added.

There has been concern that China's PMI data falling[13] in recent months is also indicative of a significant decline in industrial activity. But as we have seen, China's industrial sector includes a lot of oversupply, and a fair share of low-value manufacturing. Also, much of the private sector is still finding it tough, with their export markets having ground to a financial halt and retooling for local consumption costly.

China continues to offer a lot of opportunities for companies with the right product at the right price, but the manufacturing industry within China has to adapt very quickly to things changing fast both inside and outside China. That, as stated often before, means that China's industry needs to retool, requiring some short-term pain. Dips in PMI data can also be aggravated by sectoral hiccups and cyclical drags. This is particularly the case with export manufacturing for products such as toys for the Western Christmas market and certain clothes and footwear – highly seasonal business. Whatever happens, China will get more expensive to live, work and make things in. That is supposed to be a good thing, worth going through some pain for, because without it China will stagnate at "nearly-but-not-quite developed status" and face all kinds of economic gloom, while the rest of the world will lose the hope that China provides the global economy the kind of consumer-driven boost it needs.

> China continues to offer a lot of opportunities for companies with the right product at the right price

The myth of cost advantage

Something that has emerged recently in discussion about China's trade is how it is losing its cost advantage. However, this all very much depends upon what you think of as an advantage. Cheap plastic Christmas trees are an advantage for the middle-class US and UK families wanting some sparkle in their Yule. But the working conditions in the factory that made those plastic Christmas trees at such a stupendously cheap price were not so great. So the advantage was for the consumer, not the worker. This is fine for the consumer living thousands of miles away completely unaware how those cheap plastic Christmas trees get made, so long as they are so dazzlingly cheap. But, consumers living in the same country as the people working on a minimum wage (if lucky), doing long hours, probably locked in to stop them wandering off for a cigarette or toilet stop whenever they feel like it – thus raising fire risks – with no protective equipment and probably handling some pretty nasty chemicals, might feel a bit more awkward.

Even those super-rich Chinese, for whom the Chinese economic miracle was a freeloading ride over the flotsam and jetsam below, cannot escape the environmental woes that have come from this "economic miracle." Although they probably can hop on a Lear jet and escape to the south of France for the "season." The point is, the trade "advantage" was not a long-term benefit, certainly not for its mass of low-paid workers; it was a short-term expedient to get to the next stage, where life can get a bit better yet. Previously, it was a case of getting from dirt-poor to not so dirt-poor; now it is getting from beginning to consume to being full-blooded consumers. And that means industry has to provide better quality, more social responsibility, less pollution, more choice, less fakery, etc. In short, value-added. And Chinese consumers are becoming more empowered to demand better.

China is not losing a cost advantage and having to face losing business investment to "near-shoring"[14] in other cheaper countries (India/ Mexico), or even "home shoring" as they lose cost advantage. China is choosing a new economic path. It may have been cajoled in this direction, but it has 1.3 billion people to sell to, from rural farmers in Guizhou buying basic commodity goods, to super-rich Ferrari drivers in Shanghai. Who needs to sell to Americans anymore, they're all up to their armpits in debt anyway?!

The other common complaint made about China is its supposed complete lack of trading morals. The protectionism and price fixing are indeed problems, but not atypical of a developing country – it's just that China is so big, and exports so much. And let us not forget that such lack of trade morals was not confined to China, unless the Opium Wars could be considered moral trade practice.

History is important in understanding China's trade. Zhejiang, Fujian and Guangdong provinces – the three provinces making up China's eastern "tummy," with a crinkly coastline of coves and tiny islands – were throughout much of history home to many pirates and tax-dodging traders. Under the Confucian class system the merchant class came at the bottom of the hierarchical pile, below even common peasants, and their social ratings did not improve under communism. They may have bent the rules, but they got things done and made money, often against the odds. And it was they whom Europeans and Americans (among others) saw as mercantile like-minds in China, where morals were something for missionaries to dispense.

This rather forgetful view about how China (shorthand for Chinese companies and trade bodies) flouts international trade rules (as if developed countries never did) is not uncommon. There will be complaints about how Chinese export trade associations set up price-fixing cartels[15] that give their members an unfair competitive advantage in the vitamins trade. They are fixing prices and finding an unfair competitive advantage because they will most likely get away with it for a long time, deny everything and let the Chinese courts settle things. More fool you for not paying due attention!

I have been watching foreigners come into China for about 20 years and I have seen many of them act as if China is just like everywhere else, where people play by the rules, appear very nice and say all the right things. But foreign companies are still getting burned in China. A case in point being Caterpillar, as discussed in Chapter 6.

It all comes back to advantage, and the taking thereof. The factory workers of Guangdong may be lying in their death beds coughing up chemical poisoning, but someone will have made a buck taking their advantage, cost or otherwise. There was no real advantage to China, just to certain Chinese with the ability to make it rich before getting found out, or moving onto the next new product the West demanded, at cheap-as-chips prices. However, those days are receding. Now the advantage China has is that its society is demanding better for itself.

No trade collapse

Many China pundits saw the May 2013 trade data to be signs of a sharp decline in the country's trade. But much of that drop in numbers was due to the government cracking down on people making fake trades through Hong Kong to take advantage of exchange rate differences, while others were going through natural cyclical downturns. Prior to the crackdown, China's exports to Hong Kong grew by about 93 per cent in March, and 57 per cent in April, much higher than the Hong Kong government import statistics. Not only was this a case of exchange rate arbitrage, but it was also linked to value-added tax (VAT) rebates. After the crackdown by the authorities, exports from China to Hong Kong grew by just under 8 per cent in May 2013. This was not a collapse of China's export traders, but the unruly edges of Chinese commerce getting its wings clipped, temporarily. But it further called into question the voracity of China's trade data and has increased scepticism[16] that the trade figures are wrong.

In this period of economic flux, there are certainly difficulties being felt in the export trade sector in China, especially the private sector. While the HSBC PMI figures for May 2013 were a sickly 49.2, the official government PMI index,[17] which, unsurprisingly only tracks SOEs, actually went up to 50.8 in the same month. All at once we see where the plan of increasing private involvement in the economy, to raise efficiency and the retooling of China's economy towards domestic consumption, is leading. The companies that are suffering the most are probably the ones best positioned to adapt, but are likely finding adapting very hard under conditions where obtaining financing for retooling is scarce – because the banks are relending to local authorities to roll over old debts with new ones. However, the government now appears to be trying to encourage banks to keep the liquidity taps open for private SMEs, and to encourage them to grow faster, so now the tide is changing.

Meanwhile, China's import trade continues to grow as the country continues to consume vast amounts of raw materials in the endless quest to build castles on sand – cities such as Lanzhou New City,[18] which may become a lovely place to live, but probably not. China is still buying imported metals and minerals from countries such as Australia and Brazil,[19] not to forget soya beans, rice, luxury goods, timber, oil,[20] wine, etc. China is increasingly important as importer from other countries and therefore other countries are increasingly relying on China as a consumer market. But if China's consumer economy begins to slow, this could create problems for foreign manufacturers already looking at poor prospects in other markets.

China's trade data is also difficult to rely on because of underreporting or overreporting of data, which leads to distortions of growth rates.[21] This makes growth comparisons difficult to rely upon, which affects not only sourcing but also investment sentiment. If investing sentiment is weak because of bad data, yet manufacturing and exporting is robust, there can be mismatches between industrial capital need and supply.

But measuring the scale of domestic demand and the potential for exports into China continues to be made more difficult by poor trade data, not just on the Chinese side, but also because of systemic inaccuracies in international trade data anyway. Take, for example, the International Energy Agency (IEA),[22] which stated in its February 2013 Oil Market Report that measuring the oil trade is "more of an art than a science." But the IEA, in measuring China's apparent domestic demand, a proxy measure for consumption based on Chinese refinery output plus net imports and less exports (which are negligible), has not been keeping an eye on changing levels of inventory in the market, and now admits that "a step change in Chinese refining capacity has dramatically increased the potential for product swings." That is, the inventory swings are getting more significant, and so this simple proxy measure is more likely to be significantly off. Considering China represents about 10 per cent of global oil consumption, and 40 per cent of global demand growth, the size of the China market is actually quite important. Underestimate the size of China's demand and production will be too low, leading to heightened demand and prices rising. Overestimate and you could have a supply glut and prices falling.

Getting a clearer picture of real volume and value of trade is not just a challenge for China but also for trade worldwide in these increasingly global times. One solution has been devised by the Organisation for Economic Cooperation and Development (OECD) in conjunction with the World Bank, which focuses on measuring trade on a value-added basis,[23] rather than simple volumes in and out. This makes sense, given the vast amounts of outsourcing of product assembly for re-export that goes on, both globally and in the context of China.

According to the first set of data published in Paris in January 2013, including data on 18 key industries across 40 countries, this value-added approach puts China's trade significance in a new light. For instance, the new OECD/World Bank measure for China's trade surplus with the US in 2009, which had been calculated at US$ 176 billion, shrinks in value by a quarter, rounding it down to US$ 132 billion. The value-added aspect means that much of the real value of China's exports is created outside China, estimated by the OECD/World Bank measure at about 30 per cent of total value in 2009. This affirms a growing number of those with the opinion that because China's exports have remained largely low down in the value-added part of the final production line, its significance within global trade is actually overinflated, as is its trade surplus.

Not so much of a surplus

Another area where caution in regards to China's trade figures is wise, is where hot money inflows,[24] disguised as trade payments, distort the real trade numbers and the real size of China's trade surplus. According to Lu Ting, an economist at the Bank of America Merrill Lynch in Hong Kong,[25] during the first quarter of 2013, if the value of fake transactions passed off as trade deals is deducted from official trade surplus data, the real figure would stand at about US$ 6 billion, or 10 per cent of official trade surplus data, with much of this money being used to make investments into real estate and the financial sectors. This would mean this was China's leanest trade surplus figure during a January to April period since the country suffered a trade deficit during that period in 2004.

This outstanding claim by Lu Ting is that China is cooking its trade books and falsifying its trade surplus to raise its international status and protect the corrupt crony–capitalist élites that run China, much in the same way that it could be arguably said happens pretty much worldwide. Noted economist Dr Enzio von Pfeil, who gained notoriety for calling the 1997 Asian Economic Crisis as early as 1995, in the face of the prevailing trend at the time, went as far as describing China's trade surplus as "fictitious" during a Bloomberg/Businessweek interview[26] in May 2013. During the interview, Dr von Pfeil also noted that, in regard to the Chinese economy being run by local government officials who cook the books to make money and keep their cronies in power, the country is ungovernable. One could equally argue that a US Senate's entire government budget being held ransom, by a minority bent on repealing a law Senate had already passed by a majority, also points to a country with a significant level of "ungovernable."

Summary

China's trade data cannot be absolutely correct because there appears to be a significant amount of trade that goes uncounted, and some of that which is counted is faked. The reality could be that China is less of a demon exporter than its official figures might claim, or it could be more of a demon exporter, but with more of its trade gliding in under the wire. The two factors might accurately cancel each other out, but that's unlikely. Most likely is that the trade data is inflated, but to what degree is anyone's guess, without insider knowledge from China's customs authorities.

Again the take-away from this is to believe nobody and to make your own investigations and judgement calls. Often the most important data for those working in China is the micro-level data pertaining to a niche sector of interest, so such macro-level data has little practical use, and it is therefore largely pointless for most people to try to make arguments about it.

chapter 9

Retooling China's Industry to Drive Domestic Consumption Growth

Grab a value-added spanner!

Retooling China's economy[1] away from export manufacturing and investment-led economic growth should reduce demand for commodities used in construction, heavy manufacturing, manufacturing machinery, transportation and other investment-heavy sectors. In its place, the government wants China's domestic consumer economy to grow in significance, and with it demand for consumer goods. Growing the domestic consumption part of China's economy will rely partly on how well the Chinese government redistributes the wealth created among consumers, either through improving wages and employment, or through taxing industry to boost fiscal cash flows to be used in financing the building of a more comprehensive and effective social security net, which effectively improves the value of wages and provides employment.

So, which sectors (you ask) now show strong consumer demand? Arguably, fresh air and clean water. If you think that's a daft idea, then consider Chinese millionaire entrepreneur, philanthropist and serial media stunt progenitor Chen Guangbiao, who in February 2013 launched a line of fresh-air-in-a-can products[2] selling in a variety of tantalising scents such as "Pristine Tibet" and "post-industrial Taiwan."

China's consumers are desperate to buy food that they know is not contaminated or fake. What the food scares represent in the context of this discussion is the great unquantifiable of consumer mistrust. Not trusting that the food they are giving their child won't make them seriously sick or even kill them. Companies that manufacture and process food by resorting to cutting corners, using dirty ingredients, lacing food with cancerous colourants, etc. are making products that consumers don't want and creating competitive skews in markets to the detriment of companies that play by the rules and make good products. This creates yet more inefficiency masked within the manufacturing numbers.

Better manufacturing and better products means paying more. Where they have the money to do so, Chinese consumers will pay a premium to have better products, particularly food, that won't harm them. But this is where the challenge to step up the value-added ladder gets complicated for China's companies. For there to be more value-added products made by better manufacturers, there must be more compliance with quality regulations and capital available to those companies improving their businesses and products. There is no lack of regulations in China, but there is a significant lack in policing and enforcement. This allows regulation-dodgers not only to continue but to flourish, often with collusion from corrupt officials, stealing away market share and profits from the legitimate companies that do pay for improvements to increase their value-added.

We hear about tough sentences being passed down to corporate law breakers, but just as it is impossible to take large swathes of Chinese officialdom to court on corruption charges, it is likewise impossible to take to court all the corrupt corporate leaders of grubby manufacturing companies who ride the system, dodging standards and producing goods that harm people. Conducting show trials, and encouraging citizens to name and shame via online blogs, as they increasingly are doing, helps. But it is unrealistic to think the government of China will simply hand over a function of the police to the masses. They may let this kind of activity go on for as long as it keeps corrupt officials and bosses from overtly flouting the rules, but this kind of mass demonstration of judicial power online is something the government will very quickly (and probably is already doing) put a lid on before it gets too successful and powerful.

But consumers in China have another power – that of choice. They don't need to name and shame companies to get bosses sacked and tried for corruption; they can judiciously avoid buying the products of those companies and choose to pay for products from companies they can trust. They can also share positive and negative product and service reviews. This power of choice has come from growing incomes.

But consumers in China have another power – that of choice

Generating wealth – the future of China's wage packet

What Chinese consumers want is better-quality products to fill their homes with and to wear. To pay for these more expensive, better-quality products, they need to have higher wages. While the economy is slowing, the job market, although tougher, is still generating opportunities, particularly for experienced, and therefore higher-paid workers. There is also evidence that unskilled labour is increasingly being sought.

As renewed demand for employees has risen, so wages have begun to recover from relatively low growth in 2012. Add to that,[3] local governments have been raising their minimum wages, such as in Zhejiang and Guangdong, where minimum wages increased by 12 per cent and 13 per cent respectively in 2012. The central government is also considering an average minimum wage growth of 40 per cent. The German Chamber of Commerce[4] agreed that wages would rise significantly in 2013, based on its annual poll of German companies in China, and suggested that white-collar and blue-collar wages would go up by 8.1 per cent and 9.9 per cent respectively in 2013, while wages for some key qualified jobs might rise by as much as 50 per cent, given the competition to retain talent.

Higher wages and higher spending power should lift the quality expectations of Chinese consumers, and with it the expectation for product and company accountability, sustainability, reduced pollution, efficiency, better resource use, more recycling, more environmental protection, and worker rights being not only enforced but improved. In short, better rule of law and greater regard for ethics. But while progress has been slow, promotion of the rule of law and a revival of social ethics is something already being addressed by the new Chinese leadership. Higher wages will also mean more people will invest more in their children's educations, forming the basis of a better-educated workforce in the future so that China can continue up the value-added ladder.

Is China likely to price itself out of the market? As discussed later in the book in regard to China reaching its Lewis Turning Point (LTP), the Chinese economy is fast approaching the point where it can no longer create wealth by simply converting cheap labour into added-value. Added-value will then have to come from innovation and increased higher value, higher technology production. China probably still has another decade or so before reaching that point. This means that average wages in China are likely to continue to grow. But will China price itself into trouble with such fast wage increases? According to a 2011 report published by Accenture titled "*Wage Increases in China: Should Multinationals Rethink Their Manufacturing and Sourcing Strategies?*", wages in China are actually still relatively quite low, despite having grown very fast, and even quite significant hikes in salaries do not significantly put a dent in profits.

But not everyone agrees that the jobs market in China is as robust as it may seem. In Stephen Green's "*On The Ground China – The Smog in Beijing*" report for Standard Chartered, published in June 2013, there is company survey data from Manpower and Standard Chartered Research that shows job demand among employers is weak and getting weaker across the industrial sectors, not stronger. There have often been news stories in the press about high levels of unemployment among university graduates in China. But, as the Standard Chartered report points out, China reports unemployment among graduates every June (as they graduate) and then again in September, and the report quotes 21st

Research Education director Yang Dongping[5] as saying in a Caixin article[6] that the figures are unreliable because they are reported at the wrong time, and should only cover graduates still unemployed after a year.

It is also not clear what graduates are being asked. Are they being asked if they are unemployed, or are they asked whether they are still seeking employment? If the latter, then there are plenty of graduates taking jobs to keep themselves in cash while they continue to seek jobs that are better suited to their qualifications. For example, I have no doubt that the barristas at the Starbucks I have been into often in Shanghai are graduates. It is also possible that many graduates have too-high expectations in terms of the positions and wage levels they expect to gain on leaving university, with a head full of facts but little experience and few skills.

To get a clearer picture of how the shift in the economy is really affecting industry and employment, what is needed are better employment and unemployment/underemployment data, but the official figures published remain almost surreally unchanging. As discussed later in Chapter 10, they are officially manipulated to create the idea that there is not a problem. The central government will most likely know what the real situation is, but does not publish that data because it would cause the kind of reaction that the graduate unemployment figures seem to create, with one press article after the other inflating the size of the problem. But it would arguably be better for all concerned if the real numbers were published.

Creating jobs to keep a lid on social ills

The main reason for the central government remaining tight-lipped on real unemployment figures is that it is concerned with maintaining "social harmony." The reality would increase public demand that the government creates new jobs to rectify the problem. But to do so would be to take a step backwards towards command economy politics. Perhaps the logic of the central government in suppressing the real unemployment figures is to restrain itself from following its natural urge to create jobs to reduce the significant job losses in some areas of the economy that retooling the economy inevitably causes, particularly in manufacturing sectors fast becoming twilight industries. It would also be disingenuous of the government to rely on state-owned enterprises (SOEs) to sponge up unemployed people and create jobs, because that would only add yet more inefficiency in the state sector. Already many graduates are, in the face of a tough job market, playing it safe[7] by taking state-sector jobs.

Allowing the employment market to work within market forces is a highly sensitive political step to take, but a necessary one. The jobs should follow the money into the companies that are successful in creating added-value, and those will be the ones that respond to the increasing demands for quality among consumers. A temporary peak in unemployment as the country retools is something the country needs to go through if there are to be longer-term improvements in working conditions, company efficiency and productivity, and a better consumer market.

Poor workplace safety standards

If demand for skilled labour is increasing again, and wages are increasing, this is good for China's market and workers. No more should they be expected to work in poor conditions, for long hours and low wages. In 2010, the suicides of ten workers at Foxconn's massive factory in Shenzhen sparked intense media interest in working conditions in China, and some long-needed soul-searching by those abroad who have enjoyed the benefits of cheap Chinese manufacturing of consumer products, such as Apple iPhones, unaware or unconcerned about the people working under poor conditions who make them.

Foxconn was already struggling with falling sales by 2009 and 2010, and faced accusations of overworking its employees and providing low wages and poor working conditions. Foxconn was forced to fully comply with Chinese labour laws, with a deadline of July 2013. It was removed from the Hong Kong benchmark Hang Seng Index in June

2011 and the company was forced to bring in the US-based Fair Labor Association[8] (FLA) after Apple, Foxconn's biggest customer, revealed abuses of labour[9] at the company's factories. These included employing people under the legal age for full-time employment, violations of safety rules and forcing workers to work long hours. The FLA and Apple then set out a 15-month action plan for Foxconn to sort out its labour abuse issues, stipulating 360 recommended changes, of which the FLA reported the company had complied with 284 by August 2012.

Foxconn is not an isolated case. Samsung[10] was also charged with "illegal and inhumane violations" at its manufacturing plants in China by China Labour Watch, based in New York. And these are the big multinationals. There are even worse abuses going on among many Chinese companies. According to official figures for 2010,[11] there were 79,552 work-related deaths in China, an average of 218 per day. Clearly, the government cannot allow such abuses and violations of the law and of human rights to continue in the name of economic growth, and is trying to stamp out such abuses. But in a competitive market like China, where markets are so fragmented, rules so rarely policed and corruption rife, policing the labour laws is a mammoth task. A task not helped by local governments which have "almost complete disregard of safety standards", according to Geoffrey Crothall from China Labour Bulletin.

Improving worker conditions costs money, and so without the law being enforced, companies continue to flout the law. This was highlighted tragically once again in the case of the Jilin chicken processing factory fire in June 2013, which killed about 120 people because emergency exits were locked[12] to stop workers taking breaks. In an article in the *China Daily* entitled "*China has much to do to improve workplace safety*,"[13] the paper demanded that the causes of the fire be thoroughly investigated and those responsible for any wrongdoing be brought to justice according to the law. The case highlighted the issue of local government officials charged with enforcing companies' regulation compliance continuing to take bribes to turn a blind eye to infringements, resulting in workplace deaths remaining commonplace – apparently 27,700 either died or went missing[14] at work in the first half of 2013, amid over 226,000 workplace accidents, according to official data.

Cutting corners in quality standards

It is not just the lives of workers that are at stake either. Companies in China have also been caught out cutting corners in terms of product quality for many years, producing products for market that are potentially harmful to those buying them, let alone making them. The list of examples is too long to go into here, but what is important to note is that the problem is still significant. It is another example of inefficiency – thinking that saving money to make bad products is more efficient than making better products that can be charged more for (value for money).

For instance, in May 2013 the European Union (EU) published statistics from its rapid alert system for dangerous goods (known as RAPEX), showing that of the 2,278 notifications of seized dangerous goods that posed risk to consumer health and safety in 2012, 1,126 notifications were for products sourced from China and Hong Kong, representing 58 per cent. The total number of notifications in 2011 was 1,803, of which 839 were due to products from China, representing 54 per cent of the total. The EU was quick to say that China is a major source of imports in the EU anyway, but clearly Chinese manufacturing is still cutting corners to undercut competition, and the problem is getting worse.

European Commission data for 2008 counterfeit import products show that 55 per cent of counterfeit products seized entering the EU that year were from China, and this rose to 73 per cent of the 115 million articles seized by EU country customs officials in 2011.[15] The proportion of goods not seized cannot easily be ascertained, but the risk of them being potentially harmful is high. Businesses investing in China and importing from it need to understand that while China professes to provide a level playing field in law, in reality this can often be far from the case. And while it can provide cheap products, cheap is not necessarily good, and is often a false economy.

Obviously the situation causes concern for consumers who might be harmed by such products. But it also increases concern that many of China's manufacturing industries remain fixated on being the cheapest by cutting corners and breaking the rules, rather than complying with the rules and giving consumers, both in China and abroad, the value-added quality assurance that they are willing to pay for. But to rise up the value-added chain, Chinese companies must produce goods that rival those imported from foreign companies, and to achieve that they need to be able to innovate.

Is China able to innovate?

China's growth to date has come mainly from cheap labour and investment, with one-time-only boosts from events such as the offloading of public housing, the closing down of thousands of SOEs in the 1990s, etc. These cannot be repeated, and potential new big events such as these are few – possibly *hukou* reform and removal of the One Child Policy. Much of the value China has added has come from bringing in foreign expertise through the operation of joint ventures, where Chinese companies partner with foreign counterparts, the Chinese side offering cheap labour and the foreign side offering expertise and technology.

But to build a more sustained domestic consumer economy, Chinese companies need to get inventive, and come up with more of their own innovations. I have always argued that Chinese people are just as smart, inventive and innovative as any other nation. For example, the man who built his own dialysis machine[16] because he couldn't afford the treatment that would keep him alive. That is inventiveness and innovation, and if he remains well, that could be the basis of a good business. What the Chinese people lack is an environment that encourages and nurtures innovation.

As evidence I would point to how quickly Chinese people have embraced the internet and online technologies, their recent rapid economic and social changes having made them quick and ready to adapt to new technology and adapt technology to their own ends. A great example is Chinese online supermarket (now majority-owned by Walmart) Yihaodian, and its virtual walk-in stores. The idea is that at certain points in Chinese cities, you will, with the aid of a smartphone, be able to view a virtual store where you can walk in and buy goods, pay for these by credit card and have them delivered to your door.

What I think is most important to emphasise here is that there is the ability to innovate in China, but the current environment does not always encourage it, because of corruption, cartels and cronyism. Nor do censorship of the internet, the lack of reliable copyright protection, or the inefficiency in industry. There are many systemic blocks working against innovation, creating a situation where people tend to play it safe. That will change, and it seems the government is beginning to shake down these systemic blocks and encourage its people to take more risks by starting to create a social security net to help them when they fall. But these things take time.

There are too many systemic blocks working against innovation, creating a situation where people tend to play it safe

Summary

In short, like the volume of industrial output and trade itself, the important point about data on China's trade and industry is that there is a lot of quantity, but not all of it is quality.

Part III

Citizen Consumers

chapter 10

Population, Employment, Income and the Middle Class

How many Chinese people are there really?

That China has a huge population is common knowledge, but concept familiarity perhaps dulls people's real perception of just how huge that population is, and therefore how colossal a task measuring it is. It's worth stepping back from China's total population figure to really appreciate just how big it is. At the 2010 census, the figure stood at roughly 1,339.72 million people. That is slightly under one fifth of humanity. The figure represents a continent within a country. According to the United Nations Department of Economic and Social Affairs, the total size of the population of Europe stood at 739 million in 2011 – a number representing about 55 per cent of the total population of China.

Now imagine that some 300 million (about the same as the population of the USA) of those people are economic migrants within the country, moving from place to place in search of the next big construction project or new factory opening. Keeping track of such a mobile population, even with the *hukou* residency registration (more on that later) system in China, is not easy. It is easy for people in China to fall off official registers, either because they are economic migrants to cities where they are not registered citizens, or because China's One Child Policy means many children go unregistered by parents avoiding punitive economic consequences for having more than their allotted progeny.

The perception of the Communist Party of China (CPC) being omnipotent, with a tight control over its people, is false. The CPC is a very big organisation, but even it cannot completely control 1.3 billion people. It has enough trouble keeping a party of 82.6 million members under control. To put that in perspective, the population of Germany is 81.7 million, and the CPC's membership represents only 6 per cent of the total population. The last census in 2010 had a zero-hour of 1 November 2010, but census data was not published until 28 April 2011. Given that 18 million babies were born in China in 2011, at 49,000 or so per day, in the 189 days it took to complete and publish the census data, about another 9 million Chinese people were born – about the population of Belarus. At best, calculating the population of such a vast and constantly growing country as China is going to be an estimate.

However, some estimates are better than others. According to the 2010 census in China, Shanghai's total population (including rural regions) was just over 23 million. Of that, according to National Bureau of Statistics (NBS) data, Shanghai's urban population within the main city, was 14.12 million. Yet, according to a Shanghai Demographic Survey, Shanghai's population in 2008 was apparently 18.88 million – a number generally assumed to have been chosen for its string of auspicious "8s" rather than statistical accuracy.

Chongqing is often mistakenly cited as being the world's largest mega-city, with a total population of 33 million according to the NBS Yearbook in 2012, which contests with the 2010 census result of 28.85 million, and would mean Chongqing's population grew by 14.5 per cent between 2010 and 2012! However, Chongqing municipality covers an area just larger than Scotland, much of which is rural. The actual urban population of the "province" was 15.4 million in 2010, of that about two-thirds lived in Chongqing city proper, not including outlying towns, and the city grandees are apparently planning to reach 12 million by 2020.

Even the seat of China's governmental power, Beijing, cannot agree on its own population size. The census said 19.16 million in 2010 (20.18 million by 2011), but the City Statistics Yearbook of China published by the NBS shows the population as 12.58 million, of which 11.87 million lived in the city proper, while the NBS Statistics Yearbook in 2011 (containing 2010 data) gave the total number as 12.78 million.

Just like the gross domestic product (GDP) data, if you add up the national total and the sum of the provinces, we find more discrepancies in the data. The official data includes nearly 5 million people whose residence is "difficult to determine." This is like saying nobody is quite sure where the population of Norway has gone. The disparity between central and provincial figures does seem to be expanding, but is not significant (see Table 10.1).

So there are slight anomalies in the data, China simply being a big country with any slight margin of error seeming to generate big numbers. But more local population inaccuracy, such as not knowing the size of the migrant worker population, skews any per capita data at a local level. The top-line numbers also do not reflect that the way China's population is changing will likely have profound effects on its future social structure and economy.

Table 10.1 Population of China by broad type, 1999–2011

	Military	Residence difficult to determine	National total	Provinces total	Provinces % of national total
1999	2.52	2.85	1,238.18	1,232.82	99.57
2000	2.50	3.01	1,248.12	1,242.61	99.56
2001	2.48	3.17	1,256.36	1,250.71	99.55
2002	2.46	3.34	1,265.61	1,259.82	99.54
2003	2.44	3.50	1,274.87	1,268.93	99.53
2004	2.42	3.67	1,284.12	1,278.04	99.53
2005	2.40	3.83	1,293.38	1,287.15	99.52
2006	2.38	3.99	1,302.64	1,296.27	99.51
2007	2.36	4.16	1,311.92	1,305.41	99.50
2008	2.34	4.32	1,321.21	1,314.55	99.50
2009	2.32	4.49	1,330.51	1,323.70	99.49
2010	2.30	4.65	1,339.72	1,332.77	99.48
2011	2.23	4.81	1,347.46	1,340.42	99.48

Source: NBS China Statistical Yearbooks.

The One Child Policy

The changes in China's population within an economic and social context must be framed by discussing the significant effects that the One Child Policy has had, and continues to have. Launched in 1979 after the population topped one billion, China's One Child Policy remains the CPC's most audacious attempt at social engineering. China's fertility rate dropped from 5.8 children per woman in 1970 to 2.7 in 1978, and the government believes the One Child Policy curtailed population growth by preventing 400 million extra births (approximately the total population of China in 1937).

But implementation has always been patchy. Today, a surprisingly low 20 per cent of children under 14 are from single-child families according to the State Population and Family Planning Commission (SPFPC). However, the policy has been most effective in cities rather than the countryside and consequently the number of one-child families is far higher, at above 80 per cent in most tier 1 and 2 cities.

In urban China, residents have faced heavy fines and can lose their jobs if they have a second child. Many increasingly financially stretched couples in towns and cities now prefer to have fewer children and cannot afford, nor have room for, more. But in the countryside, where parents depend on children to help and support them in their old age, especially sons, resistance has been widespread and continual. Rural families in China have been targeted with inventive campaigns to encourage family planning, including being paid not to have more children.

The One Child Policy has slowed population growth, but would repealing it really mean China's population would rebound, or would it simply continue to slow? Many seem to think that it would continue to slow.

Urban China is increasingly middle-class and career-obsessed, so children are now more of a "nice to have" than a necessity. Meanwhile, a significant proportion of rural adults are migrant workers in cities, many of whom have never done a day's farm work nor have any interest in the farm other than its land value. Many have little interest in passing on the land to their children, and would rather sell their lease rights to the growing number of large-scale farming cooperatives that buy up adjacent land parcels to farm more efficiently, using more mechanisation, to create more productive and profitable agro-industry. Farming is becoming a business in China thanks to previous land-law changes, and new changes will likely mean that process accelerates.

So the incentive to have children used to be that the children would take over the family farm and look after the parents in their old age. But Chinese families and society are faced with modern realities that vie with their traditional family and societal values.

A word on the concept of Confucian filial piety

China has a long tradition of filial piety that was amplified by the teaching of Confucius. Confucius's teaching laid out respective roles that people of different ranks and trades should play within society, and how they should interact with others to maintain a harmonious society, all the way up from peasant farmer to the Emperor. A key social relationship covered by Confucian philosophy is that between family members, especially children and parents. In this relationship, parents are responsible for the care, upbringing and education of children, who must remain obedient to their parents and care for them in old age.

This concept has been a cornerstone of Chinese social philosophy and culture for centuries, and the idea of filial piety, and respect and care for one's elders is deeply engrained. This is why people with elderly parents feel a strong obligation to provide for them, on top of what their parents can provide for themselves, if not a strong sense of duty to do so.

The duty of care

Because China's economic development now means that many people live far away from their parents,[1] this duty becomes increasingly difficult to perform. Add to that the effects of the One Child Policy, and many only children are left with the burden of caring for elderly parents by themselves. This can put immense pressure on those with elderly parents, and for those who find they cannot cope, there is a deep sense of shame for not being able to help their aged parents more. This sense of duty also makes it hard for those elderly parents, who begin to feel guilty for becoming a burden on their children.

This changing situation is forcing Chinese society to face the fact that it must rethink how it is going to look after so many more elderly within its population. Children cannot be left on their own to look after the old, so not only will government need to step in to help more, but more old and elderly people in China will have to find places in retirement homes, and plan their finances to pay for the care in old age that their children will not be able to provide. Yet not enough of these homes exist for the numbers of retirees, so spaces are oversubscribed and costs are high.

Providing these kinds of care services, either residential or in the elderly person's own home, will become increasingly necessary, even if not desirable. Retirees, those planning their retirements and those planning for having retired parents all must save heavily from their incomes to cover future costs of health care, accommodation and care services. This will perhaps be one of the most significant future opportunities in the services sector in China in coming years.

The late part of 2012 and early part of 2013 saw increased speculation that China's government was starting to take seriously the idea of scrapping the One Child Policy. Open debate among some leading state-connected think tanks and key political figures has increased. This included an uncommonly public battle between former State Councillors Song Jian (whose population projections formed the basis of the One Child Policy) and Peng Peiyun (who for a decade from 1988 to 1998 was head of China's Family Planning Commission, and therefore in charge of One Child Policy implementation). Peng advocated to the new Chinese leadership a gradual phasing out of the One Child Policy, arguing that China would economically founder if its population remained bound by it and aged before it became rich enough to support itself. Song, argued that removal of the Policy would lead to a baby boom and rampant population growth that could equally create economic woes for the country. The debate led to an adjustment of the Policy after the CPC Third Plenum in late 2013, but no repeal.

In early 2014, the government tweeked the Policy to allow couples among who only one partner was an only child to have more than one baby. Much journalistic expectation of a baby boom ensued, but it remains unlikely there will be a baby boom, and most likely that China will continue to grow older.

Demographic dementia – China's aging population

China's population growth is still slowing. If we look at the rate of population growth since 2000, we see the rate continues to fall, and will soon be half the rate in 2000. But even this data is open to interpretation. For instance, the NBS data for 2011 and 2012 were still close to 0.6 per cent, but, according to a World Bank report[2] published in 2012, China's population annual growth rate was 0.47 per cent, and according to the Central Intelligence Agency (CIA)[3] it was 0.48 per cent in 2012. Others have agreed more with the NBS and put the 2012 rate at 0.56 per cent (see Table 10.2).

Table 10.2 China percentage annual total population growth, 2000–2012

	% annual growth of total population
2000	0.80
2001	0.66
2002	0.74
2003	0.73
2004	0.73
2005	0.72
2006	0.72
2007	0.71
2008	0.71
2009	0.70
2010	0.69
2011	0.58
2012	0.56

Source: NBS China Statistical Yearbooks.

Whatever the rate, the population is soon going to stop growing, despite mini baby booms as was supposed to have happened in 2012, a Dragon year being very auspicious for the birth of a baby. Again, according to the NBS, the birth rate in China appears stabilised at about 12 births per 1,000 population, but this is not fast enough to stop the population from aging, and will have significant effects on China's economy (see Table 10.3).

Whatever the rate, the population is soon going to stop growing

There continue to be figures that seem to contradict. For example, the One Child Policy has been more effective in cities rather than the countryside, so the number of one-child families is far higher, at above 80 per cent in most tier 1 and 2 cities, while many rural households have more than one child. So the numbers on fertility and family size appear self-contradictory at times. The data also rather busts the myth that China's One Child Policy has been a resounding success. Family average size does appear to be shrinking, as the NBS household survey data shows, and assuming this to be largely accurate in most respects, and failing any other better data, we have to assume this is so (see Table 10.4).

Table 10.3 China decline in birth rate over 20 years, 1992–2011

	Births/1,000 population		Births/1,000 population
1992	18.2	**2002**	12.9
1993	18.1	**2003**	12.4
1994	17.7	**2004**	12.3
1995	17.1	**2005**	12.4
1996	17.0	**2006**	12.1
1997	16.6	**2007**	12.0
1998	15.6	**2008**	12.1
1999	14.6	**2009**	12.0
2000	14.0	**2010**	11.9
2001	13.4	**2011**	11.9

Source: NBS China Statistical Yearbooks.

Table 10.4 China average urban and rural family sizes, 2002–2011

	Urban household average size Persons	Rural household average size Persons
2002	3.03	4.12
2003	3.01	4.10
2004	2.98	4.08
2005	2.96	4.07
2006	2.95	4.05
2007	2.91	4.03
2008	2.91	4.01
2009	2.89	3.98
2010	2.88	3.95
2011	2.87	3.90

Source: NBS China Statistical Yearbooks.

China's rapidly changing demographic profile with a falling birth rate and enhanced longevity demands the country's population pyramid will logically trend towards an older society in the coming decades. The NBS has indicated it expects that China's population of 12–19-year-olds will drop by a significant 18.2 per cent between 2010 and 2020. China's teenage population is set to decline further still to approximately 9.1 per cent of the total population in 2050, from 13.8 per cent today.

Because of such demographic trends, the central government has been slowly repealing the One Child Policy in China's major cities (though to a far lesser extent in the countryside) by introducing various exemptions. But the aging of China's population will continue whatever happens now or in the future to the One Child Policy. According to Zhu Yong, Deputy Director of China National Committee on Aging, speaking in the Chinese press[4] in October 2012 on the problem of the aging population, some 200 million Chinese people will be over age 60 as of 2013. To put that in perspective, 200 million people is roughly equivalent to the combined populations of Germany, France and Italy. Nearly three out of ten Chinese people will be older than 60 by 2040, according to a United Nations forecast.

This marks a significant future decline in the number of people expected to be economically active in contrast to the proportion of the elderly dependents. In an article in China.org,[5] in July 2012, Zheng Bingwen, head of the Chinese Academy of Social Sciences (CASS) Global Pension Fund Research Center, was quoted as saying that between 2010 and 2050, China's population of working age will reduce by 100 million people down to 870 million, having peaked at 998 million by 2015. However, Li Jun, an expert with the Institute of Quantitative & Technical Economics under CASS, thinks China's working age population will be reduced to 710 million by 2050, a decline of 230 million compared with 2010. Either way, employees are about to become a much more precious (and expensive) resource in China (see Table 10.5).

But perhaps the entrepreneurs of the future in China will be its retirees. Free from the kind of pressures young Chinese face from the investment expectations placed upon them by their parents and grandparents, and

Table 10.5 The population of the over-60s in China, 2000, 2005, 2010 and 2015

	2000	2005	2010	2015
As a % of the Chinese population	10.66	13.01	14.85	16.91
Number of people (mn)	132.49	167.42	197.97	233.06
Number of women (mn)	66.59	85.50	100.24	116.96
% women	50.26	51.07	50.64	50.18
Number of people (mn):				
60–64	39.35	50.70	66.37	85.64
65–69	37.18	42.72	45.89	51.77
70–74	27.90	34.48	37.37	38.04
75–79	16.06	22.01	26.70	32.30
80–84	8.25	11.84	14.09	16.71
85–89	2.76	4.25	5.79	6.74
90–94	0.87	1.16	1.33	1.36
95+	0.13	0.25	0.42	0.50
Total	**132.49**	**167.42**	**197.97**	**233.06**

Note: 2015 figures are author's own estimates.

Adapted from source: NBS China Statistical Yearbooks.

with an economic incentive to try to keep earning, it could be that more elderly Chinese turn to back-yard inventing and establishing home-run businesses, instances of which are already common.

Pushing back the retirement age

Because of China's aging demographics, and the pressure this will have on the country's future economy, the Chinese government has been considering pushing back the age of retirement, which currently stands at age 60 for men, 50 for women workers and 55 for women cadres. Back in March 2011, in an article for the *China Daily*,[6] Yin Weimin, minister of Human Resources and Social Security, expressed that the government was considering pushing back the retirement age to 65 to reflect how more people are living longer. In the same article, Fan Ming, director of the Institute of Market Economy at Henan University of Economics and Law, indicated that by 2035 every two taxpayers would have to pay the social security expenses of one retired person, compared to 3.5 taxpayers paying for each retired person now. There are also those who want to lower the retirement age to create job vacancies for the many unemployed young people, although how they are supposed to create the wealth to pay for all those additional pensions is not explained.

Yet, since then, the Chinese government has not instigated a change to the retirement age, despite it being quite low compared to that of many other countries. There are likely three key reasons for not doing so. Firstly, many retirees are actually continuing to work, often setting up their own small businesses, and remain contributors to the economy, if in a reduced way. Secondly, many people in labour-intensive jobs would not wish to work even longer before they can retire. Thirdly, people have to pay into a pension for at least 15 years before they can retire, but many pension plans are still too young, and their contributors have not had time to accumulate enough of a pension pot.

So, rather than arbitrarily set new retirement ages, the Chinese government appears to be considering a range of different retirement ages suited to the rigours of working in different sectors. It would also make sense to allow employees who feel they still have a contribution to make in the workplace the right to negotiate to stay on. This would also mean companies could retain experienced staff members, perhaps on reduced hours, who could help train up new staff, thus improving efficiency rather than losing that experience completely.

In July 2012,[7] at a workshop on coping with its aging population, He Ping, director of the Social Security Research Institute under the Ministry of Human Resources and Social Security (MoHRSS), announced a proposal to introduce retirement mechanisms in China whereby employees would be encouraged to retire at a later age and companies would make allowances for that. His proposal was to begin implementing the policy in 2016, gradually increasing the retirement age, possibly by one year every two years over a ten-year period.

Reaching its Lewis Turning Point (LTP)

According to the NBS in 2012, the much-anticipated decline of China's working age population began in 2011, when the size of the 15–59-year-old cohort shrank by 3.45 million year-on-year, their share of the total population falling to 69.2 per cent from 69.8 per cent in 2011. This turning-point was bound to happen eventually, but what is harder to know is what the effects will be on China's society and economy in the coming years.

This gradual aging of the population, contemporary with China's sharp increase in the minimum wage and growing average incomes, is pushing China away from an economic model based upon low-skilled manufacturing towards a higher value-added industrial base and workforce. Because China has scant social security provision (forcing Chinese workers to save a very large proportion of their salaries) and faces increasing living costs, the Chinese government has recently had to significantly increase its spending on health care and education to avoid the so-called "middle income trap."

China's big problem with its aging population is that it faces getting old before it gets rich. China has gone through the period of rapid industrialisation based upon a vast pool of cheap, unskilled labour drawn from its rural population, leading to massive urbanisation. The point when the pool of excess rural labour becomes fully absorbed into the industrialised sector, and where continued capital accumulation leads to rising wages expectations, is most commonly called the "Lewis Turning Point" (after Nobel-Prize winning economist Sir Arthur Lewis). At this point, the economy can no longer create wealth by adding cheap labour to create value. New added-value must then be created through increased efficiency, innovation and higher-value, higher-technology production. China faces this LTP soon.

According to International Monetary Fund (IMF) economists Mitali Das and Papa N'Diaye[8] in a new working paper published in January 2013, China will reach its LTP in the early 2020s. Its economy is running out of the high-octane fuel (cheap labour employed in cheap manufacturing, aided by imported technology) that has kept its economy motoring along at fast growth rates. The vast pool of rural underemployed labour peaked in 2010, and in 2011 the population of working age began to shrink and the total population became 51 per cent urban. According to Das and N'Daiye, China will reach its LTP when wages begin to rise as excess labour is exhausted somewhere between 2020 and 2025.

It is difficult to be precise about these things as many factors can influence trajectory. But before the LTP arrives, China needs to raise its value-added game. Companies and industries in China should prepare themselves for continued rises in labour costs, which will add costs to all products and services, driving up the cost of living, which won't be so bad if you're already rich, but for squeezed middle-incomers things will get less exuberant. Those still just above the poverty line can expect to go back under again. The LTP situation therefore creates an extraordinary economic challenge for the new Chinese leadership.[9]

China's gender skew

Another factor resulting from the One Child Policy is the growing gender imbalance within China's population. An historical preference among the majority Han nationality Chinese for a male "heir," coupled with the One Child Policy, led to a sharp rise in selective abortions of female foetuses. The result, over the One Child Policy's 30-plus-year history, is that China's population has continued to become increasingly skewed towards a ratio where men outnumber women (see Table 10.6).

The figures below are at birth. Women tend to live longer than men, and China's population is aging. Thus, whereas the overall gender skew in the total population is that there are about 105 men for every 100 women in China (a figure that is mentioned in the NBS Statistical Yearbook), this skew is not even across the age groups. The biggest difference is in the under-40s, with men in 2011 representing 29.5 per cent of the population, and women just under 27 per cent – the gender skew in the under-40s is actually 109.6 men for every 100 women – nearly twice as large as in the overall population (see Table 10.7). But as China's population ages, this skew will likely become exacerbated.

Too many frustrated young men are never good for society. It has been argued that significant natural disasters (including two major floods of the Yellow River) and famine during the nineteenth century, which hit the weakest members of the population hardest (women and children), led to a gender skew then. The subsequent swell in the disaffected

Table 10.6 Increase in gender imbalance in China over 20 years, 1992–2011

	Gender ratio at birth (female = 100)		Gender ratio at birth (female = 100)
1992	108.8	**2002**	118.7
1993	109.8	**2003**	115.7
1994	110.5	**2004**	119.4
1995	111.5	**2005**	119.5
1996	112.4	**2006**	117.7
1997	113.3	**2007**	120.4
1998	114.2	**2008**	120.1
1999	115.1	**2009**	119.5
2000	116.5	**2010**	117.9
2001	120.9	**2011**	117.8

Source: NBS China Statistical Yearbook 2012.

Table 10.7 China population aged under 40 by gender, and gender imbalance, 2006–2011

Millions	2006	2007	2008	2009	2010	2011
Men aged under 40	381.0	377.3	371.2	368.9	363.8	395.3
Women aged under 40	361.3	357.0	348.9	344.5	337.4	360.7
Women = 100*	105.5	105.7	106.4	107.1	107.8	109.6

*Author's own estimations.

Source: NBS China Statistical Yearbook 2012.

and unemployed young men across China fuelled the creation of the Taiping rebellion, a civil war and social cataclysm that caused the deaths of between 20 and 40 million Chinese people, depending on different estimates. The Taiping Rebellion also contributed to the downfall of the Qing Dynasty itself, opening the way for a century of incursion by other foreign powers (the UK, France, Germany, Russia, the US and Japan) in China (the Qing were themselves Manchus, not Chinese).

In the future things look hard for China's men in finding partners. Already young Chinese men face increasing demands to achieve high incomes, buy homes and own a car before they can even consider entering the marriage market. Meanwhile, becoming an ever-more scarce resource, Chinese women are becoming choosier in who they pick as a mate. A growing cohort of frustrated young men is accumulating at the same time that income inequality has become even more apparent in China. Meanwhile, because of the switch in economic development model away from cheap, labour-intensive export manufacturing, and more towards a higher value-added one aimed at raising productivity and quality, so requiring more technical skills in the workplace, jobs for unskilled labour are becoming scarcer. All of this creates a highly volatile mix of social instability that could lead to increased rates of violent crime, or worse.

What's so funny about peace, love and urbanisation?

Since coming to power, the CPC has tried to fast-track China's economy out of poverty and into a "proletarian utopia," both for the sake of its population (long ravaged by war, disease, famine and natural disasters) and to prove its own legitimacy. This it began by passing laws creating more equality, changing land ownership rights, bringing equal marriage and inheritance rights for women, equality of employment, etc. Then, to supercharge that development, the CPC launched the Great Leap Forward to collectivise industry and agriculture and streamline production. This was then exacerbated when Mao Zedong, judging the failure of the Great Leap Forward to having been caused by "reactionary elements," promulgated the Great Proletarian Cultural Revolution.

The stick approach to rapid economic growth failed, so after the death of Mao, and the subsequent trial of the Gang of Four, Deng Xiaoping tried the carrot approach, by making it possible for farmers to grow their own crops over and above their tithe to the state, and for small-scale entrepreneurs to begin setting up businesses making things to sell for the export market. This worked well for a while, creating new, if modest wealth among more people, but production remained inefficient, prices began to rise and inflation created social unrest.

Then, the CPC began to seriously push for greater industrialisation. To achieve that, it had to greatly increase the urban population, knowing that urban population concentrations are much better at creating added-value to the economy than widely distributed rural ones. The more value added to the economy, the higher average wages could grow and the better that would be for social harmony and the legitimacy of the CPC as China's ruling party.

For this to happen, the CPC had to break the so-called "iron rice bowl" of jobs for life at state-owned enterprises (SOEs), with all housing, education and welfare provided, and condemn inefficient sunset industries to close. This was done both to eradicate the crippling social welfare burden and jobs-for-life culture that stymied efficiency in industry, and to release more of the workforce into jobs with companies that concentrated on adding value to the economy, rather than destroying it. This led to the closure of whole tranches of rust-belt factories during the late 1990s, and the bargain-price sell-off of the state-owned housing stock to its incumbent residents.

Meanwhile, the government began rebuilding China's cities, knocking down old, decrepit infrastructure and replacing it with new commercial and residential districts, linked by new roads and public transport systems. China's cities mushroomed. For example, Beijing went from three ring roads in the late 1980s to five now, and counting. The result was rapid urbanisation.

When I first went to China to study in 1988, three-quarters of China's population lived in rural areas. Ten years later, in 1998 (according to NBS data), that figure had decreased to two-thirds. Another ten years later, in 2008, the rural population was 54 per cent of the total population, and by 2011, China reached the historic point of becoming a majority urban population, with nearly 52 per cent of people living in urban areas.

With that massive shift in population has come the massive growth in China's industrial output. This led to very rapid growth in average incomes (see Table 10.8).

Table 10.8 China's population by urban/rural split, 2002–2011

	Urban population Millions	Rural population Millions	Urban population % of total	Rural population % of total
2002	494.7	765.1	39.3	60.7
2003	516.7	752.2	40.7	59.3
2004	536.2	741.8	42.0	58.0
2005	556.0	731.1	43.2	56.8
2006	571.9	724.4	44.1	55.9
2007	589.6	715.8	45.2	54.8
2008	603.5	711.0	45.9	54.1
2009	619.9	703.8	46.8	53.2
2010	665.8	666.9	50.0	50.0
2011	693.1	647.3	51.7	48.3

Source: NBS China Statistical Yearbook 2012.

For the Chinese government, urbanisation remains a focal point of socio-economic policy, helping to draw more labour into more efficient means of economic wealth generation. As more consumers are concentrated into urban populations, they are more easily reached by retailers and service providers, raising consumption as contributors to the economy. But paying for continued urbanisation is problematic, given rising local government debt. In a May 2013 article in Reuters,[10] central government insiders indicated that Li Keqiang had rejected a National Development and Reform Commission (NDRC) draft proposal to fund further urbanisation by RMB 40 trillion, to help raise China's urban population to 60 per cent by 2020 and so keep the economy chugging along at around 7 per cent per annum. Apparently, Li has concerns about finding the money not just for infrastructure, but also an improved social security net and reform of the urban resident registration (*hukou*) system.

The signs that the *hukou* system would surely change came when a *New York Times*[11] article released news that the Chinese government actually plans to urbanise 250 million rural Chinese over the next 12 years. Where the money to do this will come from is not yet apparent, nor (at time of writing) was the urbanisation plan official. But if this does go ahead, then reducing investment as a proportion of GDP, and with it building whole new cities and suburbs, will be difficult. It will be hard to maintain rapid urbanisation without continued investment, and making more people urban will not ensure growth in domestic consumption. Public spending issues such as land rights, increased congestion, rising costs of health care, education and pensions will also not go away quickly.

The *hukou* skew – a brief introduction

Simply living in a city in China does not make a person "urban." China has in place, and has since its early dynasties, a household registration system, known as "*huji* 户籍" under which each household is registered to where it lives at registration, giving it a "*hukou* 户口" or registration status. This *hukou* status means people are allocated employment, education, health care and social benefits at the place of that *hukou* registration. Those who are from the countryside, but working in a city, or indeed someone from one city working in another, are not entitled to government social benefits where they actually work, but only where their *hukou* is registered.

The 163–200 million migrant workers, whose labour has helped build China's new cities and industries, are mostly not entitled to receive social welfare benefits where they live and work. Adding in the families of those migrant workers, there were about 234 million urban dwellers without an urban *hukou*, approximately one-third of the urban population. Their work status is usually transitory, they often live in very poor circumstances and face prejudice and discrimination. It is a situation that has long been debated as needing change. *Hukou* system reform was promised under the government's Third Plenum document in late 2013, offering more rights of abode in cities to migrant workers, including access to the same benefits offered to local city dwellers. It will likely be implemented on an incremental basis, where the longer workers remain actively working in a city, the more benefits they will receive, until they eventually achieve full city *hukou* status after a certain number of years.

Such a change would mean more of the population is given the chance to become economically active, contributing to the utilised pool of working-age people at a time when the working-age population is shrinking. It would also help keep rising labour costs from spiralling due to a reduced workforce, and improve productivity by keeping more people in permanent jobs, rather than floating from one job to the next, and so accumulate skills. Given more access to health care and education, the migrant workforce would also be healthier, losing fewer days to illness (improving productivity for companies and reducing loss of income for workers), and better educated – allowing again for accumulation of skills.

A change in the *hukou* status that allowed migrant workers to receive social benefits such as health care and education would also mean more families could stay together, rather than living apart from their spouses and children, as is the case for about 63 per cent of migrant workers.

For those living with their children, 88 per cent of those children attend schools established specifically for migrant workers, and are usually of a low standard and often illegal. Of these children, about 83 per cent will end their education at completion of middle-school (the basic legal requirement), meaning most will end up in low-paid menial jobs. This is also a waste of future potential working-age people when China needs more skilled workers involved in higher-value production by a better-trained and educated workforce.

A formal *hukou* status would also help protect migrant workers from being underpaid, overworked and only employed on a non-contractual basis, leaving them at risk of being fired if they complain about poor work and safety conditions, etc. At the present time, they also have no protection should they become ill. Having little access to health care services, they rarely take time off to recover from illness as they risk losing their job to someone else, meaning many continue to work even when they are not fit to do so, raising the risk of workplace accidents.

It is the inequalities faced by migrant workers that have fuelled many significant instances of social unrest. Reforming the *hukou* system will require a lot of investment in schools, social services, pensions, etc., and this will be a cost that will have to come out of taxes and the wealth created in the economy. But the long-term economic outlook for China would likely be that the costs associated with reform of the current system would be vastly outweighed by the gains to the economy, as well as in social contentment.

Another key benefit would be the much greater ease of labour movement around the country, allowing skills to move to meet demands in different industries and different companies where they are most needed, without the hurdle of residence restrictions. This would increase productivity and skilled labour supply across the country, helping more private companies to find the workers they need, and push China's industrial complex up the value ladder. Precisely where it needs to go if China is to remain competitive.

Finally, creating a fairer job market for migrant workers would help them to earn better wages, accumulate more skills, better educate their children and ensure more skilled workers for the future to create more value in the economy and become significant consumers themselves. Lifting one-third of the urban population out of poverty and into significant consumption will be crucial to sustained economic growth.

Employment and un(under)-employment

The official rate of unemployment has been stuck in a 4 per cent groove since about 2002, prior to which it persisted at 3 per cent. The unemployment figures of the 1990s did not show any real fluctuation, even when the government closed down many SOEs. The reason is that government unemployment figures are very selective, not including people laid off from SOEs, nor counting men over the age of 50 or women over 45. Also, those who are not registered for unemployment insurance and therefore do not qualify for benefits will not register themselves as unemployed because there is simply no point. Only about 13–14 per cent of migrant workers have unemployment insurance. Migrant workers tend not to be counted in the unemployment data anyway. It is also likely that local government officials massage their regional unemployment figures down to hide problems for which they may receive blame.

Tom Orlik, writing in the *Wall Street Journal* in December 2012, highlighted the results of a survey of 8,000 Chinese households,[12] run by Gan Li, an economics professor at South Western University of Finance and Economics in Chengdu. In the survey, Gan found that the unemployment rate among China's migrant workers had risen sharply to 6 per cent by June 2012, up from 3.4 per cent in August 2011, suggesting 10 million unemployed as a result of the sharp slowdown in exports and real-estate construction. The survey also suggested that the real urban unemployment rate was 8.05 per cent in June 2012, up from 8 per cent in August 2011 and nearly twice as high as the official 4.1 per cent rate.

The rate of unemployment is a useful indicator (if reasonably accurate) of wage pressures, and therefore cost of operation for companies. It is also an indicator of the amount of inefficient use of the workforce, which harks back to the issue of the *hukou* system discussed above. The lack of employment mobility, skills and education in the workforce created by that system is likely a significant cause of the high unemployment rates among migrant workers, and therefore the workforce in general. The graduate unemployment situation discussed earlier also points to lack of job mobility being a contributing factor. That many graduates are looking more at jobs in the state-owned sector because of better pay and job security also means private enterprises face problems finding the skilled and educated people they need to make their businesses grow.

As China's economy has slowed, many companies have had to lay off workers. What often happens is that companies will offer workers either a statutory severance package or they choose to resign and get a larger payment. This method of encouraging workers to take redundancy helps companies to avoid conflict with workers, but also helps the government unemployment figures, which do not include anyone taking voluntary redundancy. So, when the government counts the official unemployment figures, those made redundant by this means are not counted. In an article for *Foreign Policy*[13] in September 2009, Huang Yiping, chief Asia economist for Citigroup, estimated that the real numbers of those losing their jobs following the loss of export trade that year was probably double the government figure.

The official press continued to publish articles in which the unemployment rate remained at 4.1 per cent up to the end of 2013. What the figures fail to include are the numbers of people underemployed in China. There are many rural workers who are underemployed at the lower end of the scale, but also many graduates who fail to find work better suited to their qualifications and end up serving coffee at Starbucks or flipping burgers at McDonalds. The lack of credible published figures on un(under)-employment means it is hard to gauge just how inefficient the employment market in China is, and therefore how much potentially could be gained in the economy by better use of its labour force. Harking back to the issue of the aging population again, and the shrinking size of the labour force, more efficient use of labour has to be an imperative, but designing policy to improve the situation can only come from better data – and the much-anticipated reform of the *hukou* system.

The Gini coefficient and income disparity

The demographic and employment trends detailed above mean that costs and prices will continue to rise, and this will amplify the growing inequality between rich and poor. How deep the disparity is between China's rich and poor, and the gap between the developed urban coast and rural hinterland, was not fully known until very recently, although much had been written about the growing income gap.

The Gini Index of income disparity is a standard statistical measure of income equality. If the Gini score is zero, then everyone has a completely equal share of the wealth of the economy. If the score is one, then the entire value of the economy is held by one person.

In January 2012, the NBS admitted it had been collating Gini coefficient figures since 2000, but had not published them because data on high earners was inaccurate. In January 2013, the NBS published its first set of Gini figures. In those figures, the Gini score for 2012 was 0.474, down from a peak of 0.491 in 2008. To put that in perspective, according to a Unicef Social and Economic Policy Working Paper entitled "*Global Inequality: Beyond the Bottom Line,*" compiled by Isabel Ortiz and Matthew Cummins, in 2008 the whole of Asia had a Gini coefficient of 0.404, while the worst region for inequality was the Caribbean and Latin America at 0.492.

There are dissenters though. In a report[14] by Chengdu Southwestern University of Finance and Economics' Chinese Household Finance Survey Center published in December 2012, it was claimed that China's Gini coefficient was actually as high as 0.61 in 2010 compared to an average of 0.44 across all countries monitored by the World Bank. Credence for this comes from the officially admitted standpoint that the incomes declared by higher-income households are often well below the reality due to people in those households significantly underdeclaring their real incomes and assets.

Whatever the actual figure, it is clear that inequality is an issue in China. Without the statistics, the news stories of young sons and daughters of high-ranking officials and people who have made millions in the rapid growth of years past showing off their immense wealth, flouting the rules, writing off expensive sports cars and generally being obnoxious, while most Chinese continue to struggle on relatively low incomes, are enough evidence to prove that the inequality is there. The scale of the inequality also breeds a growing amount of resentment.

Inequality creates growing anger

The number of Chinese people living in extreme poverty[15] (defined as living on less than US$ 1.25 per day) fell from 835 million in 1981 (or 84% of its population) to 156 million in 2010 (down to 12% of the population), according to a World Bank paper ("*The State of the Poor: Where are the Poor and where are they Poorest?*" – April 2013). According to the paper, China's share of the extreme poor population of the world dropped from 43 per cent (making it the largest contributor of the extreme poor population) in 1981, to 13 per cent by 2010.

China has therefore achieved an historic success in the past three decades by probably being the single country that has lifted more people out of poverty than any other, ever. But while fewer people have remained poor, and more have been elevated into a more comfortable "*xiaokang*" (living comfortably if modestly) existence, the rapid economic growth of the country has created an ever-widening wealth gap. That wealth gap hurts the economy. Not only because many of China's rich are increasingly moving their cash offshore and out of the Chinese economy, but also because it weakens the growth in incomes among those lower

> China has... probably... lifted more people out of poverty than any other, ever

down in the pecking order, and creates growing social resentment and disillusionment.

A central tenet of the book *The Spirit Level* (Allen Lane, March 2009) by Richard Wilkinson and Kate Pickett is that economic growth and extreme wealth do not a happy nation make, and that violent crime, a plague of the US (the world's wealthiest economy) is created by inequality, despite its wealth. This points to many of the growing problems in China. According to an Associated Press article in June 2010, violent crime in China jumped 10 per cent in 2009, perhaps due to a correction in the data published by official sources, perhaps a result of economic slowdown, but also just as likely a reflection of growing resentment at inequality, frustration with lack of justice and desperation among the many in China's population who have not reaped the benefits of the country's economic growth. The growing gender skew,[16] with about 30 million more men than women, is also another likely contributing factor. The economist Ena Edlund has estimated that every 1 per cent increase in gender imbalance creates a 6 per cent increase in the rate of violent and property crime.

There have been several high-profile cases of men running amok and killing people indiscriminately in schools and kindergartens in China in the past few years, echoing the kinds of crimes seen in the US over recent years. China is also suffering from a dramatic rise in its suicide rate. According to an AFP article in September 2011,[17] the Chinese government and state media published figures that put China's suicide rate at 22.23 people out of every 100,000, based on data from the Centre for Disease Control and Prevention, which would give the country one of the highest suicide rates in the world. The rate is especially high among women.

More generally, there also appears to be a rising current of mistrust among the Chinese population. In February 2013, the Chinese Academy of Social Sciences published its "*Annual Report on Social Mentality*,"[18] which was based on a survey of respondents' trust towards different people and organisations, and concluded that the level of trust among China's population was not only poor, but had worsened, reaching 59.7 points out of 100, down from 62.9 points in 2010.

Even the NBS's consumer confidence index on the economy shows that while people continue to be generally optimistic in their confidence in the economy and their expectation of future economic growth, their satisfaction level is weaker. This indicates a lack of satisfaction in the way economic growth has converted into actual improvement in people's lives. Should economic growth expectation and confidence be weakened due to the slowdown in the economy, that satisfaction level would also likely decline ahead of the two other indices (see Table 10.9).

In December 2012, continuing concern about the lack of equilibrium in the Chinese economy prompted 100 academics to write an open letter[19] to the government in which they pressed for urgent reforms to the political and economic system to prevent the stagnation of progress in Chinese society. The letter also warned that official corruption and dissatisfaction in society could "boil up to crisis point" and that China could miss its opportunity to continue peaceful reform and "slip into the turbulence and chaos of violent revolution." This is quite a stark warning to make so publicly, but it underlines the urgency with which the Chinese government is having to tackle the underlying fundamental flaws in the current system.

Part of the problem with the current system is the reliance on indicators such as those above, and the official Gini coefficient, which do not give a true picture of how unfair Chinese society has become. To rectify the problems in China's society, and make it more equal, the Chinese government is being urged by many[20] to rectify its economic policies, and (it appears) is doing so. Policies seeking to reduce income inequality are perhaps the most important in order to reduce social unrest that such inequality breeds.

The middle class myth

Thankfully, a central plank of the CPC current leadership's policies is social harmony arising from a fairer distribution of wealth and investment in a stronger social security net, including raising the

Table 10.9 NBS Consumer Confidence Index, June 2011–June 2013

Date	Consumer expectation index	Consumer satisfaction index	Consumer confidence index
2011.06	111.4	103.2	108.1
2011.07	111.8	96.2	105.6
2011.08	110.4	96.9	105.0
2011.09	108.9	95.2	103.4
2011.10	106.3	91.8	100.5
2011.11	101.7	90.0	97.0
2011.12	105.3	93.2	100.5
2012.01	109.3	95.8	103.9
2012.02	110.9	96.1	105.0
2012.03	106.6	90.2	100.0
2012.04	108.5	94.7	103.0
2012.05	108.9	97.1	104.2
2012.06	103.2	93.3	99.3
2012.07	101.5	93.3	98.2
2012.08	103.7	93.0	99.4
2012.09	104.0	96.0	100.8
2012.10	109.3	101.2	106.1
2012.11	109.4	98.6	105.1
2012.12	107.6	97.8	103.7
2013.01	110.1	96.1	104.5
2013.02	113.3	100.6	108.2
2013.03	107.9	94.5	102.6
2013.04	108.1	97.1	103.7
2013.05	102.7	93.4	99.0
2013.06	100.5	91.7	97.0

Source: NBS China Statistical Information Network (www.stats.gov.cn).

provision of education, health care and pensions. This is meant to help free up spending by China's so-called established and emerging middle class of consumers, to become free to save less to cover these needs.

China's nominal middle classes are the lynchpin of the new Chinese economy that is based upon domestic consumption growth rather than export manufacturing and investment-fuelled infrastructure projects. Until about a decade or so ago, the middle class in China did not exist, or was at least officially unrecognised. Now it is officially the whole reason behind the retooling of China's economy towards domestic consumption.

Understanding this economic powerhouse (the so-called middle classes of China) is also fraught with difficulty due to the poor definition of who actually counts as "middle class," "middle income," "established consumers," or whatever we shall call them, as is what they are really earning and spending their money on, and how much grey income they really have. Articles, reports and books abound on the middle classes in China, but there is little consistency in the definition or inclusion criteria of who counts as middle class in China. This means that sizes and projections about the middle class are also often widely different. And this is significant because the middle class of China is often cited as, and indeed probably is, increasingly important to the future growth of the global economy.

According to John Ross,[21] a senior fellow at the Chongyang Institute for Financial Studies at Renmin University in Beijing, a meaningful definition of middle class for China should make sense both in Chinese and Western terms, and should include ownership of a home and a car and the ability to take an annual foreign vacation or significant domestic vacation. This is quite a useful definition as it neatly sidesteps the issue of putting a number to the income bracket, which has shifted upwards rather rapidly in recent years, and is constantly changing.

According to a new bilateral study *"US–China 2022: Economic Relations in the Next 10 Years"* by the China–United States Exchange Foundation[22] (CUSEF) written by a panel of US and Chinese economists and published in May 2013, by 2022 China's middle class is expected to reach 630 million, an increase from 230 million in 2012. This chimes close to what Helen Wang, author of the book *The Chinese Dream: The Rise of the World's Largest Middle Class and What It Means to You,*[23] cites, that is, according to McKinsey Global Institute, the Chinese middle class are those people with annual incomes, in terms of purchasing power, in a range from US$ 13,500 to US$53,900. CASS released a report in 2004 defining the Chinese middle class as families with assets valued from US$ 18,100 to US$ 36,200 (RMB 150,000 to RMB 300,000). The official data from China's NBS defines the Chinese middle class as households with an annual income ranging from US$ 7,250 to US$ 62,500 (RMB 60,000 to RMB 500,000). Helen Wang herself uses a combination of these definitions in her book, including urban professionals and entrepreneurs from all walks of life, who have college degrees and earn an annual income from US$ 10,000 to US$ 60,000. Wang believes this to be over 300 million people, or 25 per cent of China's population in 2010.

According to Kenneth Rapoza in Forbes,[24] within a generation the middle class in China will be roughly four times the size of the US middle-class population, citing the United Nations (UN) Population Division and Goldman Sachs. By 2030, China should have approximately 1.4 billion middle-class consumers (roughly the entire current Chinese population now) compared to 365 million in the US, and 414 million in Western Europe. To me this seems more than a little optimistic. Also rather overoptimistic was the Asian Development Bank report "*Key Indicators for Asia and the Pacific 2010*,"[25] which defined the Asian middle class as spending between US$ 2 and US$ 20 per day, by which criteria the middle class in China numbered 800 million people.

The Organisation for Economic Cooperation and Development (OECD)[26] bases its measure of middle-class inclusion on an income of between US$ 10 and US$ 100 spending per day at PPP (Purchasing Power Parity). By this measure, the OECD says that the US middle class numbers some 230 million people (73%) of the population, while China's middle class is measured at "up to 10 per cent" of the population (up to about 134 million people, or about 44 million households), expected to rise to 20 per cent by 2020.

Meanwhile, Dragonomics estimate that in 2012 there were 107 million "established consumer" households (roughly multiply by three for population), growing at 20 per cent per year during 2005 to 2012, falling to 15 per cent growth over 2012 to 2015 and down to 9 per cent each year between 2015 and 2020. This estimate was broadly based on Boston Consulting's definition of middle-class income as US$ 7,500 and above in 2010.

While running Access Asia, we defined the Chinese middle class as those people who are urban, invariably white-collar workers and have a narrower household income of approximately US$ 9,000–30,000. This bracket was deliberately narrower because we felt that the US$ 10,000–60,000 range was too big, and that those on US$ 30,000 and over should really be counted among higher-income consumers. That gave us about 25–30 million households in China falling into the middle class between 2010 and 2012, or approximately 13.5 per cent of all urban households in China, and between 6 per cent and 7 per cent of all households.

In February 2013, Yuval Atsmon, who is principal in McKinsey's Shanghai office, stated that the proportion of people in China earning between US$ 17,000 and US$ 35,000 a year (that is, the middle class) is set to increase from just 6 per cent in 2010 to 51 per cent in 2020.[27] While I can agree with the 2010 figure, I am much more sceptical about the forecast size of the middle class in China. But his figures coincide with the CUSEF[28] figure of about 630 million middle-class consumers in China by 2022, up from their estimate of 230 million in 2012. In the McKinsey Quarterly[29] published in June 2013, a figure of 174 upper and mass middle-class households (roughly 522 million people) with annual incomes between US$ 9,000 and US$ 34,000 was given for 2012, rising to 272 million households by 2022, about 816 million people, or nearly 60 per cent of the population.

What all these different estimates show is not that everyone is wrong, or that the different definitions are wrong, but that the situation is changing so fast that it is hard to be accurate. This is where China continues to confound even the best informed pundits, and why making claims about the current size of China's market and its future growth is such a dangerous game – an art rather than a science. For my part, I shall put my head on the block and predict 40 per cent of

China's households will be middle class by 2020, and I shall publish my definitions for China's middle class in 2020 to prove that I was right!

Income, savings and investments

What really drives middle-class growth is both average wages growth and willingness to spend rather than save. According to the NBS,[30] the average urban resident's per capita disposable income grew by 9.6 per cent after adjustment for inflation in 2012, compared to 2011. While I can agree that this is still strong growth, I would argue that given the rising cost of living in China, even with likely continued strong income growth, the real income threshold needs to also increase to remain meaningful, and so the criteria for middle-class inclusion will also need to be raised, especially given the high cost of housing in much of urban China, home ownership being a prerequisite for inclusion as middle class.

Wage inflation, as China's industrial sector meets its LTP, is likely to increase. The increased need to meet safety and quality standards will also push up food prices, which are a key contributor to overall consumer prices. Caixin Online[31] estimates that wages for unskilled workers will double in the five years from 2013 to 2018, and skilled workers' average salaries will grow at about 12 per cent, although wages in the state-owned sector are likely to be kept in check through government intervention.

This could have the effect of pushing more graduates to look for work in the private sector rather than in the state-owned sector, and thus more talent into more innovative companies, thereby raising labour productivity. Increased productivity would combat the likelihood of stronger inflation as China shifts towards an economy more heavily reliant on domestic consumption than export manufacturing.

Higher incomes would also increase demand for better-quality goods over low-quality goods, creating more demand for companies to improve their productivity, efficiency, innovation and competitiveness

Table 10.10 Total retail sales, average urban wages, total household savings and net new savings, 2000–2012

RMB trn	Total retail & wholesale trade	% annual growth	Average urban wage (RMB)	% annual growth	Household savings	% annual growth	Net new household savings	% annual growth
2000	3.4		9,333		6.4		0.47	
2001	3.8	10.1	10,834	16.1	7.4	14.7	0.94	100.19
2002	4.2	11.8	12,373	14.2	8.7	17.8	1.31	39.43
2003	4.8	13.3	13,969	12.9	10.4	19.2	1.67	27.07
2004	6.0	25.0	15,920	14.0	12.0	15.4	1.59	–4.60
2005	6.7	12.9	18,200	14.3	14.1	18.0	2.15	34.87
2006	7.6	13.7	20,856	14.6	16.2	14.6	2.05	–4.46
2007	8.9	16.8	24,721	18.5	17.3	6.8	1.09	–46.69
2008	10.8	21.6	28,898	16.9	21.8	26.3	4.54	314.28
2009	12.5	15.5	32,244	11.6	26.1	19.7	4.29	–5.44
2010	15.5	23.3	36,539	13.3	30.3	16.3	4.25	–0.83
2011	18.1	17.3	41,799	14.4	34.4	13.3	4.03	–5.17
2012*	20.7	14.3	47,183	12.9	40.1	16.6	5.71	41.57

*Author's own estimates for 2012.

Source: NBS China Statistical Yearbook 2012.

to meet compliance with increased consumer demand for quality, and government policing of quality standards.

But wages growth can only fuel stronger consumption if the government really begins to increase social welfare spending in a much bigger way. Providing higher levels of health care, education and pensions, not just basic coverage spread across the widest population, would encourage more households to save less and spend more. Reform of the *hukou* system is also likely to help migrant workers gain fairer wage growth. According to the NBS, monthly migrant worker wages rose 11.8 per cent year on year in 2012 over 2011, reaching RMB 2,290 per month, down from 21.2 per cent growth at the end of 2011. If *hukou* reform does come into place, this could be a major contributor to more rapid growth in the size of the middle class in China, as indicated by some estimates (see Table 10.10).

Income reporting and "grey income"

Defining China's middle classes, or significant consuming classes, is also blurred by the lack of clarity on what people in China really earn. For example, savings statistics do not include investments, and household income (although supposed to include all non-wage income) is generally known to be significantly underreported.

Back in October 2010, I was alerted to the findings of a research report on the grey economy (as in undeclared income, not old people) in China by China Reform Foundation deputy director Professor Wang Xiaolu.[32] In this report, Professor Wang suggested that China's grey income could amount to as much as "RMB 10 trillion, or 30 per cent of GDP," coming from non-wage earnings from property deals, side-line trades, private money-lending, etc. This immediately sparked debate about how big the significant consumer market really was in China, and its real spending power. He declared that big-ticket items were the biggest beneficiary of this grey money, and that over 60 per cent of that cash is in the hands of just the top 10 per cent of urban households. That is, the middle class and above.

This made sense because comparing the average incomes at the time for even the higher-income brackets did not square with the conspicuous rise in consumption of luxury goods. Clearly there were more people earning more money than they were declaring for there to be so many luxury brand outlets successfully opening across China at the time. While taking the opinion that Professor Wang's estimates were probably overblown, GavKal Dragonomics used half of his estimated distortion from the grey market to come up with their own figures for the size of the middle class and their spending power for the first quarter 2013 edition of the *China Economic Quarterly*, in which they estimated that in 2012 there were 107 million "established consumer" households.

So, there are anywhere between 100 million and 260 million middle-class Chinese at present, with an additional RMB 3 trillion in real income and spending power based on the Dragonomics adjustment of Professor Wang's estimate, meaning that split evenly between them each middle-class person had between RMB 11,500 and RMB 30,000 (approximately US$ 1,850 and US$ 4,800) in additional, unrecorded income.

What is most striking is the level of inaccuracy in both the real income levels recorded in official statistics and the real size of the middle class, which points to an even greater level of inequality between the upper- and lower-income households in China (and a lack of real understanding of the size of the issue), which further highlights the potential for animosity within Chinese society. But the data also shows that potential average income and spending power could be greater than the official records suggest, which points to continued positive potential growth in the consumer market in China despite the slowing GDP growth rates.

China gets a Volvo, a lawnmower and a NIMBY attitude

But are the middle classes of China happy? They're certainly not happy with chemical plants, battery factories and tanneries being built in their neighbourhoods, like any other middle-class NIMBY (Not In My Back

Yard) household anywhere else in the world. And, just as the working classes of Britain's Industrial Revolution eventually rose up the value-added chain and became middle class, so will the Chinese, and with it will come the righteous indignation at anything that rocks the castle of contentment of so much of Middle England and Middle America.

Better educated than many, well informed through constant media feeds wherever they go and with property and position to protect, China's middle classes are political sceptics with seemingly deep suspicions about the motives of the very politicians and corporate cadres who helped to create the white-collar workers' Utopia we see in China today, with all its luxury goods, entertainment outlets, cars, pollution, corrupt politicians, pollution, mega-rich embezzlers, pollution, lack of public civility and pollution.

What is also of importance is how China's middle class is growing together, agglomerating in satellite towns and new suburbs, the same way that the country's economy has, from small islands of economic activity and consumption, into whole regions, and now deeper into tier 3 territory, and beyond.

From isolated islands of consumption to the scramble into lower-tier cities

China's economy grew from the opening-up of its economy in the early 1980s primarily in the special economic zones (SEZs) of the south coast and in the key cities of Shanghai, Beijing and Tianjin. These places became islands of economic growth amid a sea of continued poverty and a planned-economy-induced economic trance. Gradually, these islands of economic growth spread into their surrounding regions, and new cities and provinces began to open up economically. This is a process that is still ongoing, with ever larger areas becoming economically significant, and new areas emerging.

Until recently, the Pearl River Delta (PRD), Yangzi River Delta (YRD) and Bohai Rim regions were the main economic blocks in China, but these have begun to join up – the first two through growth in export manufacturing in Fujian and Zhejiang, and the YRD and Bohai Rim have agglomerated together thanks to the spread of economic activity into Jiangsu and Shandong provinces. Along the Yangzi River, Wuhan, Chongqing and Chengdu have all emerged as areas of rapid economic growth, drawing wealth generation into the interior regions of China. Anhui, between Wuhan and Shanghai, has also grown rapidly recently thanks to being a relatively low-cost manufacturing and logistics base in-between the upstream Yangzi River economic hubs and the YRD region. Meanwhile, economic development has spread along the south coast westwards into Guangxi and Yunnan. Northeastern China's provinces of Liaoning, Jilin and Heilongjiang have also seen economic growth spread out from their major cities.

China's economic growth can be thought of in terms of being isolated islands of significant economic consumer activity that have gradually joined together, with new wealth gradually creating new towns and cities, new industrial areas and development zones, in-between. Economic development and wealth in China therefore depends very much on where you are talking about. Certain regions and provinces of China remain largely backwaters of the economic revolution, as yet, such as mostly agricultural Jiangxi in the east, mountainous Guizhou in the southwest, agricultural and mountainous Hubei in the centre and the coal-extraction-blighted Shanxi to the south of Beijing. Heading west, Shaanxi with its wealth of tourist sites (in the ancient capital of Xi'an) also remains further behind in the economic growth stakes, but with great recent growth potential. Then in the sparsely populated "hinterland" provinces and autonomous regions of Gansu, Inner Mongolia, Qinghai, Tibet and Xinjiang, economic growth has been slow due to the great distance from the main regions of established economic activity.

China has about 12 cities with populations over 2 million, another 22 cities with populations of between 1 and 2 million, another 160 cities with populations between 500,000 and 1 million, and then another 468 other smaller cities – about 660 cities in total. Despite having studied and researched China for about 30 years, while I can put a pin in the map for quite a few of these cities (possibly about 30–40, perhaps more), the rest I may have heard of, but have never looked up on the map, to my shame. To my shame because China has about 160 cities with populations bigger than Edinburgh, which to me as a child growing up in a small town in Scotland, was a BIG city – but it had fewer than 500,000 residents in 2011. I really should know more about these cities, not just because of their population sizes, but because they are where China's new economic growth is really coming from. Shanghai is old hat these days, it's Pingdingshan that's where it's at!

Indicative of how important these cities are becoming is evidenced by the fact that both Carrefour and Walmart are leading the modern grocery retail charge into these lower-tier and interior hinterland cities, along with KFC and McDonalds, and one assumes inevitably the likes of Starbucks, Zara and Uniqlo. After slower outlet growth in 2012, both of these leading supermarket and hypermarket chains have decided that development in lower-tier cities and into western provinces is where the new front of market expansion is going to be. And this makes sense given that economic growth has been much faster in these places recently than in the more developed eastern seaboard cities.

What is really exceptional about these lower-tier cities is that due to many leading brands and chains not yet having established a physical presence, online retailing is already as prevalent in these lower-tier cities as it is in higher-tier cities. Also, because many people in lower-tier cities are more likely to be connecting to the internet via mobile devices (smartphones and tablets) than PCs or laptops, mobile online retailing is a key facet of the brand extension strategy for many companies heading into the interior and down into the lower tiers.

The lower-tier cities are also where small- and medium-sized companies are competing more successfully by imitating the leading fast-moving consumer goods (FMCG) goods brands, using local knowledge to build customer bases that the leading companies have not yet reached, having continued to take a wait-and-see approach to the lower-tier cities until quite recently. That is all about to change, thanks in large part to the growth in modern, organised retailing by the likes of Carrefour and Walmart in these cities.

It is for this reason that macroeconomics begins to lose its meaningfulness, as gauging the market potential of these smaller cities has more to do with understanding local market environments and less to do with national trends. As well as the usual socio-economic numbers, successful market entry in these local markets relies much more heavily on local market factors, and judging the importance of these comes down to getting a much more intimate understanding of what makes each place tick.

Climate, geography and culture – that which econometrics cannot measure

What statistics about China, and often the analysis of its various markets, fail to quantify is the effect that location has in the way people live and act as consumers. China stretches from the subtropical southwest to the sub-arctic northeast; it covers colossal mountain ranges and deserts, huge river systems, prairies and forests, areas of very high population density and areas where practically nobody lives for most of the year. To expect the people living in each of these different parts of China to live homogenous lives, with homogenous lifestyle needs, is a nonsense.

> *What statistics about China often fail to quantify is the effect location has on how people live and act as consumers*

Each city has its key industries, leading retailers and manufacturers, as well as its own combination of first-entrant leading national competitors, be they retailers, FMCG manufacturers or luxury brands. Just because the islands of consumption in China are joining up into larger blocks of consumerism does not mean they will all be the same. On the contrary, for many years to come many of China's regional markets will remain quite distinct, with their own regional characteristics.

For example, if you look at the organised grocery retail markets in Beijing and Shanghai, two of China's most developed cities; the retail landscapes in these two cities are still very different from each other, simply because of the physical layout of each city. Beijing's wide boulevards and massive blocks are less conducive to pedestrian traffic than Shanghai's smaller roads, lanes and blocks, and hence the convenience store sector in Shanghai is much more developed than it is in Beijing, even after so many years.

Summary

As more companies and brands reach further into lower-tier cities, China's consumer market is only going to get more diverse, not less so. What much of the data on China fails to represent is that diversity. That is because China is not one market, for most sectors, but a collection of regional markets, each with very distinct characteristics. The sooner companies trying to do business with "China" grasp this, the more likely they will succeed in finding the right market within China for their goods and services. Being in China does not mean you have a potential market of 1.3 billion people. Arriving in Shanghai and expecting to be able to sell in Chengdu is like opening a shop in London and expecting to sell to Muscovites.

chapter 11

Retail Sales

A bottle half empty, or half full?

China is undergoing the shift from an economic model driven by export manufacturing to one more driven by domestic consumption. This is good news for any companies trying to sell into the Chinese consumer market, if they can negotiate the extremely fragmented nature of those markets, the high level of counterfeit goods, the throng of jostling competitors and the confusing market size data.

When looking to benchmark the potential market within China, it is imperative that companies understand that the official figures used to measure the domestic consumer market in China are not offering the kind of measures that they may appear to do. Not only do the retail sales top-line figures appear confusingly similar to the overall consumer spending figures, but they are also inconsistent in their definition.

Because of this, the official "retail" statistics miss the real retail market size by a long way, and have done for years. Businesses using the official figures to make investment decisions in China have therefore been doing so based on a set of figures that overstate the real market size. Most of my research experience with China data has been in working with the market sizing, sectoral breakdown and company shares of retail sales of consumer products and services to Chinese consumers, and particularly, more recently, the emerging "middle classes."

When running my own company, Access Asia, our retail sales statistics were calculated as the sum of individual markets within the retail sector. We researched each of the sectors of the market individually, using industry and company sources, as well as national statistics. Our figures therefore did not match the oft-quoted government retail statistics, which, as well as being worked out in a totally different way, include such non-retail commercial activity as wholesaling, catering and other services, along with sales of cars and fuel.

In 2005, following a survey of the growth in private enterprise in the services sector, the Chinese government revised the value of the nation's gross domestic product (GDP) by nearly 17 per cent. This move threw out many historical figures, including retail sales. This forced me to completely re-evaluate China's total retail market value, based on comparisons made with other countries in the Asian region, and a re-evaluation of each of the individual sectors within. In 2006, I took a sabbatical from report writing for about six months to completely re-calculate each of the sectors within China's retail market, food and non-food products. The motive was growing concern, both my own and among others, that the official market size figures for domestic consumer expenditure and retail sales, as published by the Chinese government, were significantly misleading for the unwary.

The results of that work became the backbone of Access Asia's reporting on China's retail markets, and were also published in the fourth quarter edition in 2006 of the *China Economic Quarterly*. One of the headline findings of that research, summed up in that article, was that China's retail sales in 2005 were at most US$ 450 billion, which was about half the value of the commonly cited "total retail sales of consumer goods" number given by the National Bureau of Statistics (NBS). This meant that anyone or any business investing in a consumer product market in China using the official retail sales figures were basing their business plans on numbers twice the size of the retail market reality! This probably

> anyone... using the official retail sales figures were basing their business plans on numbers twice the size of the retail market reality

went a long way to explaining why so many foreign companies in China, at that time, were struggling to meet revenue targets they had projected on market entry based on the confusingly defined retail market figures.

And official definitions and number series continue to change. Looking at the chart below from catering upwards, the combined catering and retail sales numbers can be seen adding up to what is now described by the NBS as retail and wholesale trade. However, this retail and catering sum adds up to more than NBS figures for total household expenditure, which does not make sense. What the NBS counts as retail sales only is so close to total private household expenditure that they are spookily similar. Also, note that the retail sales data from the NBS used to coincide with the retail and wholesale trade data, but the difference between the two from 2010 is basically the numbers for the catering trade.

My own retail sales figures represent a composite value of all the retail food and non-food sectors, built from known domestic production figures, plus imports less exports, cross-checked with company trade association data and expressed in retail values. But these only represent one-fifth of GDP. It is likely that much of what is expressed as sales through official channels misses the uncountable trade in counterfeit goods known to traverse the Chinese economy, while the official figures themselves include much non-retail, just to add confusion.

There is another national level set of retail statistics announced by the NBS, the "total sales value of retail trade." The scope of this wholesale and retail trade data for 2006 and 2007 covered enterprises and establishments above a designated size, covering only retail enterprises with at least 60 employees and annual revenues of at least RMB 5 million, according to the NBS Yearbook. For the designated size for 2008–2011, the indicator was based on income from principle business, while for other years it was based on total sales or turnover and engaged persons. This figure is lower than the total size of the retail market quoted by the NBS, in Table 11.1, because it only covers those enterprises that meet or exceed the qualifying statistical size criteria.

Table 11.1 Chinese government retail and wholesale trade and household consumption versus real retail sales figures, 2008–2012

RMB bn, current prices	2008	2009	2010	2011	2012
Total GDP	30,067.0	33,535.3	40,151.3	47,156.4	51,932.2
Total final expenditure	15,342.2	16,927.5	19,411.5	22,856.1	26,433.5
– % of GDP	51.0	50.5	48.3	48.5	50.9
Government consumption expenditure	4,175.2	4,569.0	5,335.6	6,361.6	7,737.9
– % of GDP	13.9	13.6	13.3	13.5	14.9
Total private household expenditure	11,167.0	12,358.5	14,075.9	16,494.5	18,700.0
– % of GDP	37.1	36.9	35.1	35.0	36.0
Urban household expenditure	8,399.3	9,457.9	10,878.4	12,755.1	14,467.3
– % of GDP	27.9	28.2	27.1	27.0	27.9
Rural household expenditure	2,767.7	2,900.5	3,197.5	3,739.5	4,232.7
– % of GDP	9.2	8.6	8.0	7.9	8.2
Retail & wholesale trade	9,119.9	10,541.3	15,455.4	17,578.9	20,716.7
– % of GDP	30.3	31.4	38.5	37.3	39.9
Retail sales (NBS)	9,119.9	10,541.3	13,691.8	16,068.3	18,388.4
– % of GDP	30.3	31.4	34.1	34.1	35.4
Catering sales	1,540.4	1,799.8	1,763.6	2,054.3	2,328.3
– % of GDP	5.1	5.4	4.4	4.4	4.5
Retail sales (author's own figures)	6,371.2	7,412.5	8,397.2	9,419.7	10,764.1
– % of GDP	21.2	22.1	20.9	20.0	20.7
Online retail sales	120.8	250.0	523.1	817.1	1,153.5
– % of GDP	0.4	0.7	1.3	1.7	2.2

Adapted from source: NBS China Statistical Yearbooks.

In 2011, this number was RMB 7.18 trillion (in Table 11.2), compared to the RMB 16.07 trillion quoted above. But using the retail sales figure based on calculating the value of the component retail sectors, as I did while running Access Asia (trended forward using NBS annual growth rates), the total for retail sales in 2011 was more likely to be RMB 9.42 trillion.

Table 11.2 Basic conditions of wholesale and retail trades, 2006–2011

Total sales (RMB bn)	2006	2007	2008	2009	2010	2011
Wholesale trade	8,759.4	10,562.0	17,026.0	15,783.5	21,912.1	28,870.1
Retail trade	2,246.1	2,712.1	3,797.0	4,333.2	5,751.5	7,182.5
Wholesale and retail trades	11,005.5	13,274.1	20,823.0	20,116.6	27,663.6	36,052.6

Source: NBS China Statistical Yearbooks, Table 17.1.

Things become all the more confusing from 2010 onwards. Up to 2009, the retail sales figure comprised retail and wholesale, plus catering, plus "other," or was broken down by urban, county town and rural. Yet, after 2009, the same data series continues with the noticeable absence both of "other" and "county town" data sets (see Table 11.3). The "county towns" were subsumed into the urban figures. But even the combined urban and county towns prior to 2010 was significantly below the 2010 urban figure, yet took a significant jump (29.9%) upwards in 2010. And the retail and catering total less the "other" data also enjoyed a significant jump (34.6%) in growth in 2010.

While readjustments for the sake of accuracy are to be welcomed, the lack of published reasoning behind it means the data simply becomes that much more unusable, particularly in calculating historical growth trends.

The effects in terms of nominal growth rates are better seen in Table 11.4.

Also highly suspect is the way that, in 2010, the margin of disagreement between urban/rural breakdown of retail sales and retail/catering suddenly disappears down to zero. Then there is the fact that the data series for rural retail sales shows a 19.7 per cent decline in 2010. If we look at the "retail and wholesale" trade figures below and the "retail sales" figures, we see that up to 2009 they are identical, but from 2010 onwards, they are quite different (see Table 11.5).

So what happened in 2010 to create this fault line in the data? The culprit was an economic census in 2009 conducted by the NBS, which refined the coverage of the retail and services sectors, including an RMB

Table 11.3 Official breakdown of retail trades, 2007–2012

RMB 100 mn	2007	2008	2009	2010	2011	2012
Retail	75,040	91,199	105,413	136,918	160,683	183,884
Catering	12,352	15,404	17,998	17,636	20,543	23,283
Other	1,818	1,885	1,932			
Urban	60,411	73,735	85,133	133,689	156,908	179,318
County town	9,944	12,213	14,220			
Rural	18,856	22,540	25,990	20,865	24,318	27,849

Source: NBS China Statistical Yearbooks.

Table 11.4 Year-on-year growth of official breakdown of retail trades, 2007–2012

RMB bn	2007	2008	2009	2010	2011	2012
Retail sales*	7,504.03	9,119.85	10,541.32	13,691.82	16,068.25	18,388.39
YoY % +-	16.7	21.5	15.6	**29.9**	17.4	14.4
Catering	1,235.20	1,540.39	1,799.75	1,763.55	2,054.33	2,328.27
YoY % +-	19.4	24.7	16.8	**–2.0**	16.5	13.3
Urban	7,035.45	8,594.77	9,935.27	13,368.89	15,690.83	17,931.76
YoY % +-	17.2	22.2	15.6	**34.6**	17.4	14.3
Rural	1,885.55	2,254.00	2,599.00	2,086.48	2,431.75	2,784.91
YoY % +-	15.0	19.5	15.3	**–19.7**	16.5	14.5
Retail/catering TOTAL	8,739.23	10,660.24	12,341.07	15,455.37	18,122.58	20,716.66
YoY % +-	17.0	22.0	15.8	**25.2**	17.3	14.3
Urban/rural TOTAL	8,921.00	10,848.77	12,534.27	15,455.37	18,122.58	20,716.67
YoY % +-	16.8	21.6	15.5	**23.3**	17.3	14.3
Degree of variation** (%)	2.08	1.77	1.57	0.00	0.00	0.00

Notes: *Not including catering – was called retail and wholesale trade up to 2007.

**Of urban/rural total over retail/catering total.

Source: NBS China Statistical Yearbooks.

1.3 trillion revision upwards of the previously much underreported services industry. This represents progress for the future. With services now more accurately counted in, the picture of the size and shape of the domestic consumer market should become more accurate. However, the historical data trends have to be understood in the context of how

Table 11.5 Comparing official retail and wholesale trade and total retail sales percentage of GDP, 2007–2012

RMB bn, current prices	2008	2009	2010	2011	2012
Retail & wholesale trade	9,119.9	10,541.3	15,455.4	17,578.9	20,716.7
– % of GDP	30.3	31.4	38.5	37.3	39.9
Retail sales (NBS)	9,119.9	10,541.3	13,691.8	16,068.3	18,388.4
– % of GDP	30.3	31.4	34.1	34.1	35.4

Source: NBS China Statistical Yearbooks.

the research methodology changed in 2009, leading to the jump in value in 2010. The lack of published clarity on methodologies used is a major headache in making sense of all these contradictory data sets.

Retail sales or consumer expenditure or neither or both?

So the government figures described as "retail sales" should really be better termed "household consumer expenditure." That would be a neat answer, but a wrong one. It is important to realise that the official retail sales figure, which used to be called "total retail sales of consumer goods," and the most widely reported figure on China domestic consumer market, also represents significant amounts of institutional and corporate sales and wholesale transactions.

What this government figure does is to substantially overstate what is truly purchased from the retail market; that is, goods sold to consumers in shops. It is also very poor as a measure of overall consumption, because it ignores many services, which have been the fastest growing part of the consumer economy over the past decade. Retail sales in China do include building materials; only of interest in terms of such data not usually being included in retail sales, and a hangover from more command economy times. I remember a few years back the top prize for a local lottery in Sichuan was a truck-load of cement. Not as crazy as it might seem, given that many rural farmers, both then and now, are likely to build their own homes.

The other question is where are all the sales made by service sectors other than catering? No laundry services, travel agency data, real estate transaction profits, cost of private tutors, gardeners, hair and beauty salons, plumbers, electricians, taxis, theme parks, cinemas, etc. There is a great deal of the services sector in China that continues to go underreported, despite the increased coverage of services sectors in the last economic census data (which added 4.4% to GDP in 2009), and yet the private services sector is one of the strongest growth components in employment generation in the economy. It is significant that the NBS gives scant regard to coverage of such services in its retail sales data gathering surveys and also calls into question the data on real consumer incomes and spending levels.

According to the Asian Development Bank (ADB) report entitled "*Asian Development Outlook 2012 Update – Services and Asia's Future Growth*," the service sector in China remains relatively small, and indeed appears to be "smaller than expected," taking the per capita income of Chinese consumers into account. The ADB report notes that the services industry share of GDP in middle-income countries averages at about 55 per cent, and 54 per cent of total income, while in China services industries provide only 43 per cent of GDP and 36 per cent of employment.

Anyone who has visited China can see that its services sector is very much alive and well, and that people working in all aspects of the services industry are not idle. So it can only be assumed that services continue to be underrepresented within the statistical economy. Indeed, looking at the NBS urban consumer survey data for household consumption, it can be seen that 30 per cent of consumer household spending goes on services. If so, then the total domestic consumer economy as reported is too small, probably to a very large degree.

Another exercise conducted with the *China Economic Quarterly* in 2006 was to look at retail sales as a proportion of consumer expenditure in other Asian countries at the time (2005). Simply put, we compared retail spending and consumer spending and their respective contribution to GDP, allowing for the differences in average incomes and the split between rural and urban consumers. I updated this approach for this book, and the outcome of this admittedly thumbnail sketch is that the value of retail sales tends to represent between about one-third and one-half of private consumer expenditure (averaging at 40%) across Asia ex-China, and between 20 per cent and 30 per cent of GDP (averaging at 22%). Clearly China comes out quite low compared to the rest of Asia, ex-China (see Table 11.6).

If we look back at the official data again (see Table 11.7), we can see that total private household expenditure rings about true at 36 per cent, close to but still below the expected 40 per cent, but both the NBS retail & wholesale trade and NBS retail sales figures look too high, at nearly 35.4 per cent and 40 per cent respectively. My own estimate of retail sales, at 20.4 per cent of GDP looks to be more in line with the rest of the Asian economies.

This reinforces the notion that the NBS data on retail sales represents more than just retail sales. The NBS retail sales figures are too close to

Table 11.6 Household consumption and retail sales percentage of GDP across a range of Asian countries, 2007–2011

Consumption/GDP %	2007	2008	2009	2010	2011
India	62.0	61.3	60.9	60.6	60.3
Indonesia	63.5	60.6	58.7	56.6	54.6
Japan	57.3	58.3	60.1	59.2	60.3
South Korea	54.4	54.7	54.1	52.6	52.9
Malaysia	45.2	44.7	48.8	47.5	47.5
China	34.9	37.1	36.9	35.1	35.0
Average ex-China	56.5	55.9	56.5	55.3	55.1
Retail/GDP %					
India	32.8	32.3	30.8	29.6	29.2
Indonesia	21.5	19.3	19.3	19.3	18.7
Japan	26.1	26.4	28.1	28.2	28.6
South Korea	23.2	23.6	23.6	23.5	24.2
Malaysia	25.1	26.7	30.4	30.1	31.2
China (official)	27.2	30.3	31.4	34.1	34.1
China (author's own)	21.2	22.1	20.9	20.0	20.7
Average ex-China	25.7	25.6	26.4	26.1	26.4

Source: ADB/national statistics of each country.

Table 11.7 China urban and rural household expenditure compared with retail and wholesale and retail trade figures, 2007–2011

% of GDP	2008	2009	2010	2011	2012
Total private household expenditure	37.1	36.9	35.1	35.0	36.0
Urban household expenditure	27.9	28.2	27.1	27.0	27.9
Rural household expenditure	9.2	8.6	8.0	7.9	8.2
Retail & wholesale trade	30.3	31.4	38.5	37.3	39.9
Retail sales (NBS)	30.3	31.4	34.1	34.1	35.4
Retail sales (author's own figures)	21.2	22.1	20.9	20.0	20.7

Adapted from source: NBS China Statistical Yearbooks.

Table 11.8 China percentage annual growth of household expenditure compared with retail and wholesale and retail trade figures, 2009–2012

% annual growth	2009	2010	2011	2012
Total private household expenditure	10.7	13.9	17.2	13.4
Retail & wholesale trade	15.6	**46.6**	13.7	17.8
Retail sales (NBS)	15.6	29.9	17.4	14.4
Retail sales (author's own figures)	16.3	13.3	12.2	14.3

Adapted from source: Author based on NBS China Statistical Yearbooks.

total private household expenditure, so they either contain government procurement and business-to-business transactions, or also include the value of the consumer services sector, or both. My own money is on the NBS figures containing business-to-business, institutional sales and services sector sales, the details for which are simply not published.

A final set of data disparities occur among the growth rates of both retail sales and consumer spending. Referencing those data, if we look at the annual nominal growth rates across the different versions of retail sales and consumer expenditure, we find some strong areas of data suspicion. For instance, the total private household expenditure figures widely buck the trend shown in the NBS retail and wholesale trade trends in 2011 (underlined in Table 11.8). This is not helped by the 46.6 per cent growth aberration (in bold in Table 11.8) in 2010 for retail and wholesale trade.

The matter comes down to the Chinese data sets not being historically revised backwards, even once a major revision occurs, as in 2010, and hence the mighty growth rates among the NBS figures for retail sales and retail and wholesale trade. The other point to make is that each of these data sets is created in different ways, so divergence is partly down to differences of methodology.

How government household consumption surveys and retail data are gathered

Retail sales data is gathered by the NBS based on three sets of data collecting methods, all relating to how they gather information from a sample of retail companies of different sizes. The companies sampled fit into three categories. At the top of the pile are around 5,000 or more very large retail and wholesale companies whose data is fed directly to the NBS centrally in Beijing.

This is supplemented by between 130,000 and 140,000 mid- to large-sized companies fitting within the statistical threshold of having RMB 20 million or more in sales revenue for wholesalers, and RMB 5 million in revenue or more for retailers, as well as hotels and caterers whose turnover is RMB 2 million or above. The data from these sources are fed to local NBS bureaux at provincial level, then gathered up to central NBS in Beijing.

NBS also carries out a sample survey of those retail, wholesale and catering companies below the statistics threshold to gain representation for the mass of companies in this segment. The data from these companies is gathered either by sending out surveys to be filled in and returned to local NBS offices, or for local NBS interviewers to visit and interview the businesses.

Household consumption is done based on two separate surveys of households, one carried out in urban areas, the other rural. The urban survey is conducted in about 470 cities covering 65,000 households, with participating households maintaining a daily consumption diary, in the form of an issued NBS survey form, which they complete and hand over to local NBS survey personnel. Each year about a third of households are rotated out of the survey and new households added in to keep the data respondents fresh. The data is gathered, checked and passed up the chain from local NBS offices up to NBS headquarters in Beijing. The rural surveys are held in much the same way, covering about 3,000 more households and collected on a monthly basis.

A common critique of the household consumer surveys is that the higher income groups surveyed are more than likely to underdeclare their incomes, as is discussed above in regard to the research findings of Wang Xiaolu,[1] who calculated that many higher-income families have as much as 20 per cent more "grey" income (and therefore spending) than their official declared income.

That said, the household consumption surveys do give at least some insight into what is going on in China's households, and this data can be a very useful cross-checking mechanism for testing market size data claimed for certain sectors, against trends seen in the household surveys. The survey data is also available by province, although only for the latest year covered in each NBS Yearbook. However, gathering together the tables across a series of Yearbooks, and different spending trends across a wide selection of broad sectors over time and across provinces emerges, making them a useful measure of different growth patterns across the provinces, and their potential in each area of the country.

They may be biased in their coverage, but nobody other than the NBS has the resources (or permission) to gather so much data from so many households in China, and so when looking at the real retail market in China, they offer a better insight than do the official retail sales top-line figures.

Why checking retail data sources is important

Before quoting any data from China, it makes sense to look closely at who actually produced it before believing in it. For instance, to ascertain the real size of the retail market in China, one might consider looking for data from a non-government organisation, as you might in another country, such as a trade association. But all trade associations in China come under the Ministry of Commerce, and are therefore branches of the government which are obliged to use government data. Sometimes they do branch out and use data produced by, and accredited to, outside agencies, such as market research companies or consultancies. Or, at least, that's how it seems.

Before quoting any data from China, it makes sense to look closely at who actually produced it before believing in it

My own experience in searching for data on retail trends led me to the China Chain Store and Franchise Association (CCFA) published yearbook, the "2010 China Chain Store Almanac." In chapter two, pages 75, 76 and 77 detail data on rural consumption and ownership of key electrical and electronic products, as well as average incomes, all of which are sourced to the company I set up, Access Asia. A bit of foreign research credibility helps in making this government quango's data seem a bit more balanced and not so overpoweringly NBS. The problem was, of course, that all of this data originally came from the NBS, and was sourced as such in our reports. However, this sourcing was not used in the CCFA book, instead being credited to Access Asia. By turns, this data appeared through the CCFA in other published articles, further decoupling the link with the original NBS data, and thereby giving it more credence as data gathered by non-official, commercial entities (Access Asia).

Likewise, on pages 77, 78 and 79 in the same chapter, the book quotes data from Access Asia on the breakdown of sales by type of product for leading electrical and electronics retailers Guomei (Gome) and Suning, all of which should correctly have been attributed to the respective company financial reports.

Of course, the whole issue comes back to the reasons why anyone publishes data in China. In the case above, the CCFA could have used the NBS data directly, but it used the Access Asia data to make itself look more broadly based in its research sourcing. Likewise, many foreign consultancies will use the official retail sales data as it is to paint the picture that they, and the Chinese government, want. Both want to lure investment, so both use the data that looks best. If that data does not bear a modicum of scrutiny, and is challenged, then the usual defence is that it is "the official data," or platitudes are given like "Yes, we know the official data has problems but we feel the overall trajectory is solid."

While the official data has its political raison d'être for the Chinese, it can also be very useful in its neat, unmolested form for many foreign pundits in China. If, for example, a real estate investment consultancy is trying to lure large-scale investment into the China commercial property sector (with the promise of a fat percentage if the deal comes off), it will use all the bright, shiny statistics it can lay its hands on to build a case for that investment. It wouldn't necessarily raise investor caution about the possibility that use of substandard building materials might mean that much commercial property built in China may have a significantly shorter shelf-life than the sales prospectus would have people believe. It also wouldn't want to point to data showing how oversupply in certain areas of the retail market and industry are causing store closures due to consolidation. And it certainly wouldn't be showing its potential investors pictures of Dongguan's now infamous and colossal New South China Mall, a decade old and still practically empty.

It is also worth mentioning here that government incentives can have a significant effect on promoting retail sales, the free-market economy still having a significant slice of "command" left in it. There are various cases to illustrate this point. The rural home appliances subsidy scheme is one such. The scheme began in 2007, and offered rural residents a 13 per cent rebate on selected white goods and consumer electronics, and provided new sales to manufacturers facing falling demand at the time due to the global financial crisis, which severely hit their export market.

The scheme released pent-up demand for affordable household appliances and consumer electronics in the rural market, where the ownership of key white goods and consumer electronics was still low. For example, the ownership of refrigerators among rural households was only 26 per cent in 2007, compared to 95 per cent in urban households.

The scheme gradually rolled out from three provinces in 2007 (see Table 11.9), to cover most of the country by 2013, when it ended. According to China's Ministry of Commerce, in 2012 nearly 80 million units were sold, up by 22.6 per cent on 2011, running to a total value of RMB 214.5 billion in sales, up nearly 19 per cent on 2011. By the end of 2012, the cumulative effect of the scheme since its beginning in 2007 was the sale of 298 million appliances worth in excess of RMB 720 billion.

A similar market-boosting effect came from the 2009 price rebates on offer from the government for people buying fuel-efficient cars, which created a sudden surge in car sales. It is also arguably the case that many people do much personal shopping via a company account, getting corporate discounts, tax-free consumption and undeclared (and untaxed) income.

Most micro-sector data is guesswork

This is why sizing China from the bottom upwards makes more sense. If you are investing in China, you need to get to know the specific sector

Table 11.9 Rollout of the rural home appliances subsidy scheme, 2007–2013

Period	Provinces	Total provinces Dec 2007 – Nov 2011
Dec 2008– Nov 2012	Henan, Shandong (inc. Qingdao) & Sichuan Inner Mongolia, Liaoning (inc. Dalian), Heilongjiang, Anhui, Hunan,	3
Feb 2009– Jan 2013	Guangxi, Chongqing, Shaanxi & Hubei Jilin, Xinjiang (inc. Bingtuan), Gansu, Qinghai, Ningxia, Beijing, Tianjin,	9
	Hebei, Shanxi, Shanghai, Jiangsu, Zhejiang (inc. Ningbo), Yunnan, Fujian (inc. Xiamen), Hainan, Jiangxi, Guangdong (inc. Shenzhen), Guizhou & Tibet	19

Source: Ministry of Commerce of China website (www.mofcom.gov.cn).

or sectors you are investing in. The total retail market figures are not only meaningless in many respects to most businesses, they are highly contestable. By focusing on the detailed sectors, it should be easier to root out the bad data and to spot, for example, the glitches in annual percentage growth rates in a micro sector, or the steep variations in per capita consumption in that sector, and then be able to ask why the data is behaving so badly. It might just be that the sector is still so nascent that the trends are all over the place. Young markets do go haywire. It might be that strong fluctuations can be attributed to key events, such as price inflation, strong demand created by a new player in the market or new innovation. But at least it should be easier to spot the trends that matter to that market.

Of course, micro data in China has the ability to be even more unreliable than the macro data. In many sectors in China, there are literally hundreds of competing companies and brands, very few of which have a truly national reach, many only regionally significant and most only locally so. Many sectors have no overseeing trade association. Because so few companies in China really have a completely national reach, it is better to think of China as effectively a continent, with each province being a "national" market, so companies operating in China need to adapt how they operate to suit each "national" market, just as they would in Europe. Most companies operating in China will focus on certain key provinces or municipalities where demand for their goods or services is best developed. It therefore makes much more sense for them to have data on regional- or provincial-, if not city-level market sizes and wider economic trends to better identify the provincial markets within China best suited to their business.

There is often very little research data on the sectors, apart from a few reports published by Chinese research houses, and the veracity of that data (its true source, its research methodology, etc.) is often opaque. This is where employing as wide a range of research methodologies and sources as possible, to try to create a consensus, makes sense. What should be remembered is that market data in China is based on conjecture and best estimates. The data available is almost certainly from one source only, and therefore heavily biased, or is simply someone else's conjecture. When that data becomes published, it appears more credible, but this does not alter the fact that much of the available data on China's micro markets is still guesswork.

There are ways to make more educated guesses though. The best starting point is to assume that no single data source will be correct, but by comparing all the available sources it can be possible to see where common trends appear. Of course, if all the available data sources agree with each other, then you have to decide whether they are all quoting the same dubious data source, or are indeed in possession of strong data trends.

An example of the latter is China's wine market, where there are only a few domestic wineries of note, and where foreign imports play a big role in the market. Using domestic production and import data, it is very easy to get a pretty good idea of the market size. However, even in this sector, there is the issue of bulk wine imports being used to blend with domestic wines to produce hybrids, so blurring the lines. Apparent consumption data (domestic production, plus imports less exports) such as this does not allow you to judge what is actually sold, or how much remains as unsold inventory, but at least you can be more confident that you are in the right ballpark.

In most cases, strong agreement among different sources indicates that those sources are all quoting from the same prescribed text. This is where you need to compare apparent consumption data to get an idea of what the likely stock in the market is, and compare the retail data trends with apparent consumption, focusing on per capita consumption and annual growth trends. This usually highlights inconsistencies in growth patterns or raises eyebrows at the claims of per capita consumption.

A word on Chinese research companies

In the course of my work doing research on China's consumers markets, I have encountered many reports written about China's consumer products markets by local Chinese research houses. Such companies and government-aligned bureaux began emerging in the 1990s, and

I worked with and bought data from some of them. Most tend to be generalists, gathering data from government statistical bureaux at provincial and lower levels to provide more detailed data than the general government Yearbooks. Most of the reports published by these research houses hinge upon only trade side production output and factory-gate sales data, with company financials. This they then use to work out per capita sales, market shares, forecasts, etc.

Most of the analysis is only descriptive, pointing out what is obvious from the data itself, and what is apparent from simple observation of wider economic trends and how they influence any given sector. There is little concern in most of these reports with illuminating on the consumer incentives and consumption trends, and what is creating demand trends. Most trends data looks at new products and production data, very much with an industry focus.

This is all well and good, but such reports tend not to provide much more than a data set you may not have had, and a lot of other stuff you really probably couldn't care less about. There is also very little detail given about how the figures were derived, which means that the data will always suffer from a degree of uncertainty. Most of these research houses are at best data processing factories.

I have seen such companies first-hand. I visited the offices of one such in Beijing in the late 1990s, which its well-dressed and clearly well-paid CEO boasted as having substantial government backing. The offices were big, very smart and well appointed, and I remember being shown into one large room full of people where the CEO declared "in this room, everyone has a PhD!" Substantial brains they may well have had, but they were engaged, by the CEO's own admission, in sheer number crunching, not analysis. This is where my company was to come in, to work with them on developing proper analysis of the vast numbers they had in huge databases run on similarly capacious banks of computers.

And thus stood the juxtaposition: Here was a large, state-funded Chinese market research operation, manned by an army of PhD graduates, asking for advice on how to conduct research in China from a couple of blokes from the UK who worked out of their spare rooms at home. And they were very serious to know what it was that they needed to learn.

This was no isolated case either. I was also asked to address a group of about 1,000 researchers from a very large state-owned enterprise (SOE) in Beijing, organised via a leading online research aggregator who sold our reports at the time, to explain to these researchers why it is that foreign companies buy market research data, and what they use it for. That occasion was perhaps the nadir of my Chinese-speaking experiences. I presented for an hour on some quite technical research themes, in Chinese, to a bunch of (again) PhDs, despite my whole PowerPoint presentation not working on their overhead projector, and answering a barrage of eager questions at the end. All of this the morning after a rather monumental drinking session!

But that was then. Although many domestic research companies still seem to lack much depth of analysis, this is more of a reflection on the still nascent stage of market research usage among many Chinese companies. But things are changing fast, and Chinese research companies are vying for business with a whole raft of foreign research companies, and they are raising their game every year in response.

The pool of talent is also increasing, not just in numbers, but also analytical power. I have worked with many young Chinese researchers in foreign companies who display very astute critical thinking skills and analytical imagination, and I do not doubt that they will hone their skills in these companies only to take off and set up new research businesses of their own. They will have grown up in the new China, immersed in fast-track economic growth, huge technical advances and the now burgeoning growth of online retail and social media. They will be the next generation of researchers who really understand what is going on in China's consumer markets, and who won't be fooled by the numbers.

Saving face – why consumer survey data needs circumspection

The need for companies to build a market means they strive to better understand Chinese consumers and what makes them tick in terms of what they like to buy and why. Understanding consuming behaviours through consumer surveys can tell us a lot about what people like to buy and why, and why they chose one brand over another. In the West, such surveys tend to work quite well because consumer habits are often already very sophisticated, and certain key considerations can be assumed to be in place for the most part.

For example, when buying food products, consumers in the West tend not to worry hugely about whether the food they are buying has the potential to make them ill. They assume that the food industry, being well regulated and monitored, is generally clean, and that food manufacturers not only comply with the rules to stay in business, but also to protect their brands from unwanted bad press.

The situation in China is quite different though. The Chinese are deeply concerned that the food they buy might be laden with some kind of poison or other. The 2008 melamine in milk scandal was merely the most notorious of a constant rash of food poisoning and contamination issues that have been around for years, caused by systemic failures in the food processing industry in China, and which continue to create problems. So when Chinese consumers answer surveys about food, they are not merely framing their choice of products or brands based upon flavour, function, attractive packaging or convenience, but significantly based upon whether they trust a company, brand or product to provide basic safety.

This extends in a way to non-food products. Shoddy production quality of some domestic goods might help keep their price down, but shoddy goods can at best have limited functioning lives before needing to be replaced, and at worst can be dangerous.

Then there is the sheer pace of change in China's domestic economy. The majority of the current generation of adult Chinese consumers has seen massive growth in their economy throughout their lifetime. They have seen that growth drop down to high single figures, but they have no real sense of what a recession is, and they have managed to avoid being embroiled in the global financial storm so badly affecting the rest of the world.

That rapid growth has brought with it rapid and constant market entry of new products. For example, Chinese consumers largely went from no phone to mobile phone. Building telephone wire networks was deemed a waste of time when the world was beginning to take on mobile telecommunications in a big way in the late 1990s, so most Chinese leap-frogged right up to date with the latest technology, and continue to do so. That is why most Chinese would not understand if you were to talk about video cassettes, for example. It is also why they replace their phones every six months, rather than every two years as in developed countries.

The constant turnover of new goods and brands in the market means that few Chinese really develop much brand loyalty. When surveyed about which brands of drinks they have bought in the past 12 months, they will name many, and that list would probably change significantly within a year thanks to constant new innovations and new market entrants. Survey data therefore becomes out of date very quickly.

Surveys in China still face the tug-of-war between what I think of as "face" and "fear." Face is the sense in which survey respondents want to appear more sophisticated and urbane, and therefore overstate their real consumption, while fear is the natural sense of scepticism and suspicion about the "snooping" motives behind such research.

It has long been the case that companies doing consumer surveys in China have to filter the responses they get back to remove the effects of consumers being inclined to answer more positively than is the reality. One problem has always been the one of survey respondents stating what they aspire to buy when answering a question about what they have bought in the past. Respondents often exaggerate quantities or frequencies of purchasing because they feel that the answers expected from them should be as positive as possible. Also, with so many Chinese using social networking, where many swap review notes on different products or brands they have tried and liked (or disliked), there is a lot of social peer influence that can significantly skew the way survey respondents answer surveys, with them tending to cite what they have heard about products rather than actual experience, especially if they have not tried a product – admitting such ignorance would be a loss of "face."

Survey data responses are therefore often an expression of desire rather than reality.

There is also the thorny issue of sampling in conducting consumer surveys in China, not least because the country has 1.3 billion people. Again, it makes sense when conducting surveys to focus on who exactly the product or service you are dealing with is likely to be aimed at. There is not much point surveying a bunch of migrant workers from Anhui province on Coach accessories that are way above their purchasing capability.

It no longer makes sense to cover just the tier 1 cities these days, as the strongest growth in retail sales is now in tier 2 and below, right down to tier 5. If you want a good idea of where to cover, simply follow the vanguard. For example, I have met with executives from foreign supermarkets in China who have told me that they look at where certain key brands are opening stores to gauge where to look next for expansion. It might be KFC or McDonalds if you are a mass-market retailer, or Starbucks if you are aiming at a higher-income bracket, but wherever those outlets are opening (and increasingly this is in lower-tier cities), the retailers look to follow.

So survey scope has to be broad by region, but also by income bracket. It is all well and good knowing what the middle class of today are buying, but for every ten middle-class families now, you can add two more families who will be middle class next year, and another two the year after that. You need to also cover the aspirational *xiaokang* 小康 (literally, "little comfort") consumers who are up-and-coming, or risk missing the next wave.

There also needs be focus on who is a likely consumer for a particular product. This is not just whether they are men or women, or their likely age group, etc. That is too simple. What I have seen happen to the Chinese consumer market in recent years is not only growth in the numbers of significant consumers, but also the increasing variety of lifestyles and attitudes of those consumers. This is not just young people either, as many older Chinese are already exploring alternative lifestyles to those expected and prescribed to them in the past.

Many consumer surveys in China fail to capture the emerging huge amounts of variation in Chinese consumer lifestyles. The assumption is that narrow definitions still apply to China, but of course they never really did. Much has been made recently of the subculture courted by the likes of Adidas in China, which has veered away from the sportswear sector and begun to focus on the casual-wear market by targeting its marketing on China's youth culture, as if this is something innovative. That subculture has been there for decades, but it just hasn't been as visible as it is now. When I was a student in Beijing in 1988–1989, there was already a well-established alternative music, dare we call it "punk" subculture in China's capital city. That subculture has morphed and adapted through rave, house and hip-hop, drum 'n' bass, and developed its own punk-with-Chinese-characteristics genre that most foreign marketers are only just catching onto. It is the creative edges of society that create the biggest changes, those which most consumer surveys in China completely fail to garner.

Is the cap on the bottle fake?

The problem with China's counterfeit goods market is that much of what is seized is destined for export, and represents only the tip of the iceberg. The domestic market is likely to be much bigger. What is even harder to quantify is the size of the retail market that lies outside of the official economy. Estimates are few,[2] but those that have surfaced range from about US$ 16 million in 2006 to about US$ 19–24 billion in 2013. There are estimates that counterfeit goods account for nearly 8 per cent of GDP![3] Based on the 2012 GDP figure, that would amount to RMB 4.2 trillion, which would represent 22.6 per cent of the official retail sales figure. If we add that counterfeit market onto the total official retail sales figure, we would have a retail market worth around RMB 22.5 trillion in 2012, or 43.4 per cent of total GDP.

The number of overall cases of counterfeit products being dealt with by the authorities in China says a lot about the scale of the problem. A report in the *China Daily*[4] in October 2012 highlighted that in the first nine months of that year, the authorities handled 54,200 cases concerning copyright infringements and the production and sale of counterfeit products. The article quotes a spokesperson for the General Administration of Quality Supervision, Inspection and Quarantine (AQSIQ) as saying that the value of the products involved was worth RMB 3.14 billion. And these are just those cases that have been identified.

There are some sectors where counterfeit products are of specific concern to the industry and create a huge possible skew on market data. The sector where there is the greatest concern, both in China and overseas due to the significance of Chinese exports, is the drugs market. According to an assessment made by the World Trade Organization (WTO) and widely quoted in the Chinese and international press, in developed nations the counterfeit drugs market usually represents less than 1 per cent of the total national pharmaceutical markets, but in China the WTO estimates that fake drugs represented perhaps 30 per cent or even more of the domestic pharmaceutical trade.

According to the National Development and Reform Commission (NDRC) of China, and the China Ministry of Commerce, the total pharmaceuticals industry in China is estimated to be worth in the region of RMB 1.1 trillion, including both prescription and over-the-counter Western and traditional Chinese medicines. If the counterfeit trade is added to this figure, assuming that the counterfeit market is hidden from and not included in government ministry data, then the total market value could be RMB 1.43 trillion. However, it should be noted that a lot of this illicit trade goes overseas.

What the government bases its estimates on is how much of this crime it manages to uncover, of course. Often the fake drugs are hard to spot because they use stolen, recycled packaging, which includes the necessary hologram logo on the packaging, making the fakes harder to identify. The other problem is that most of the trade is for prescription drugs. Not only are prescription drugs more lucrative by value, they are also easier to pass off – doctors trusting their suppliers and consumers trusting their doctors, so fewer people find out they have been duped until it is too late.

China's research and development-based Pharmaceutical Association estimated that about 8 per cent of non-prescription drugs sold in China are counterfeit, which if correct means that if we take that 8 per cent away from the total pharmaceuticals market value, the remainder (based on the WTO estimate of 30% of total market value) would represent about 35 per cent of all prescription drugs in 2011. Many of those caught out will never be able to complain and so raise the authorities' awareness because they die from taking fake drugs. According to the International Policy Network[5] (IPN), the estimated death toll from substandard medicines in China is somewhere between 200,000 and 300,000 people each year!

Of course, the Chinese government is concerned and acting to reduce this illegal trade, making tens of thousands of arrests and seizing billions of Yuan in illegal drugs, tightening-up pharmaceuticals purchasing practices, etc., but as with so many sectors in China, policing such a large country with so many active components is a monumental task, especially when so many vested interests are involved in keeping things just as they are. All sectors are affected, from high-end drugs to trucks to honey. Yes, honey! According to a March 2013 article in the *Shanghai Daily*,[6] half of all honey sold in China is counterfeit. Yes, half! No I don't know how you make counterfeit honey.

So, when we discuss China's retail market data, what we are talking about is only the legitimate portion that comes under the government's radar, including the relatively larger, easy-to-monitor businesses that tend to be legitimate, if perhaps a bit creative with their accounting. How much goes on under the radar is a completely different story. I cannot, of course, give you any data on this, or point you in the direction of reliable data providers on the counterfeit goods market in China, because I tend to avoid association with criminals. But I can advise that if you have a market figure for your particular product sector of interest, you need to be thinking in terms of adding probably between 15 per cent and 30 per cent on top of that figure in terms of the "grey" and "black" markets, depending on how significant counterfeit goods are likely to be to that market.

And on that note, may I indulge you with my admiration for Carl Crow's book *Four Hundred Million Customers – the experiences – some happy, some sad of an American in China, and what they taught him* (Harper & Brother's Publishers, New York and London, 1937). In this superb book, which describes in vivid detail the commercial shenanigans of Shanghai in the 1920s and 1930s, Crow at one point describes exports of the very humble and cheap Chinese "horse bean." The beans, meant as fodder for pit ponies working in mines in Europe, would be adulterated to maximise profit by adding clay beans made from Yangzi River mud, which were dried and added to the sacks of real beans to bulk out their weight.

Similar stories still abound today, and there are few if any products that are not faked in China. It may not be possible to calculate the size of the counterfeit market in any particular sector with any great sense of accuracy, but it is undoubtedly there, and probably bigger than expected.

The rapid rise of online retailing

It is hard to understate just how rapidly online retailing has grown in importance to China's retail landscape, so let's begin with some data illustrations. What is interesting first of all is that there is some slight disagreement between the various reporting authorities as to the actual figures. For example, the Internet Society of China reported a total online retail market figure for 2012 of RMB 1.32 billion, more than other figures produced by the "official" China Internet Network Information Centre (CNNIC) and Ali Research Centre, but agreed with CNNIC that the online market represented 6.3 per cent of the official total retail sales figure (see Table 11.10).

Such inconsistencies are slight, and probably reflect different ways of gathering the data among each of the different organisations. It is also worth noting that, as the figures tell us, China's online retail market has grown from virtually nothing in the past decade, and continues to grow very fast. It has taken many by surprise, including much of the retail industry. So it is not really that surprising that keeping track of the growth of this new market will be difficult. There are thousands of

Table 11.10 Various sources' figures on growth of the online retail market in China, 2008–2012

	2008	2009	2010	2011	2012
CNNIC					
Total people using the internet (mn)	298.0	384.0	457.3	513.1	564.0
Number of online purchasers (mn)	74.0	108.0	160.5	194.0	242.0
% online purchasers to online users	24.8	28.1	35.1	37.8	42.9
Total online retail (RMB bn)	120.8	250.0	523.1	756.6	1,259.4
% annual growth	122.9	107.0	109.2	44.6	66.5
Per capita online spend (RMB)	1,632.4	2,314.8	3,259.0	3,901.0	5,203.7
% annual growth	39.8	41.8	40.8	19.7	33.4
China E-commerce Research Centre (CERC)					
Number of online purchasers (mn)	77.4	113.0	168.0	203.0	247.0
Total online retail (RMB bn)	128.0	264.8	554.1	801.5	1,320.0
Per capita online spend (RMB)	1,652.5	2,343.2	3,299.0	3,948.9	5,344.1
iResearch					
Total online retail (RMB bn)	128.2	263.0	461.0	786.5	1,304.0
Per capita online spend (RMB)	1,693.1	2,379.9	2,806.9	3,963.1	5,333.1
Online share of total retail					
Total retail sales (author's own figures)	6,371.2	7,412.5	8,397.2	9,419.7	10,764.1
CNNIC online retail % of total retail	1.92	3.42	6.32	8.15	11.88

CERC online retail % of total retail	2.04	3.63	6.70	8.64	12.45
CNNIC online retail % of total retail	2.04	3.60	5.57	8.47	12.30
Retail sales (NBS)	9,119.9	10,541.3	13,691.8	16,068.3	18,388.4
CNNIC online retail % of total retail	1.32	2.37	3.82	4.71	6.85
CERC online retail % of total retail	1.40	2.51	4.05	4.99	7.18
CNNIC online retail % of total retail	1.41	2.49	3.37	4.89	7.09

Source: CNNIC/CERC/Internet Society of China/AliResearch.

online retail sites now conducting millions of transactions, every day. At peak times the volume of online transactions has been so high that the logistics industry running the distribution to customers behind the screen has struggled to cope. It was astonishing to see photos during Chinese New Year in 2013, of distribution depots in China not only full to their ceilings with packages awaiting delivery, but also piled up on the forecourt outside the depot, up above the top of the depot door.

Out of interest, AliResearch has forecasted that online retail in China will grow in value to RMB 5 trillion by 2016, while CERC expected online shoppers to top 300 million by the end of 2013. But even here the various e-commerce data "authorities" do not share exactly the same numbers, despite the records for such business being electronically generated. CNNIC is usually the benchmark data set for online everything in China, but as the online retail industry grows, increasingly it is other information sources that are rising in prominence. One of the most significant retail information sources for China now comes from Taobao.

In the last five years, retailers have been piling into the online retail market. The business-to-consumer (B2C) sector of the market is now growing much faster than the consumer-to-consumer (C2C) segment, as more brands find they can reach more people faster online than they can by building store networks, and more cheaply. This has been aided by improvements to online payment security and delivery services (see Table 11.11).

Companies such as Walmart and Carrefour are looking at developing their store networks both as physical stores and as delivery depots for their online business expansion. This is especially the case for lower-tier cities where business expansion is increasingly focused on the online market, and where more people are using mobile devices to access the internet and shop online (see Table 11.12).

China is set to begin massive broadband expansion in the coming years. Broadband coverage has lagged behind developed countries,[7] with only 11.7 per cent coverage nationwide by the end of 2012, compared

Table 11.11 The comparative growth of C2C and B2C online retail sales, 2008–2012

	2008	2009	2010	2011	2012
RMB bn					
C2C	114.2	225.6	449.3	541.5	748.7
B2C	6.6	24.4	73.8	215.1	510.7
TOTAL	120.8	250.0	523.1	756.6	1,259.4
% annual growth					
C2C	129.2	97.5	99.2	20.5	38.3
B2C	50.8	271.7	202.0	191.6	137.4
TOTAL	122.9	107.0	109.2	44.6	66.5
% breakdown					
C2C	94.6	90.2	85.9	71.6	59.5
B2C	5.4	9.8	14.1	28.4	40.5
TOTAL	100.0	100.0	100.0	100.0	100.0

Note: Author's own estimates

Table 11.12 Rapid emergence of mobile online retail, 2008–2012

	2008	2009	2010	2011	2012
CNNIC					
Total people using the internet (mn)	298.0	384.0	457.3	513.1	564.0
Number of online purchasers (mn)	74.0	108.0	160.5	194.0	242.0
% online purchasers to online users	24.8	28.1	35.1	37.8	42.9
Number of mobile online purchasers (mn)	neg.	neg.	3.4	25.6	55.4
% mobile online purchasers to total online purchasers	neg.	neg.	2.1	13.2	22.9

Source: CNNIC (www.cnnic.net.cn).

to an average of 25.7 per cent in developed countries, according to the Ministry of Industry and Information Technology (MIIT), and in juxtaposition to a total internet penetration rate of 39.9 per cent of the population. MIIT is also looking to 4G technology[8] for rapid broadband expansion in the coming years. If penetration of broadband does increase as rapidly as planned, then this will mean a significant growth not just of online penetration, but also online retail sales and especially mobile online retailing. China's entire consumer economy will increasingly be shaped by online trends, and this will have a significant impact on how its domestic market can be measured. In future, the most accurate data on the growth in China's consumer products and services markets may come not from the government, or manufacturers, but from online retailers.

The rapid rise of Taobao data

Founded by the Alibaba Group in 2003, Taobao Market (淘宝网) was set up as a C2C product sales platform, similar in its genesis to eBay, but it quickly became a site for selling new products, rather than just second-hand, and a site where small- and medium-sized business became able to reach a much wider potential consumer audience. Taobao then expanded its platform to include B2C sales through its Taobao Mall site in 2008, which then became an independent business segment for Alibaba in 2011, changing its name to Tian Mao (Tmall) in early 2012. Tmall allows retailers that had not established their own e-commerce platforms in China to begin online retailing with reduced risk and investment cost – many retailers then graduate up from Tmall to have their own e-commerce sites, either with or without a continued presence on Tmall.

Taobao is important to the argument about online retail simply because it has become so big. If the total number of online purchasers in China was under 200 million in 2011, Taobao and Tmall combined had over 250 million – obviously with a significant amount of crossover.

Taobao therefore has data on the purchasing habits of a large majority of China's online shopping population. That data is not only used by Taobao, but the company also provides e-commerce trends data, right down to some very specific market sectors and subsectors. The company offers free trends data at a top-line level, and such data is increasingly quoted in press articles, not just in terms of online retail but in the wider context of retail sales trends in China. So, in a way, Taobao is becoming a new benchmark for micro-sector comparative growth and market sizing in China. Indeed, it is perhaps becoming significant enough to have overtaken the likes of NBS and the CCFA in terms of reliable trends data on the retail sector at a micro level, and will most likely, if online retail continues to grow in its significance to the total retail market, continue to rise in significance as a data source for the whole retail industry.

This is not just because online retail is getting bigger, which it is, or that Taobao's share of the market is so big, but Taobao also provides e-commerce infrastructure services to a wide array of retailers in China. Taobao's owner, Alibaba, owns the AliPay online transaction system, which is one of the most successful and reliable in China. This means that Alibaba, and hence Taobao, is providing online transaction services to wide swathes of China's retailers who are active online. They will therefore know better than most the volume of trade that retailers are doing online, and the relative successes and weaknesses of different retailers and product or service sectors outside of their own platform.

Not content with that, Taobao also has its eTao online shopping search engine, so it can track the search habits of consumers. In short, Taobao knows what consumers are searching for, what they are buying, how much money they are paying for products and through which retailers. They also know the time of day of purchase and the gender, age and purchasing history of the people who buy different products. Taobao sits on a data gold mine, in other words, and is already monetising that resource by selling online retail trends data via its Mofang.taobao.com (数据魔方 "data cube") website.

And it is not just top-line data. Taobao's data cube allows you to track micro-market sales on a day-to-day, month-by-month as well as year-on-year basis. You can see how many people are buying a narrow product sector out of how many searching for that product, which retailers are selling most, which brands are selling the best, which provinces and cities are the hot spots for purchasing of that product, and in which provinces and cities are the retailers doing most of the selling. You can even look at which specific products are selling well at any given time, their brand, their sale price, their level of discount, etc.

Summary

So, the options on what data to use in China, much like the options on the supermarket shelves, are growing exponentially each year. The smart way to approach market sizing in China is to use as many of them as possible to get the widest variety of opinions, data sources, research approaches and trends, all of which can combine to give as accurate a picture of any particular market in China as it is possible to get. Sure, there are significant weaknesses in each of the component parts alone, but when combined it is possible to create some credible trends out of the chaos of the Chinese market.

But it is the wider distribution and commercialisation of data that is of most interest to me at the moment. The fact that market data control appears to be shifting away from the government, is for me quite significant. It means that the Communist Party of China (CPC) is no longer the sole keeper of the facts on China. The internet is creating not just a commercial new reality, but also a political one. If power is won through the barrel of a gun but maintained through the control of information, then the CPC is losing direct control of some of the most important economic information to the online data miners, such as Taobao. I stress the word "direct," because the CPC can obviously still exert indirect control over that data through its control of what companies such as Taobao are allowed to do.

My thoughts on this were echoed in a Bloomberg article titled "*In China, Big Data Is Becoming Big Business*"[9] which reported on a presentation given in May 2013 at Peking University's Guanghua School of Management. The presentation was given by associate professor of marketing Meng Su, who predicted that "China will soon become the world's most important data market." To someone who has spent 20 years covering the rapid growth of China markets and their increasing global significance, reading this was bit of a "Really? You don't say!" moment, but I have to agree. Anyone who is in a position to get hold of the vast quantities of data that China's online economy is already generating, and can analyse and interpret that data, and fast, is going to be in control of some of the most valuable market data in the world, assuming that the Chinese economy doesn't collapse.

Suddenly, the state-owned research companies in the 1990s, with rooms full of PhDs, and cellars full of data processors begins to make sense as a business model. I can already see emerging a situation where the lack of reliable data on markets in China is going to be completely replaced by real-time, real-market data. No longer will we have to scrape around for scraps of information from state organs with which to piece together a likely market size or share, we will just know – year-on-year; month-on-month, week-by-week, day-after-day. What will become more important is rapid response interpretation sifted from the mass of data available.

chapter 12

Property – The Safest Investment Bet in China?

Own home, will consume

Prior to the 1990s, most Chinese people lived in state-allocated housing, paying low nominal rents. Then, in 1998, the then premier, Zhu Rongji, privatised that state-owned housing stock, selling it off at low nominal prices, creating the first private housing market in China. Very quickly, many people sought to sell off their state-provided, now privately owned homes to trade up to newer apartments, using the collateral from the home sale, plus accrued savings, which meant many could buy cash-on-the-barrel or by taking out only a relatively small loan.

As the new century opened up, so did the property market in China. Many of those who had traded-in their state-owned home for a new apartment had seen the value of their new property appreciate as much as six-fold. Thus began the rapid trading-up and speculative property purchasing that has created the rapid growth in prices.

As time has gone by, and with a markedly underperforming domestic stock market, bank deposit interest at next-to-zero and few financial products worth putting money into, most Chinese with the money to invest have continued to prefer to take a punt on the red-hot property market. But the real effects of increased housing costs are not really being seen in the government data on household spending, with residence (which includes building and building/decoration materials, rent, private housing and utilities – water, electricity and heating fuel) staying level as a percentage of overall expenditure, and with price inflation on residence recorded at an amazingly low 4.5 per cent in 2010, 5.3 per cent in 2011 and 4.9 per cent in May 2013.

At the start of April 2013, the central government brought in a 20 per cent capital-gains tax on the sale of second homes[1] and also raised the required down-payment for second homes from 60 per cent to 70 per cent and raised mortgage rates from 1.1 per cent to 1.3 per cent. The policy was not implemented across the country in equal measure, and was focused on cooling property prices in the most expensive cities, but increasing demand in lower-tier cities will also see a need for such controls to be implemented more generally across the country. However, for those investors who already hold onto significant amounts of property, the new measures are not likely to have much effect. Because China has very limited taxation on housing, those with the cash to spend can continue to buy up property, further pushing up prices, and making it harder for those on lower incomes to get a foot on the property ladder.

It will also be a challenge for the central government to keep local government investment in higher-value property development, since local governments also like to keep property prices high to make more money from the development of land. The problem for the central government will be persuading local governments to create more affordable housing rather than invest only in more valuable construction projects, and to control price rises in existing property. For example, many cities pegged home price increases for 2013 at a rate under the growth rate for average disposable incomes, but this could still lead to anywhere between 7 per cent and 13 per cent growth in property price rises depending on the city.

In July 2012, according to data published by China Real Estate Index System (CREIS) the average house price in 100 surveyed cities in China was RMB 8,717 per m^2. According to a Peking University report published in August 2012,[2] 84.7 per cent of households in China owned their homes in 2011, and the average size of those homes was 116.4m^2, a per capita average of 36m^2. This puts the average home price at RMB 1,014,660, or thereabouts. Given that the average official urban income in 2012 was RMB 47,183, based on that official income figure it would take the average urban household 21.5 years to buy the average home, assuming one wage earner per household, who spent their entire wages on paying off the mortgage. Assuming that both adults work, and are equally paid, then we can halve that to 10.75 years. But, according to SouFun Holding's[3] tracking of prices in 100 cities in China, and government data, an average-sized apartment in China's cities now costs the equivalent of 40 years' average annual income. Soufun's estimate was that the average price in December 2012 was RMB 9,715 per m^2, which is about 11.5 per cent more than the CREIS average in July 2012 above.

Tough mortgage criteria in China mean that most people pay a large percentage of their home in cash (20–30%), and pay off their remaining mortgage quickly, or simply pay cash for the full price. A 20–30 per cent deposit on the average home would therefore amount to between RMB 202,932 (this lower figure being 4.3 times the average individual wage and 2.15 times the combined incomes of a couple both earning the average urban wage) and RMB 304,398 (this upper figure being 6.45 times the average individual wage and 3.23 times the combined incomes of a couple on the average urban wage).

It is hardly surprising then that Chinese people work so hard to save as much cash as they can to get a foothold on the property ladder. Those who do take out a mortgage can expect to pay somewhere between 30 per cent and 50 per cent of their monthly income servicing mortgage debt, compared to about 9 per cent of average monthly income in the US. The general lending guideline in China is that banks should insist that borrowers' salaries be at least twice as much as their monthly mortgage repayment burden on a loan. Most mortgages from China's banks are for anywhere between five and 30 years. The lending rate for loans over five years is (at time of writing) benchmarked at 6.55 per cent. Again, these high percentages of monthly income spent on housing are not being reflected in the official rural and urban household expenditure percentages in Table 12.1, further indicating how

Table 12.1 China's rural and urban household expenditure breakdown by type, 2008–2011

% of total	2008	2009	2010	2011
Rural household				
Food	41.0	39.3	38.3	37.4
Residence	18.1	16.7	15.8	15.5
Health care and personal goods	9.0	10.4	11.4	12.3
Transport and communications	9.4	9.7	9.8	9.7
Recreation, education and culture	8.1	8.2	7.8	7.0
Household facilities, products and services	4.6	5.5	6.2	6.7
Clothing	5.4	5.6	5.6	6.1
Financial services	1.8	1.6	2.4	2.4
Other	2.0	2.0	2.0	2.2
Insurance services	0.6	1.0	0.8	0.8
TOTAL	100.0	100.0	100.0	100.0
Urban household				
Food	31.2	30.0	29.0	29.4
Residence	16.9	16.8	17.6	16.9
Transport and communications	10.4	11.3	12.0	11.5
Recreation, education and culture	9.9	9.9	9.8	9.9
Health care and personal goods	8.8	9.3	9.2	9.9
Clothing	8.5	8.6	8.7	8.9
Household facilities, products and services	5.1	5.3	5.6	5.6
Other	4.8	5.0	3.0	3.1
Financial services	2.5	2.1	2.9	2.9
Insurance services	1.8	1.7	2.0	2.0
TOTAL	100.0	100.0	100.0	100.0

Source: NBS China Statistics Yearbook 2012, Table 2.19.

inaccurate these data sets have become as an indicator of real spending behaviour. The situation also adds further evidence to the idea that China's average income numbers must be wrong, and that the declared income used by official statistical indicators do not include significant amounts of grey income. How else can people be able to afford such expensive property?

If the real incomes of Chinese people are not significantly inflated by grey income, which is likely the case among many households, then mortgage repayments are going to either take up more of monthly salary, or take longer to repay. In such a situation, there is also the risk that more people will finance their consuming lifestyles using credit cards, pushing more households closer to critical debt limits. That is a problem if house prices are kept in check, but most evidence points to continuing significant price growth thanks to high demand.

A low residential mortgage debt rate of about 16 per cent of GDP at the end of 2012, compared to 87 per cent in the US, and because buyers have to put down between 30 per cent and 50 per cent cash on a property purchase (the higher amount for second homes), mortgage lending remains proportionally low in China – only 14 per cent of total bank loans in 2012, compared to 72 per cent in the US. The debt risk is therefore manageable now, but if prices keep rising, then more buyers will either not be able to buy because they will be priced out of the market, or banks will have to start lending higher percentages of the total loans, and that will mean a higher leverage ratio. Even if the government can encourage local governments to build more low-cost housing, demand is still likely to be high and prices will soon appreciate.

Home prices will keep going up

Property prices look likely to continue with significant growth, despite central government attempts to cool house price rises. According to Dalian Wanda Group[4] (one of China's biggest property development companies) chairman Wang Jianlin, China's housing prices will very likely continue to keep going up for between 10 and 15 years. Driving the continued inflation in housing prices will be continued urbanisation creating more demand for land, which will push up land prices as available land becomes scarcer. If improvements to compensation and payment to farmers for their land come in and are enforced properly, this will also add to the cost of land.

Of course, if you trust the official National Bureau of Statistics (NBS) house price and rental indices,[5] between 2000 and 2011, urban house prices only went up 6 per cent during a period when China's urban population went from one-third urban to one-half – a clear contradiction. Meanwhile, rural house prices apparently rose by 20 per cent – which also makes no sense when so many rural people have left the land to become urban. And all the while, total rental prices went up 53 per cent – which also makes no sense when in the late 1990s practically everyone became a home-owner and property speculator. All of which presents more strong evidence that China's rural-skewed consumer price index is off the mark.

There is also the continuing problem of property speculation, where people buy up multiple units as an investment, leading to a large pool of vacant housing. According to an "*Economic Synopsis*"[6] report from the St Louis Federal Reserve in 2013, such vacant housing in China grew by 250 per cent between 2007 and 2012. To curb such stockpiling of property by investors, a pilot property tax programme,[7] which was launched in Shanghai and Chongqing in 2011, targeted those buying new second homes. In May 2013, it was extended to five coastal cities including Hangzhou and Shenzhen. The Shanghai pilot project set an exemption threshold of $60m^2$ per person, and applied tax to any space above that threshold at 0.3 per cent of the appraised value.

As more laws come in to protect the property rights of farmers, and the cost of land in the cities continues to rise due to high demand, the inflationary pressure on the property market continues to rise. At the end of May 2013, an anonymous Beijing developer paid RMB 4.6 billion[8] for a $40{,}355m^2$ plot of land near the Hongqiao Road Metro station in the Changning District of Shanghai, designated for retail or office use, at a price of RMB 29,229 per m^2, 57 per cent above the starting price, making it the highest price for a single land parcel seen in Shanghai by then. By the end of May, Shanghai had already seen land plot sales, excluding those for public use or for subsidised housing for relocated residents, rise six-fold on the same time in 2011 to reach RMB 45 billion. Over a quarter (28%) of such plots sold since the start of 2013 in Shanghai achieved over 150 per cent of their starting price at auction.

November 2012 saw the State Council back new policy changes to protect the property rights of farmers, including improving identification and registration of land ownership and from this issuing certification of ownership to farmers. The central government also allocated RMB 233.26 billion for subsidised housing projects in 2012, up by nearly 40 per cent over 2011. But, there are still worries about abusive land grabs, despite the Ministry of Land and Resources[9] having told local governments to protect farmers' land rights, and the lack of subsidised housing going to those who most need it. There is also continuing concern that the property market in China has developed into a bubble market that is set to burst.

Ghost malls and the wrong kind of sand

Other matters worth considering in terms of the property market in China are the plentiful array of ill-conceived and grandiose construction projects that have appeared in recent years. One such project, which became Access Asia's poster-boy campaign against the hubris of developers and local governments in China, was the Dongtan Eco-city[10] on Chongming Island in Shanghai. The original idea was to build a car-free, low-carbon-emission community for about 500,000 people by 2050, to be started in 2010. The developer was supposed to be the UK's Ove Arup, which traded on its eco-development credentials for years based on this non-existent project. But Arup fell out with its Shanghai City Government partners over who was funding the project. The project has been shelved indefinitely, and for the sake of the marshes on Chongming Island, internationally important for migratory birds, this is a good thing too, although the plans have not been officially scrapped.

Other effectively useless and grandiose construction projects do abound though, in different stages of completion and dereliction. Famous among these are: the New South China Mall[11] in Guangdong, declared to be the world's largest shopping mall when it opened, but which remains mostly completely empty a decade later; the town of Ordos in Inner Mongolia,[12] which was supposed to house about a million people but is likewise empty, although apparently now filling up; and Shanghai Thames Town,[13] a residential, retail and leisure complex meant to lure the rich of Shanghai with its faux-English architecture, yet serves mainly as a backdrop for nothing more than the wedding photos of young Chinese couples. These places may fill with people in the future, but when is uncertain.

There are also concerns that some of the commercial district developments in China's various cities will become marvellous white elephants rather than vibrant hubs of commerce, such as Tianjin's Yujiapu, and both Zhengzhou's and Dandong's New Commercial Districts. The problem with these developments is not so much that they were ill-conceived as they were badly timed, with minimum wages and lack of construction labour now forcing up costs of construction, and therefore property costs. Now flying in the face of monetary tightening plans, their economic viability is looking increasingly precarious.

If construction companies and the banks funding them are having concerns about their developments not finding tenants, their worries could be set to rise because some of their contractors have been cutting corners to make bigger profits. Worries about the quality of construction have been around for a while in China. For example, in June 2009, a newly built block of apartments simply toppled over in Shanghai[14] because construction piles made to anchor the building to the ground were not reinforced properly. Then in March 2013 came the news that the use of sea sand in the construction[15] of tall office buildings in Shenzhen could eventually lead to building collapse.

The actual value of the property market in China also needs deeper scrutiny because much of the property stock is built to a low level of quality. As I commented at the time in certain blogs, if the case of sea sand in Shenzhen was indicative of what might have been going on elsewhere in China, then this problem could be much more widespread.[16] The problem was that untreated sea sand contains high levels of salt that would corrode steel reinforcements over time, raising the possibility that support structures could give way and buildings collapse.

If this turns out to be more widespread than just in Shenzhen, this could be a cause of some major social unrest as people realise their life savings are invested in properties that have become worthless. Because so many Chinese people's investments focus on property, given the lack of alternatives, if such problems are widespread and significant amounts of housing stock face losing value due to poor construction, the repercussions in terms of irate citizens demanding compensation would be stark.

Summary

The most realistic appraisal that I can give is that there do seem to be regional bubbles in the housing market, but that corrective policies being implemented now can help to avert widespread crashes in it. It has also been encouraging that the leading commercial banks have been forced to increase their required credit reserves to cushion against any housing-related losses, particularly from construction companies struggling in the face of tougher credit conditions. The shadow lending market does mean that credit controls are hard to implement comprehensively, but increased taxation on home purchases should make it harder for speculative home buying to run out of control, even if some of the lending is often described as "home improvement" to circumvent such controls.

Part of the difficulty in keeping tabs on the housing market is the lack of reliable data on home price indices, both for different local markets and the overall national market. To encourage more on-record purchasing outside the shadow-lending world, and provide for better means for consumers to buy housing, a wider range of mortgage alternatives would be helpful, such as mortgage-backed securities or bonds, and mortgages could be better adapted to suit the differing needs of consumers reflecting the different market environments in each part of the country.

Lastly, the big housing caveat[17] for China's aspiring home-owning middle classes, is that nobody in China owns land but the government, and they only lease it for a maximum of 70 years. Although such leases are expected to be rolled on for residential property, this is not yet guaranteed in law, and remains a legal black hole that has spawned the concept of "castles in the air," that is, property that sits on land that cannot be owned. Also, I have heard say that the average life span for housing in China, due to the poor construction quality, is only 30–40 years!

> *a legal black hole… has spawned the concept of "castles in the air," that is, property that sits on land that cannot be owned*
>
> *the average life span for housing in China… is only 30–40 years*

Conclusion – The Continual Revolution

The preceding chapters have been a top-down approach to China's numbers. This was necessary to show how numbers on China are distorted, and to prove that China's markets are not yet free markets and that China data needs many caveats.

This approach was also necessary to explain why the current model of economic growth in China cannot continue, and why current economic retooling is necessary. This is important because the figures need to reflect the market and the market the figures, so economic reform requires reform of the statistics. The new leadership is clearly aware of this, and has been quick to outline eight priority areas of policy reform. These include reducing overproduction and structural deficiencies within industry, giving more support to rural economic development and to small- and medium-sized businesses, continuing to drive up domestic consumption and its role within the economy, gradually allowing market demand to set interest rates, creating wider diversity in the capital markets and developing the role of private capital within that. The National Bureau of Statistics (NBS)[1] also seems to be trying to tackle the issue of false reporting, at long last.

But is it too late? According to Charlene Chu of ratings agency Fitch,[2] in a mid-June 2013 article for *The Telegraph* newspaper, although the Chinese government is able to support China's banking system to pull through the current debt problems, with debt representing at least 200 per cent of GDP (probably higher), growing the economy out of this situation is going to be very hard. While Wei Yao of Société Générale was quoted as saying that the amount of company debt is now so high that the rate in growth of principal debt has come close to passing the point where the whole problem of triangular debt could create a collapse in company finances. This would put China in a position where, potentially, companies starved of liquidity might begin to fail to service debts and cause a chain of bankruptcies. China might be able to bail out companies and banks, but the threat to economic growth still looms.

Also of continuing concern is the depth of corruption, and the strong vested interests that have created and continue to protect the systemic problems that have led to China's current issues.

Statistics gathering and reporting in China has improved in some aspects, but the reporting of the "official" economy is increasingly losing coherency because the shadow economy has grown so large. The distortion in the available official data on China's markets, economy, companies and consumers means it is difficult for companies to make informed decisions when it comes to investing in China. So businesses in China now must employ a wider and more sophisticated range of data sources and research methodologies to reach a more realistic picture.

There has to be acceptance that information is always going to be open to interpretation and argument in such a big and still-developing country. The examples used throughout this book highlight not just statistical problems, but also the often large degree of inconsistency in interpretation and opinion among even some of the best-informed minds in each field of research. There is the temptation to believe that the Chinese government somehow has much better data on each facet of China's economy than the rest of us – that it hides the real data to hide the magnitude of the problems. But this is an overly simplistic view, as the government faces misreporting from its own internal agencies, and has to devise its own policies on data it knows is not always accurate.

As the economy and society of China has grown, the general lot of its people has improved; while data quality and depth of coverage to quantify those improvements, although still full of problems, is better than it used to be. The government will do all in its power to preserve those gains to ensure that China's people continue to rise out of poverty and achieve better lives. The reputation of the Communist Party of China (CPC) rests on achieving this. China's reputation also rests partly on giving credible numbers to measure its economic growth.

Outside observers of China need to understand that improving the economy is China's top priority, and measuring those improvements is as important to the Chinese government as for anyone else. Understanding how well things are improving, and identifying areas where things still need improvement are also important. But it takes time to implement improvements and for systems to bed into the culture. Vested interests can slow that progress down sometimes and impede reform, but those vested interests vie with a momentum and mass that is on a trajectory that should eventually win through. Sure, there are the corrupt cadres, high-net-worth individuals and out-and-out criminals who have taken advantage of the lack of control and accounting in parts of the economy to siphon off huge sums of money into personal bank accounts, often off-shore, but my sense is that the days of plenty for these kinds of people is coming to an end, and many will eventually be called to account.

For those conducting business in China, it is important to understand how the big economic figures are generated and where their fallibilities lie, but also to understand the finer detail of the sectors and regions and consumers they are specifically dealing with, and how quickly they are changing as the country develops at its still relatively rapid pace. They need to stop fixating on the big data, the 1.3 billion potential customers of the "China Dream" syndrome that has draped foreign economic interests in China since nineteenth-century Lancashire cotton mill owners first speculated adding an inch to the shirt tails of every Chinaman. Nor should they fixate on the temporary blips and bounces that unleash tsunamis of bearish articles and books announcing the coming collapse of China. Beware the China bears!

There is more reason now than ever to look beyond the statistics, and to understand the social, environmental, political and legal challenges. We are already seeing the democratisation of information in China, thanks to internet online forums which speed up reactions and depth of understanding among a population increasingly less tolerant of falsities. The age of big data is bringing with it direct communication between brands and consumers, making things faster, more interactive and reactive, and necessitating more responsive communication. That communication is creating more power of choice among consumers.

The fact can no longer be ignored that there is a very large grey economy in China, where money moves, like water, to fill the gaps where the official structures as yet fail to meet demand. Hence the shadow banking system, the additional "grey incomes" of many higher–income-bracket consumers, the often opaque accounting of companies, the nebulous numbers of migrant workers whose official status remains "below the radar," the factories making counterfeit goods for sale through pop-up shops and back-street wholesale markets, the unofficial education and health systems.

Reform of social, fiscal and economic policy will gradually help the country to remove the need for those grey areas of the economy, but it is implausible to demand or expect that all of those issues can be tackled straightaway. Changing laws and policies takes time to get right, as does implementing and policing those laws and policies, along with removing the vested interests of those making a living by slipping through the loopholes.

Until those reforms can bed in, China will have its grey statistical edges and its grey economy. Realising this can help companies active in China to remove the risk of underestimating the competition from that grey market, and better allow companies to protect themselves and improve their own markets by self-policing them. A good example of such self-policing is the online pharmacy retail market, where to gain credibility for a sector with a reputation for illegal companies selling counterfeit products, the leading legitimate companies formed an alliance to self-regulate the industry and root out illegal competitors.

China still presents many opportunities, but they can only be realised by a realistic approach to the market. A realistic approach rests on understanding the market at a micro level. China is not a single market yet for most businesses, but a collection of markets. These markets are separated by regions, city tier levels, logistical barriers, demographic and income groups. Knowing the detail as to which regions or cities have the right mix of population with sufficient income levels and income growth, is crucial. As is what those people actually want but are not getting from the existing market, where there is oversupply and fragmentation among the competitors in that market, etc. The devil, as they say, is in the detail.

Chinese people have enjoyed a generation of rapid economic growth. They have become used to constant change. They expect new buildings to keep going up, new cities to emerge, their neighbourhoods to be regenerated, new shops and brands to appear, new products arriving on the shelves, new technology, new media, new lifestyles, new lives. But China's economy is slowing. If it keeps gradually slowing down by a few tenths of a percent each year, as I expect it will, Chinese people will adjust and learn to cope with less dynamism. We are already seeing shifts in consumer values away from getting rich towards finding room to relax and enjoy life.

Economic and social reform, however hard to swallow, is now recognised as too necessary to avoid. The new Chinese leadership has taken over a country at the cusp of a new development trajectory requiring significant political, social and economic reform. The numbers tell us that with scant pension provision, an aging population, a slowing economy, continued state-sector inefficiency stifling the private sector and local governments struggling to pay debts with more debts, something radical has to be done.

The CPC leadership knows full well what reforms it needs to implement,[3] and that it has to enforce Party discipline to achieve them. But the self-serving local government officials, corruption, rote-learning education system and lawlessness that it needs to remove are not just a symptom of China's recent rapid economic growth. They are not even something created under the rule of the CPC. They are problems that China's rulers have faced for centuries. Bringing to bear the rule of law, creating a civil society where individual citizens can have their say and lay claim to a fair stake in the progress of China's society, producing creative and innovative new technologies and companies, letting money flow to where it is best used and most needed and creating the freedom of ideas and information needed for China to "let 100 flowers bloom" will take a complete revolution in the culture of Chinese society and politics. It will require significant reform.

If you think China's transformation over the past few decades has been miraculous, the necessary reform that now has to come, if achieved, will be perhaps even more of a miracle. It will truly be a "great leap forward." China isn't so much an economy measured with statistics, as a puzzle, played by how well you read the cryptic clues and divine your own answers. Just when you think you understand what is going on in China, you realise that everything has changed and you have to start learning all over again. And all the wisdom you might gather about China will be worth nought if you don't keep up with those changes. China being symbolised by the dragon, an ethereal water serpent in the sky, is very apt given that much of what is thought to be understood about China is actually myth.

Just when you think you understand what is going on in China, you learn that everything has changed and you have to start learning all over again

Notes

Preface

1. Mark Twain in "Chapters from My Autobiography," published in the *North American Review* in 1906. http://en.wikipedia.org/wiki/Lies,_damned_lies,_and_statistics

Introduction

1. Xin Liu, "The Mirage of China: Anti-Humanism, Narcissism, and Corporeality of the Contemporary World", Berghahn Books, New York, 2009. Chapter 4, "The Specter of Marx."
2. http://www.historynet.com/letter-from-military-history-january-2013.htm
3. http://english.people.com.cn/constitution/constitution.html
4. http://www.nytimes.com/2010/03/30/business/global/30riotinto.html?pagewanted=all&_r=0
5. http://www.washingtonpost.com/wp-dyn/content/article/2010/07/05/AR2010070500859.html
6. Page14: http://www.worldcrunch.com/tech-science/china-starts-to-come-clean-on-pollution-that-039-s-killing-its-city-dwellers/pollution-environment-greenpeace-health-pm2.5/c4s10491/#.URtMo6X2-Ag
7. http://www.uscc.gov/TheReliabilityofChina'sEconomicData.pdf
8. "*The Reliability of China's Economic Data: An Analysis of National Output*" by Iacob N. Koch-Weser (USCC Policy Analyst, Economics and Trade), the US–China Economic and Security Review Commission: "*The measurement and presentation of data in China reveals problems as well.*

Statistical work remains highly decentralized, and the quality and methods of statistical work vary across reporting units in China's vast economy. Other deficiencies are more specific. Measures of consumption rely too heavily on retail sales, while overlooking other forms of consumption. Many of the right laws are now on the books to guarantee accurate reporting of investment, but there is a lack of information to distinguish real investments from those that only exist on paper. Figures on official inflation are even more perplexing. The Chinese government continues to be secretive about the weights it uses to calculate this important measure. The consumer price index, which forms the basis of inflation measures, does not adequately factor in the role of the Chinese service sector and private industry. In addition, China's statistics undergo large and frequent revisions even after they are made public, further calling the government methodology into question."

1 The Big Numbers

1. 6 February 2013, *New York Times*, Didi Kirsten Tatlow

   This week, Chinese media reported widely on China's "phantom province," the GDP excess that resulted when the economic growth figures from 31 provinces, municipalities and regions were added up and compared to the different, national GDP figure that the government uses. In 2012, the discrepancy reached a remarkable RMB 5.76 trillion, its biggest ever and the equivalent of the output of Guangdong province, itself an economic powerhouse, the media said. http://rendezvous.blogs.nytimes.com/2013/02/06/the-phantom-province-in-chinas-economy/
2. blogs.wsj.com/chinarealtime/2013/09/06/naming-and-shaming-chinas-stats-bureau-finds-its-voice/?mod=WSJBlog
3. http://www.thetimes.co.uk/tto/news/world/asia/article3624853.ece
4. http://english.caixin.com/2013-03-25/100506113.html
5. http://www.globaltimes.cn/content/763346.shtml
6. http://www.chinadaily.com.cn/china/2013-02/25/content_16255262.htm
7. The latest data from the Ministry of Finance showed that the country spent 1.13 trillion Yuan on government procurement in 2011, or 11 per cent of the country's fiscal expenditure. It was a huge expansion from the 100.9 billion Yuan spent in 2002. Government procurement spending is

also expected to have grown at least 10 per cent in 2012 from the previous year, analysts said. "The more than 1 trillion Yuan procurement amount was a conservative calculation," said Gu Liaohai, chief legal counsel of China Society of Economic Reform and a specialist in government procurement law. "If data on other projects including education, health care, railways and government-subsidised home construction projects is included, the country's government procurement spending would be around 7 or 8 trillion Yuan, making China the largest public procurement market in the world," Gu said. http://www.globaltimes.cn/content/763346.shtml
8. http://www.econ.ucdavis.edu/faculty/woo/9.Wang-Woo.Hidden%20 Income%20in%20China.2010-12-25.pdf
9. http://www.imf.org/external/np/sec/pr/2013/pr13192.htm

2 Fiscal Fudging – Tax, Balancing the Government Books and Paying for Social Harmony

1. http://www.theepochtimes.com/n2/china-news/tax-evasion-in-china-exceeds-one-trillion-yuan-263590.html
2. http://blogs.reuters.com/david-cay-johnston/2011/12/13/wheres-the-fraud-mr-president/
3. http://www.globaltimes.cn/DesktopModules/DnnForge%20-%20 NewsArticles/Print.aspx?tabid=99&tabmoduleid=94&articleId=692619& moduleId=405&PortalID=0
4. www.globaltimes.cn/content/770919.shtml#.UWVxVJMjySo
5. www.marketplace.org/topics/business/last-minute-tax-tips/chinas-national-sport-tax-evasion
6. http://finance.ifeng.com/a/20130620/8149283_0.shtml
7. http://usa.chinadaily.com.cn/opinion/2011-11/22/content_14138169.htm
8. http://www.nytimes.com/roomfordebate/2011/11/01/is-china-facing-a-health-care-crisis/chinas-health-care-reform-far-from-sufficient
9. http://articles.marketwatch.com/2012-05-20/industries/31788683_1_insurance-system-illness-basic-insurance
10. http://www.nbcnews.com/business/economywatch/china-sliding-faster-pensions-black-hole-6203544
11. http://www.economist.com/node/21560274
12. http://www.economist.com/node/21560274

13. http://english.caixin.com/2011-12-23/100342018.html
14. http://www.scmp.com/business/china-business/article/1205797/chinas-national-pension-fund-records-7-cent-investment
15. http://www.wantchinatimes.com/news-subclass-cnt.aspx?id=20121025000016&cid=1102
16. http://www.scmp.com/business/china-business/article/1205797/chinas-national-pension-fund-records-7-cent-investment
17. http://english.cri.cn/6909/2012/07/10/2982s711079.htm
18. http://english.caixin.com/2013-06-20/100543779.html
19. http://www.ecns.cn/business/2013/04-26/60894.shtml
20. http://www.globaltimes.cn/DesktopModules/DnnForge%20-%20NewsArticles/Print.aspx?tabid=99&tabmoduleid=94&articleId=777640&moduleId=405&PortalID=0
21. http://finance.sina.com.cn/china/20130503/221015345379.shtml
22. page 47; http://english.people.com.cn/90001/90781/6571410.html
23. http://online.wsj.com/article/SB10001424127887324678604578340530200654140.html
24. http://www.nytimes.com/2013/02/17/business/in-china-families-bet-it-all-on-a-child-in-college.html?pagewanted=all&_r=0
25. http://english.cntv.cn/program/china24/20130901/101515.shtml

3 Red Ink on the Red Carpet – China's Barely Hidden Debt

1. http://www.ft.com/cms/s/0/adb07bbe-a655-11e2-8bd2-00144feabdc0.html#axzz2RRn9xM2i
2. http://english.caixin.com/2013-03-27/100507111.html
3. http://epaper.bjnews.com.cn/html/2013-06/11/content_438899.htm?div=-1
4. http://www.bloomberg.com/news/2013-05-07/china-said-to-tighten-approvals-for-local-government-bond-sales.html
5. http://www.bloomberg.com/news/2013-05-07/china-said-to-tighten-approvals-for-local-government-bond-sales.html
6. http://www.heraldsun.com.au/news/central-bank-buys-up-chinese-government-bonds/story-e6frf7jo-1226629015818
7. http://articles.marketwatch.com/2012-03-13/markets/31159984_1_japan-bonds-hong-kong

8. http://www.ft.com/intl/cms/s/710ea3da-1f14-11e1-ab49-00144feabdc0,Authorised=false.html?_i_location=http%3A%2F%2Fwww.ft.com%2Fcms%2Fs%2F0%2F710ea3da-1f14-11e1-ab49-00144feabdc0.html&_i_referer=#axzz1uHxCFDtl
9. http://blogs.wsj.com/chinarealtime/2013/03/01/hard-landing-ahead-for-chinas-local-governments/
10. http://english.caixin.com/2013-05-28/100533866.html
11. http://www.deloitte.com/assets/Dcom-India/Local%20Assets/Documents/Thoughtware/Funding_the_InfrastructureInvestment_Gap.pdf
12. http://blogs.wsj.com/privateequity/2013/03/28/chinas-governing-bodies-ndrc-csrc-tussle-over-private-equity/
13. http://english.caixin.com/2013-05-20/100530194.html
14. http://www.audit.gov.cn/n1992130/n1992150/n1992500/3291665.html
15. http://online.wsj.com/article/SB10001424127887323291704578202551007144578.html
16. http://online.wsj.com/article/SB10001424127887324461604578193010002390962.html
17. http://www.zerohedge.com/news/2012-11-22/whither-china-end-extrapolation
18. http://www.businessweek.com/articles/2012-11-15/corporate-chinas-black-hole-of-debt
19. http://www.ft.com/cms/s/0/e76db82e-0a4d-11e3-aeab-00144feabdc0.html?siteedition=intl#slide4
20. http://economy.caixin.com/2013-05-13/100527413.html
21. http://www.telegraph.co.uk/finance/china-business/10120716/China-braces-for-capital-flight-and-debt-stress-as-Fed-tightens.html
22. http://www.businessweek.com/articles/2012-11-15/corporate-chinas-black-hole-of-debt
23. http://www.businessweek.com/articles/2012-11-15/corporate-chinas-black-hole-of-debt
24. http://www.forbes.com/sites/jackperkowski/2012/10/29/chinas-smes-access-the-bond-market/
25. http://edition.cnn.com/2013/04/22/world/asia/china-activists-detained
26. http://www.globaltimes.cn/content/778714.shtml#.UYxiObUjySo
27. http://www.forbes.com/sites/kenrapoza/2013/01/28/is-china-next-to-suffer-a-debt-crisis/

28. http://qz.com/23091/asia-might-be-heading-for-a-second-debt-crisis/
29. http://www.breakingviews.com/china%E2%80%99s-next-debt-crisis-will-be-a-local-affair/21069229.article
30. http://www.abc.net.au/worldtoday/content/2013/s3739782.htm
31. http://articles.marketwatch.com/2009-11-30/markets/30742768_1_credit-card-debt-report-china-data
32. http://www.theepochtimes.com/n2/china-news/credit-card-debt-rises-in-china-23114.html
33. http://news.xinhuanet.com/english2010/business/2010-11/25/c_13622402.htm
34. http://www.researchinchina.com/Htmls/News/201203/31973.html
35. http://europe.chinadaily.com.cn/business/2013-03/18/content_16315361.htm
36. http://www.chinapost.com.tw/china/china-business/2012/04/30/339466/First-time-credit.htm
37. http://www.china.org.cn/business/2010-08/12/content_20695173.htm
38. http://www.businessweek.com/articles/2013-05-02/credit-card-companies-battle-in-china
39. http://edition.cnn.com/2009/BUSINESS/11/10/china.credit.debt/
40. http://www.chinasmack.com/2013/stories/schoolboy-moves-bricks-for-8-days-to-repay-apple-iphone-debt.html
41. http://www.globaltimes.cn/content/771485.shtml#.UZxAarUjySo
42. http://europe.chinadaily.com.cn/business/2013-04/10/content_16388630.htm
43. http://news.xinhuanet.com/english2010/business/2010-11/25/c_13622402.htm
44. http://finance.caixin.com/2013-09-03/100577401.html
45. http://www.bloomberg.com/news/2013-09-04/china-finance-minister-says-risk-of-local-debt-default-not-great.html

4 Monetary Policy

1. http://www.chinaeconomicreview.com/china-makes-biggest-ever-weekly-cash-withdrawal
2. http://www.imf.org/external/np/sec/pr/2013/pr13192.htm
3. http://www.wantchinatimes.com/news-subclass-cnt.aspx?id=20130124000097&cid=1502

4. http://www.china.org.cn/business/2012-07/13/content_25903847.htm
5. http://www.bloomberg.com/news/2013-05-13/china-shadow-banking-poses-systemic-risks-to-banks-moody-s-says.html
6. http://www.chinaeconomicreview.com/huaxi-bank-citic-trust-citic-bank-wealth-management-products-CLSA
7. http://www.cnbc.com/id/100599193
8. http://online.wsj.com/article/SB10000872396390443507204578020272862374326.html
9. http://www.businessweek.com/magazine/chinas-superrich-buy-a-better-life-abroad-11222011.html
10. http://economictimes.indiatimes.com/markets/commodities/china-gold-imports-to-keep-growing-after-hitting-record-high/articleshow/20430476.cms
11. http://www.reuters.com/article/2013/03/20/us-usa-congress-china-idUSBRE92J11U20130320
12. http://english.caixin.com/2013-05-16/100528769.html
13. http://english.caixin.com/2013-05-07/100524732.html
14. http://english.caixin.com/2013-05-28/100533923.html
15. http://english.caixin.com/2013-05-07/100524732.html

5 Manufacturing Measures

1. http://www.frbsf.org/publications/economics/letter/2013/el2013-08.html
2. http://finance.sina.com.cn/chanjing/cyxw/20130417/145515179486.shtml
3. http://www.forbes.com/sites/jackperkowski/2012/10/29/chinas-smes-access-the-bond-market/
4. http://www.businessweek.com/articles/2013-04-25/regulating-chinas-shadow-banking-system-isnt-easy
5. http://www.businessweek.com/articles/2013-04-25/regulating-chinas-shadow-banking-system-isnt-easy
6. http://english.caixin.com/2012-07-16/100411518.html
7. http://www.forbes.com/sites/russellflannery/2012/07/01/peak-issues-profit-warning-as-china-sportswear-industrys-woes-continue/
8. http://www.ft.com/cms/s/2/8e2a74e4-eac0-11e1-984b-00144feab49a.html#axzz2Qn7Uia00
9. http://www.wantchinatimes.com/news-subclass-cnt.aspx?id=20120103000099&cid=1102

10. http://blogs.swisslog.com/2012/12/07/chinas-cold-chain-logistics-set-to-improve/
11. http://www.reuters.com/article/2012/05/20/china-bond-default-idUSL4E8GE74820120520
12. http://www.china.org.cn/top10/2012-09/06/content_26443931.htm
13. http://www.chinaeconomicreview.com/us-match-china-cost-manufacturing-2015
14. http://english.people.com.cn/90778/8135629.html
15. http://business.time.com/2012/02/15/are-chinas-big-state-companies-a-big-problem-for-the-global-economy/#ixzz2Sx14wFlK
16. http://www.forbes.com/sites/dougguthrie/2013/01/07/understanding-chinas-leadership-transition/

6 Cooking the Corporate Books

1. http://www.chinamoneypodcast.com/2013/02/05/paul-gillis-three-accounting-frauds-most-chinese-companies-use-to-cheat-foreign-investors
2. http://www.brandchannel.com/home/post/2013/03/28/Volvo-China-Business-032813.aspx
3. http://www.chinadaily.com.cn/business/2012-03/24/content_14905119.htm
4. http://www.china.org.cn/business/2012-06/04/content_25559722.htm
5. http://english.caixin.com/2013-05-13/100527317.html
6. http://bpi.transparency.org/bpi2011/results/
7. http://mobile.reuters.com/article/idUSBRE91908Q20130210?irpc=932
8. http://www.financierworldwide.com/article.php?id=8480
9. http://www.theglobeandmail.com/report-on-business/industry-news/the-law-page/former-sino-forest-brass-may-face-84-million-in-penalties-osc-says/article6273364/
10. http://www.sec.gov/news/press/2011/2011-241.htm
11. http://www.chinadaily.com.cn/bizchina/2012-07/17/content_15590365.htm
12. http://finance.ifeng.com/stock/special/sdgwzj/index.shtml
13. http://online.wsj.com/article/SB10001424127887324743704578442422720766046.html?goback=%2Egde_4551639_member_238314022
14. http://www.smh.com.au/business/carbon-economy/suntechs-downfall-may-have-european-origin-20130403-2h6yu.html

15. http://online.wsj.com/article/SB10001424127887323975004578502610078088482.html
16. http://english.caixin.com/2012-12-04/100468694.html
17. http://english.caixin.com/2013-05-14/100527957.html

7 Red Chips

1. http://www.bloomberg.com/news/2013-08-01/china-s-stock-market-dysfunctional-amid-ipo-freeze-neoh-says.html
2. http://english.caixin.com/2013-05-20/100530156.html
3. http://online.wsj.com/article/SB10001424127887323864304578318101227205828.html
4. http://www.reuters.com/article/2013/05/25/usa-auditing-china-idUSL2N0E51NW20130525

8 Trade Measures

1. https://reportingproject.net/underground/index.php?option=com_content&view=article&id=9
2. http://english.caixin.com/2013-06-17/100542037.html
3. english.caixin.com/2013-08-02/100564883.html
4. http://www.forbes.com/sites/gordonchang/2013/06/09/chinas-may-numbers-disappoint-no-remedies-in-sight/
5. Standard Chartered Global Research, Economic Alert, 10 June 2013, "China- No pick-up, but no reason to panic".
6. CLSA Sinology, 10 June 2013 "Stabilizing".
7. http://www.reuters.com/article/2013/06/09/us-china-economy-idUSBRE9580GE20130609
8. http://www.forbes.com/sites/kenrapoza/2013/06/09/chinas-economy-firing-blanks-second-quarter-seen-worse-than-first/
9. http://www.bloomberg.com/news/2013-06-09/china-s-leaders-face-test-of-growth-resolve-after-may-slowdown.html
10. www.nytimes.com/2013/08/04/business/global/coin-of-realm-in-china-graft-phony-receipts.html?_r=1&
11. http://www.cnbc.com/id/100651692
12. http://online.wsj.com/article/SB10001424127887324767004578488233119290670.html

13. http://www.cnbc.com/i d/100783164
14. http://www.chinaeconomicreview.com/us-match-china-cost-manufacturing-2015
15. http://english.caixin.com/2013-04-10/100512356.html
16. http://www.bloomberg.com/news/2013-01-13/china-export-surge-spurs-data-skepticism-at-goldman-ubs.html
17. http://www.shanghaidaily.com/nsp/Business/2013/06/03/HSBC%2Bfactory%2Bindex%2Bat%2B7month%2Blow/
18. http://www.telegraph.co.uk/news/worldnews/asia/china/10123620/From-sand-to-skyscrapers-Inside-Chinas-newest-city-as-400-million-move-to-towns.html
19. http://ftalphaville.ft.com/2012/03/26/936551/china-as-the-worlds-unreliable-importer/
20. http://www.ft.com/cms/s/0/d33b5104-84a1-11e2-aaf1-00144feabdc0.html#axzz2Mcgp4vWE
21. http://www.bloomberg.com/news/2013-10-11/china-export-gains-understated-as-fake-data-distort-comparisons.html?goback=%2Egde_2387236_member_5794275577934405632#%21
22. http://en.ecoalchina.com/info/nyhy/shhy/1057090.shtml#nogo
23. http://english.caixin.com/2013-02-07/100490609.html
24. http://www.chinadaily.com.cn/china/2013-05/22/content_16517767.htm
25. http://www.tothetick.com/china-fakes-trade-surplus
26. http://www.businessweek.com/videos/2013-05-08/chinas-trade-surplus-is-fictitious-von-pfeil

9 Retooling China's Industry to Drive Domestic Consumption Growth

1. http://www.mckinsey.com/Insights/Asia-Pacific/Winners_and_losers_in_Chinas_next_decade?cid=china-eml-alt-mip-mck-oth-1306
2. http://newsfeed.time.com/2013/02/01/chinese-millionaire-fights-pollution-with-fresh-air-in-a-can/
3. http://blogs.wsj.com/chinarealtime/2013/03/15/china-the-jobs-report/
4. http://www.chinadaily.com.cn/china/2013-03/15/content_16309616.htm
5. As Yang Dongping, director of 21st Research Education, points out, the numbers are not only questionable but put together at the wrong time (*"Daxuesheng 'zui nan jiuyeji' nanzai hechu"*, Caixin, 3 June 2013). The universities have targets for their graduates to find jobs, which not only leads, Yang argues, to the numbers being unreliable, but also

wastes teaching time. Far better, he argues, to move to something like the US system, which reports numbers of those who have left college for at least a year. China currently reports as students graduate each June and then again in September. Southwestern University's survey last year of employment by education suggests that graduates have one of the lowest unemployment rates and highest wage levels ... even if it takes some time for them to find work.

6. http://magazine.caixin.com/2013-05-31/100535511.html
7. http://online.wsj.com/article/SB10001424127887324678604578340530200654140.html
8. http://www.bbc.co.uk/news/business-19340128
9. http://www.bbc.co.uk/news/business-12477756
10. http://www.bbc.co.uk/news/technology-19504381
11. http://www.thenational.ae/news/world/asia-pacific/chinas-workplace-safety-scrutinised-in-new-report-showing-over-200-deaths-a-day
12. http://www.bbc.co.uk/news/world-asia-china-22749938
13. http://english.peopledaily.com.cn/90882/8269895.html
14. http://www.business-standard.com/article/pti-stories/over-27-700-dead-missing-in-china-workplace-accidents-in-2013-113073000536_1.html
15. http://ec.europa.eu/taxation_customs/resources/documents/customs/customs_controls/counterfeit_piracy/statistics/2012_ipr_statistics_en.pdf
16. http://www.telegraph.co.uk/news/worldnews/asia/china/9817855/Chinese-man-kept-alive-by-self-built-dialysis-machine.html

10 Population, Employment, Income and the Middle Class

1. Page107: http://www.chinadaily.com.cn/opinion/2012-10/23/content_15838049.htm
2. http://www.tradingeconomics.com/china/population-growth-annual-percent-wb-data.html
3. https://www.cia.gov/library/publications/the-world-factbook/fields/2002.html
4. http://english.sina.com/life/2012/1018/517654.html
5. http://www.china.org.cn/china/2012-07/02/content_25785258.htm
6. http://www.china.org.cn/china/2011-03/22/content_22190715.htm
7. http://www.china.org.cn/china/2012-07/02/content_25785258.htm

8. http://www.imf.org/external/pubs/ft/wp/2013/wp1326.pdf
9. http://www.bloomberg.com/news/2012-11-13/china-s-new-leaders-face-an-economic-turning-point.html
10. http://www.reuters.com/article/2013/05/23/us-china-economy-urbanisation-idUSBRE94M0NA20130523
11. http://www.nytimes.com/2013/06/16/world/asia/chinas-great-uprooting-moving-250-million-into-cities.html?pagewanted=all&_r=1&
12. http://online.wsj.com/article/SB10001424127887323316804578164784240097900.html
13. http://www.foreignpolicy.com/articles/2009/09/03/how_china_cooks_its_books
14. http://english.caixin.com/2012-12-10/100470648.html
15. http://www.worldbank.org/content/dam/Worldbank/document/State_of_the_poor_paper_April17.pdf
16. http://edition.cnn.com/2012/11/14/opinion/china-challenges-one-child-brooks
17. Page119: http://www.theworldofchinese.com/2013/03/the-last-resort-chinas-growing-suicide-problem/
18. www.chinadigitaltimes.net/2013/02/trust-among-chinese-drops-to-record-low/
19. http://www.bbc.co.uk/news/world-asia-china-21597752
20. http://online.wsj.com/article/SB10001424127887323549204578317633183827770.html?mod=rss_about_china
21. http://english.cri.cn/6909/2013/05/22/2281s766371.htm
22. http://www.uschina2022.com/
23. http://www.forbes.com/sites/helenwang/2010/11/24/defining-the-chinese-middle-class/
24. http://www.forbes.com/sites/kenrapoza/2011/09/05/within-a-generation-china-middle-class-four-times-larger-than-americas/
25. http://china.org.cn/opinion/2010-09/03/content_20859345.htm
26. http://online.wsj.com/article/SB10001424127887323628804578345342201524964.html
27. http://europe.chinadaily.com.cn/china/2013-02/08/content_16214640.htm
28. http://www.prnewswire.com/news-releases/chinese-middle-class-to-triple-by-2022-new-study-by-us-and-chinese-luminaries-charts-opportunities-for-bilateral-economic-growth-208380651.html
29. http://www.mckinsey.com/insights/economic_studies/three_snapshots_from_chinas_next_chapter?cid=china-eml-alt-mip-mck-oth-1306

30. http://www.chinadaily.com.cn/business/2013-01/18/content_16137453.htm
31. http://english.caixin.com/2011-04-26/100252511.html
32. http://www.econ.ucdavis.edu/faculty/woo/9.Wang-Woo.Hidden%20Income%20in%20China.2010-12-25.pdf

11 Retail Sales

1. http://www.econ.ucdavis.edu/faculty/woo/9.Wang-Woo.Hidden%20Income%20in%20China.2010-12-25.pdf
2. According to an article on www.stnn.cc on 31 July 2007, the value of China's fake products crossed US$ 16 billion in 2006. http://www.chinadaily.com.cn/opinion/2010-07/03/content_10054025.htm

   The market value of pirated and counterfeit goods produced in China is estimated at between US$ 19 billion and US$ 24 billion a year in 2003. http://factsanddetails.com/china.php?itemid=356=9=61
3. In terms of China's domestic market, a study in 2001 by the People's Republic of China (PRC) State Council Research and Development Centre reported that the PRC economy was flooded with between US$ 19 billion and US$ 24 billion worth of counterfeit goods (Chow, 2006; Pei, 2005). Today, counterfeiting in China accounts for almost 8 per cent of Gross Domestic Product (GDP) and is even the main source of support for some local economies. http://www.hrmars.com/admin/pics/1154.pdf

   Counterfeit Products within China – A New Twist to an Old Problem: Imitation Apple Retailers Richard J. Hunter
4. 'China's quality authorities handled 54,200 cases concerning infringements of intellectual property rights as well as production and sale of fake products in the first nine months of the year. The value of the products involved was worth 3.14 billion Yuan (US$ 498.41 million)', Li Yuanping, spokesman for the General Administration of Quality Supervision, Inspection and Quarantine (AQSIQ), said at a news briefing Tuesday. http://www.chinadaily.com.cn/business/2012-10/31/content_15859687.htm
5. http://www.rsc.org/chemistryworld/News/2007/May/18050701.asp
6. http://www.shanghaidaily.com/nsp/Metro/2013/03/13/Fake%2Bhoney%2Bsales%2Bcalled%2Brampant%2Bhard%2Bto%2Bdetect/
7. http://techcrunch.com/2013/03/21/china-broadband-laggin/
8. http://english.caixin.com/2013-05-07/100524715.html

9. http://www.businessweek.com/articles/2013-05-29/in-china-big-data-is-becoming-big-business

12 Property – The Safest Investment Bet in China?

1. http://www.chinaeconomicreview.com/new-policy-property-real-estate-china-rising-prices
2. http://www.chinascopefinancial.com/en/news/post/14984.html
3. http://www.bloomberg.com/news/2013-02-19/china-housing-slaves-helping-property-rebound-mortgages.html
4. http://www.nbd.com.cn/articles/2013-05-28/745098.html
5. *"How Badly Flawed is Chinese Economic Data? The Opening Bid is $1 Trillion"* Christopher Balding, associate professor HSBC Business School Peking University, 14 August 2013.
6. http://research.stlouisfed.org/publications/es/13/ES_13_2013-05-03.pdf
7. http://companies.caixin.com/2013-05-30/100535165.html
8. http://www.shanghaidaily.com/nsp/Business/2013/05/30/Highest%2Bprice%2Bfor%2Bland%2Bparcel/
9. http://english.caixin.com/2013-05-16/100529013.html
10. http://www.cnu.org/cnu-salons/2013/04/dashed-dreams-eco-city-failure-dongtan-eco-city-chongming-island-china
11. http://www.businessinsider.com/new-south-china-mall-tour-a-ghost-mall-2013-3?op=1
12. http://www.time.com/time/photogallery/0,29307,1975397_2094498,00.html
13. http://shanghaiist.com/2013/05/13/vice_visits_shanghais_thames_town.php
14. http://www.telegraph.co.uk/news/worldnews/asia/china/5685963/Nine-held-over-Shanghai-building-collapse.html
15. http://www.wired.com/design/2013/03/poor-quality-chinese-concrete-could-lead-to-skyscraper-collapses/?goback=%2Eamf_4551639_114737765%2Egmp_36656%2Eamf_36656_114737765%2Egde_36656_member_225280883
16. http://www.scmp.com/comment/insight-opinion/article/1194958/high-stakes-involved-shenzhens-concrete-scandal
17. http://www.chinaeconomicreview.com/china-land-lease-property-law-ownership-rights

Conclusion – The Continual Revolution

1. http://blogs.wsj.com/chinarealtime/2013/09/06/naming-and-shaming-chinas-stats-bureau-finds-its-voice/?mod=WSJBlog
2. http://www.telegraph.co.uk/finance/china-business/10123507/Fitch-says-China-credit-bubble-unprecedented-in-modern-world-history.html
3. http://www.bloomberg.com/news/2013-09-03/xi-says-china-s-slower-economic-growth-is-result-of-adjustment.html?utm_source=The+Sinocism+China+Newsletter&utm_campaign=3b0716541e-Sinocism9_4_2013&utm_medium=email&utm_term=0_171f237867-3b0716541e-29615021

Index

Printed and bound by CPI Group (UK) Ltd, Croydon, CR0 4YY